This book is an invitation to 'grab a coffe *you about the God who has been my clos* *factor – not about the author and her e* *was always there, in the dark moments c* It is a book about culture, about gospel communication, about dealing with change and, above all, about the adequacy of God in all of life. It is a book that will cause you to smile, to reflect, to be amazed, to be encouraged. And remember to grab some tissues when you pull up that chair.*

Bruce Dipple
Former Australia/East Asia Director of SIM
Former Director of the School of Cross Cultural Mission, SMBC

Ruth has been an inspiration to many and a wonderful example, teacher and counsellor to her New Zealand colleagues. From her many years in Somalia and Ethiopia coupled with her qualifications as a psychologist, she has been invaluable in preparing and caring for new and returning missionaries in her ten years of annual visits to New Zealand. Her visits with her colleague Dr Kath Donovan, and peppered with her unique sense of humour, were always a welcome highlight for us.

Murray Dunn
Director of SIM New Zealand, 1986–96

Ruth pioneered the use of psychological assessment for missionaries in Australia, overcoming initial suspicion from the mission leaders with her professionalism, integrity, warmth, spiritual depth and wit. She, together with Kath, became a loved and highly respected team across Australia. Their model of assessment and debriefing was the gold standard and they became internationally recognised as world leaders in this field. Ruth was the inspiration for me to train as a psychologist. She was a tower of support and encouragement throughout my degree, and then generously mentored me in the art of psychological assessment. Today Ruth's influence continues as I pass on much of what I learnt from her to my students. I have rarely met someone who has such empathy and inclination to find something positive about even the most 'difficult' of people. Her friendship is one of my most treasured possessions.

Barbara Griffin
Associate Professor and Director of Organisational Psychology training
Macquarie University

Oetje: *Not only was Ruth a great teacher, she also possessed an enormous love for the Lord and for the Somali people. Besides learning the language, I gained deep insights into the Somali culture from Ruth. She taught me how to live among the Somali people and to be a witness for the gospel.*

Michael: *Ruth's down-to-earth wisdom, derived from her varied experiences, provided me much needed spiritual realism. Her emphasis on perseverance in the life-long marathon of sharing the good news with Somalis was particularly helpful.*

Over the past three decades, Oetje and I have been blessed by frequent letters and emails of encouragement from Ruth, sharing our frustrations, challenges and joys as we see the gospel of Jesus Christ advance among the Somali people.

Michael Madany
Coordinator, The New Life website and Project Consultant,
The Voice of New Life broadcast
Oetje Madany
Social Services, World Relief Seattle

This personal account resonates with passion for God and people. It bounces with life, with joy and humour, and Ruth shares sadness and pain as well. Like Ruth herself, the book is open, honest, joyful. It is a continuation of that great saga of God's mission which started in the Acts of the Apostles and continues as God works today through his Spirit. Read it and rejoice. Read it – and be warned. You might be called to write the next chapter.

Colin Reed
Former missionary in Africa
Former staff member, NSW Branch of the Church Missionary Society

We found through our many years of missionary service that debriefing was a necessary and helpful means of putting difficulties and successes into perspective when we returned for home assignment and at the end of our term of service. Ruth provided us with a safe and secure place to cry when we needed to express our hurts and affirmation when we needed encouragement. And she was there to rejoice with us in joys and successes. We felt listened to and cared for and we could trust her with our confidences.

Helen and Len Salisbury
SIM missionaries

The Lord bless you Stuart & Margaret
Ruth 20/11/2016

WHEN THE
LIGHTS
GO OUT

Memoir of a Missionary to Somalia

RUTH MYORS

ACORN PRESS

Published by Acorn Press Ltd ABN 50 008 549 540
Office and orders: PO Box 258
                         Moreland VIC 3058
Australia
Tel/Fax: (03) 9383 1266
International Tel/Fax: 61 3 9383 1266
Website: www.acornpress.net.au

National Library of Australia Cataloguing-in-Publication entry:

Creator: Myors, Ruth, author.
Title: When the lights go out: memoir of a missionary to Somalia/
                Ruth Myors.
ISBN: 9780994616609 (paperback).
                9780994616616 (ebook).
Subjects: Myors, Ruth.
                Nurses – Somalia – Biography.
                Missionaries, Medical – Somalia – Biography.
                Women missionaries – Somalia – Biography.
                Missions, Medical – Ethiopia.
Dewey Number: 610.73092.

Unless otherwise noted, Bible quotations are taken from THE HOLY BIBLE, NEW
INTERNATIONAL VERSION®, NIV® Copyright © 1973, 1978, 1984, 2011 by Biblica,
Inc.™ Used by permission. All rights reserved worldwide.

Bible quotations marked KJV are taken from the Holy Bible, King James Version.

Some names and identifying details have been changed to protect the privacy of
Somali individuals.

The poems 'Quest' (p. 91), 'Appointed' (p. 158) and 'Worship' (p. 204) were first
published in Ruth Myors, *Joyful in My God*, SIM International, 1983. Used with
permission.

Editor: Owen Salter, Barnabas Editorial Services and Training.
Cover design and drawings: Peter Rugendyke, PR Art Services,
                         www.facebook.com/PRArtServices/.
Text layout: Ivan Smith, Communiqué Graphics.

Dedication

*I dedicate this book to my Somali co-workers
who remain among my closest
friends along with my siblings, and to the
memory of Kath who is now rejoicing
in the presence of the Lord.*

Acknowledgements

Thank you to Acorn Press for agreeing to publish this
book and your professional help; Ed Wright, Beverly
Richardson, Carol Lukins, Margaret Douglass and
Owen Salter for his meticulous editing; my amazingly
gifted nephew, Peter Rugendyke, for the cover, map and
sketches; and the Lake Macquarie U3A Creative Writing
group, with Kathryn Fry at the helm, who week
by week kept me going.

Last but not least, thank you to my faithful friends like
Sylvia Pickford, Yeoval, who at every meeting never
failed to say 'When will you finish that book?'

CONTENTS

LIST OF FIGURES

LIST OF ABBREVIATIONS

APS   Australian Psychological Society
ELMDS   East Lake Macquarie Dementia Service
FGM   female genital mutilation
KGV   King George V Hospital for Mothers and Babies
LBI   Lebanon Bible Institute
RPA   Royal Prince Alfred Hospital
SIL   Summer Institute of Linguistics
SIM   Sudan Interior Mission
SMBC   Sydney Missionary and Bible College
WHO   World Health Organization

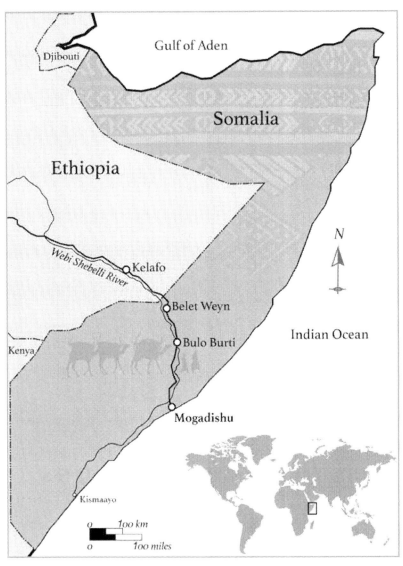

Map of Somalia

AUTHOR'S NOTE

The doors to work in the Somali Republic opened for expatriate missionaries in 1954. By early 1973 they were closed again by the newly formed socialist government. We never dreamed the time would be so short. The cost was heavy but every day given to us there was a precious gift. What I have written about is a few short years unique in the history of a land currently racked by pain. Warren and Dorothy Modricker led the SIM[1] team. Because of their vision and passion, the only years that were open to ministry by foreign missions were grasped.

Did we use our time wisely? Only eternity will tell. The light has gone out for foreign missionaries to be there in person but also for the chance for suffering Somali people to live in peace and security. Currently for Christians, Somalia is considered one of the most dangerous countries in the world, second only to North Korea.

INTRODUCTION

'Quickly, quickly, get the lanterns lit. It's nearly 10.00 pm.' This was a nightly scramble in our hospital at Bulo Burti. Unless there was a major crisis, the generator that provided lights for houses and hospital would be turned off exactly at 10.00 pm. Deliveries of babies and all other routine care of patients had to be carried out by lamplight. Without our lamps, clean glass, adequate wicks and a supply of kerosene we were abandoned to the darkness.

Sometimes in life the road ahead seems to be shrouded in darkness. During my years among the Somalis and after, there were times when government decisions, coups, communist takeovers, natural disasters, sudden deaths and my own failings left me feeling I was groping blindly. Plans were disrupted and unexpected changes enforced. But God's word says, 'Even in darkness light dawns for the upright' (Psalm 112:4) – not flickering, hurricane-lantern light but his light. Jesus, the Light of the World, promised that when we follow him we will never

---

1   Then known as Sudan Interior Mission.

walk in darkness but have the light of life (John 8:12). Remembering, in order to write a book after many years, has shown me how, even after the darkest periods, there is a light that shows the way ahead.

Miroslav Volf, the well-known author and theologian, has written graphically about his experiences under the communist government in his native Croatia. He describes the ability to make 'painful memories a wellspring of healing rather than a source of deepening pain'. He also says that the memories that make us are a patchwork quilt, the structure of which depends on the memories we feature, the ones we discard and what we choose as a background. 'We are not shaped by memories; we ourselves *shape* the memories that shape us.'[2] It has been enriching for me to go back over the years. Remembering has been an emotional journey but also a time of healing.

I worked with a wonderful team in Somalia and the members still living are among my dearest friends. Each one would tell it differently, but this is my story. I have chosen what to include and what to leave out. What I have written is the truth as I see it.

I heard the voice of Jesus say,
'I am this dark world's Light;
Look unto Me, thy morn shall rise,
And all thy day be bright.'
I looked to Jesus, and I found
In Him my Star, my Sun;
And in that Light of life I'll walk
Till travelling days are done.[3]

2 Miroslav Volf, *The End of Memory*, Eerdmans, 2006, p. 25.
3 Horatius Bonar (1808–1889).

GOODBYE

Early on 24 March 1977, we stood at the edge of the airstrip outside the village of Kelafo in the Ogaden Desert, waiting for the Missionary Aviation Fellowship single-engine Cessna to come and fly us away. The ground, usually so dry and dusty, was still cracked and wrinkled from the water that had flooded the area a year before. We hoped it was safe for the plane to land. Ethiopian soldiers surrounded us with rifles at the ready in case Somali freedom fighters were still in the area.

We, five adults and two children – Pat and John Warner with Michelle and Robyn, Christel Voll, Geoff Clerke and I – spoke very little as we waited. Gratitude that our lives had been spared conflicted with the awareness that we would not be returning. All of us except Geoff had invested years of our lives in this remote Somali village. They had been good years. We had made many friends and seen people grow in their knowledge of the Lord Jesus. But war had come and the locals had fled. No time for goodbyes. It was unlikely we would ever see any of them again.

Quietly through the trees appeared two middle-aged Somali men. Both had worked for us. One was Shafi'i. Through my years in Kelafo he had cleaned my house, washed my clothes, cooked meals and amused me with his homespun philosophies and spicy humour. Thought to be too outspoken by some, he and I had made a good team, with the occasional sparks flying. His companion was Duuro, the house worker for the Twidales, who were currently on holidays. Duuro was quiet, steady and solid. They had come to see us off.

As we talked, our means of transport landed. We said goodbye, climbed into the plane and, after an initial creaking and groaning of the aircraft along the uneven runway, we were airborne, swept away forever.

Goodbye, dear friends; goodbye Kelafo; goodbye hospital, school, houses. Goodbye scene of flood, war, gospel ministry, healing the sick, delivering the babies, weeping with those who wept and laughing with those who laughed. Goodbye to the place where smallpox was eradicated from the world, hopefully forever.

The pilot, aware that we were in a war zone, wasted no time. Our luggage was minimal. Just the clothes we had on, our passports and a few treasures rescued from our trashed houses.

As we rose into the air, I looked out the window at the rocky prominence where the year before Christel, Gwen Carter and I had sat for four days and nights while the floodwaters swirled around us. I saw the trees missionaries had planted around our houses and then we were gone over the desert to Addis Ababa.

For me it was the end of an era. The years of medical work in Somali villages were over. There had been isolation, medical emergencies without a doctor, answered prayers, cherished friendships and times of loneliness. A new life and new work lay ahead. I would be looked after. The heartbreak was for those we were leaving. Most of our Somali friends ended up in refugee camps in Somalia, uprooted from their homes and birthplace. We had done what we could. How we would have loved to be able to do more.

1

FAMILY SECRETS

'You remember that fellow I told you about the other day?' asked my visitor. He was a senior deacon from the local Baptist church and had come to spend time with me in my parents' home. I was on leave from Somalia.

'Yes, I know him,' I replied.

'Well, he was conceived out of wedlock and yet God has used him,' the elderly deacon continued.

I can't remember how I responded. I know I was astounded. I was conceived out of wedlock – so what? Paul said that as part of God's family we have been chosen in Christ before the foundation of the world. The circumstances of our birth, our family background, ongoing experiences and faith story are all individual. Surely the outcome depends on how we respond to the situations that confront us. I was always aware of a Heavenly Father looking out for me.

Years after the above conversation, and after I had permanently returned from Africa, the subject of my conception resurfaced. I was studying counselling as part of my training as a psychologist.

'Beware of family secrets and make sure there are no skeletons in the cupboards. Get rid of them!' said the teacher of one course. He added, 'Secrets are the plaque that blocks the arteries of family communication.' That was a totally new thought to me. My generation was given to secrets. A common mandate for us was: 'This stays within the family.' There were clear boundaries between topics that were for public information, those to be discussed in the family and those that were taboo.

I had known about the circumstances of my birth for over 30 years. My mother's only sister, Jessie, had told me when she was angry over some family matter.

'Did you know your mother was pregnant with you before she married your father?' Jessie said.

I was then in my early 20s. Although the thought had entered my head, I had not allowed it to take root. Now I was thoroughly enlightened. Jessie told me how my mother, who had grown up in Albury, had been teaching in Molong where my father had been born and had always lived. His father had been mayor of the town and a leading businessman. His mother, the Lady Mayoress, was the founder of the local Country Women's Association. She was also an avid gardener and the maker of the wreaths for all the town funerals. Dad, who had left school early, was working as a postal clerk. Some of his siblings were still at the school where my mother taught.

My mother, Isobel (Belle) Simpson Williams, was the longed-for first daughter after four boys, followed by a little sister, Jessie. Her father was prominent in Albury as an alderman and president of the hospital board, as well as being an elder of the Presbyterian Church. He owned a business and could afford a maid to help his wife. Mum was school captain and went to university and teacher training. She was a few years older than Dad. Although there were many common factors between the two families, culturally and in communication styles there were obvious differences. I believe the maternal relatives felt they were on a higher plane. I know my father adored my mother and always appreciated her family, but I am not sure the opposite was true.

The teacher and the postal clerk fell in love, and in December 1933 I was conceived. It was not such a remarkable story, but it had always been a family secret. I continued to guard it for many years. I never told a soul until that counselling lecture in the 1980s. I shrank from telling my parents that I knew. But I thought about what we had learned in the lecture.

The desire to deepen our relationship and enrich communication kept needling me. So one evening I girded the loins of my mind and said to my mother, 'Can we have a chat?'

Her response sounded apprehensive. 'You're not thinking of going back to Africa are you?' she asked as she followed me to the back verandah. 'No, no, no,' I reassured her.

I began, 'I just want to tell you that I know you were pregnant with me before you married Dad. I have often thought about what you must have gone through to have me. I wondered what it must have been like to tell Nanna.'

I thought telling Nanna, my mother's mother, would have been the steepest, most painful peak to climb in the ordeal of premarital pregnancy in the early 1930s. I considered our maternal grandmother to be a proud, authoritative, slightly snobbish matriarch. She invariably dressed in black, and although she must have been in her 50s when I was born, she always seemed old. The single daughter, Jessie, stayed home and cared for both parents. I never saw our grandmother do anything more strenuous than sweep the front verandah and water the potted palm.

Most afternoons she held court in the lounge room. High tea would be served to a few select friends, with Jessie handing around the bone-china cups. Nanna officiated at the teapot. If we as children were visiting we would be called in to make an appearance. We would hear *sotto voce* comments from the guests such as 'What a big girl for her age!' or 'Nothing like her mother' in a disappointed tone before we were banished without a taste of the delicacies on the tray.

'You must have dreaded telling Nanna you were pregnant,' I said to Mum.

'Not at all,' Mum responded. 'She was wonderful! She came down from Albury and told us to meet her in Sydney, where she arranged the wedding. She took complete control.'

I drew a deep breath and then shared the second thought that had been weighing on my mind.

'But Mum, I ruined your life. You had to give up teaching to get married. You must have been so disappointed.'

'Oh Ruth,' she said, 'you were such a beautiful baby. When I wheeled you down the street, people stopped me so they could peep at you in your pram. We were so proud of you.'

My second misconception was shattered. I had felt guilty for years, thinking I had been born at the wrong time, imagining myself as the source of disappointed dreams, a veritable nuisance for my parents. I struggled to keep the tears back as I heard that I was welcomed with open arms and admired by all who saw me.

Then my mother related how Nanna again left Albury and arrived in Trundle, where they were then living, for the birth. I could not envisage the Nanna I knew packing a suitcase, boarding a train and travelling by night alone to the nearest railway station to Trundle to attend her daughter's confinement. But that's what she did. Mum told me I was a difficult breech birth, born in the middle of a terrible storm. Nanna was there, a strengthening presence, taking control and making it all right.

Just as we reached the part about the breech birth my father appeared. Noticing that we were deep in conversation he began to move away. 'Don't go,' I urged. 'Come and sit down,' and I began to tell him what we had been discussing.

'Two of my older brothers got their girlfriends pregnant before they were married and I was so angry with them,' he responded. 'I thought the whole town would be talking about our family. I felt even worse when it was me and my girlfriend.' Then he talked more about the family dynamics. 'Before our Golden Wedding I asked our doctor for some counselling. Because we were going to have a party, I was frightened that when you realised the wedding date you would despise us.'

I repeated to him that I had known for 30 years and my only reaction was to feel sad about what my conception had cost them. As we continued talking, I was welcomed into a heart-piercing depth of sharing with both parents. It was just as I had been told. There was a rich reward for taking the step of courage to open a cupboard door and pull a skeleton out.

The next morning when I saw her, my mother said, 'You will never know what you did for us last night.' She told me that after I left, she and Dad continued to talk long into the night. My dealing with a taboo subject had a ripple effect for my parents. A door opened for them to return in memory to the precious, early days of their love for one another.

That's the beginning of my story. Firstborn of four.

Conceived in Molong: a village of about 2000 people, 300 kilometres west of Sydney, with a railway station, a museum and a wheat silo; the birthplace of my father and the former site of my paternal grandmother's magnificent, tiered rose garden.

Born in Trundle: a village of between 600 and 700 people, 421 kilometres west of Sydney, the centre of a wheat-growing area, famous for one of the widest main streets in the country, planned, I was told, so the bullock drays could turn.

2

OLDEST OF THE PACK

It has been a great joy for me over the last 30 years, working in my post-missionary profession as a psychologist, to sit and listen to people's stories as part of carrying out psychological assessments and debriefings. The old discoloured whiteboard on the wall of my office has been the recipient of a thousand or more histories. A favourite approach of mine was to use a genogram (a family map) to explore how significantly past family dynamics continue to dictate current opinions, behaviour and reactions.

For example, I asked one missionary couple, while debriefing them on their first leave, 'What was the most stressful factor in your first term of service overseas?'

'Being told by our leaders we had to have visitors to our area stay with us,' they both answered without hesitation.

'Why do you think that was so difficult?' I asked.

'Well, neither of us grew up in families where we had people come and stay. We weren't used to sharing bathrooms and the various things that happen in homes.'

I have personally gained much from these discussions. While listening to others' stories, I have experienced many insights into my own reactions, specifically spawned by memories of my family of origin.

A recurring theme for me has been my discomfort in new groups. When relating to people as a newcomer and aware that most of them know each other, I used to be aware of emotional vulnerability and difficulty in entering into the conversation in a natural manner. One day when this was happening the penny dropped. 'Hey!' I said to myself. 'You are acting just the way you used to when you were a newcomer at a new school.'

The coping strategy I then developed was to change my self-talk from 'This is horrible!' to 'I am no longer a school child. I am an adult. I have good communication skills. Leave the childish behaviour behind. Act your age.' Most of the time it works.

Other people's family situations are sometimes similar to mine, sometimes the opposite. No matter what our family background is like, however, it significantly influences how we view the world. Gaining increased self-awareness in this way is vital in the process of changing thinking and growing in maturity.

My father, John Daniel (better known as Jack), was the fifth of nine children. The brother either side of him had serious health problems with the result that parental attention for Jack was scanty. My grandparents' importance in the social hierarchy of Molong kept them busy, and any spare time my grandmother had apart from her two sick boys was spent in her garden and making wreaths for most of the town's funerals. Two older sisters brought up the little ones. Expressions of affection and appreciation between family members were minimal.

My father was an outstanding tennis player, winning championships while still at school. 'No one ever came to watch me play,' he told me one night. With rare insight he continued, 'I think that is why I have this obsession to win at everything I'm involved in. I'm a rotten loser. It even affects my driving. If there is a car in front of me, I can't rest until I've passed it. I hate to stay behind.'

This disclosure helped me understand why my father hungered for reassurance. A deep void within was never satisfied. Even though I know he loved me, he found it difficult to express his fatherly love to me, his firstborn, because he had never experienced such love from his own father. This also shed light on my difficulty in experiencing God as a Father figure and my need to make a positive impression on male leaders and teachers.

Leaving school in his early teens and employed by Australia Post, Jack worked hard and progressed through the ranks: from delivering telegrams to postman, then to serving on the counter, second in charge and finally postmaster. Each promotion involved moving to a different town. Because of this, we did not live long near any of our relatives. Instead we faced constant uprooting, settling into different houses, meeting new people and the discomfort of being confronted with another crowd of strangers in new schools.

Concerns about finance were another regular theme. It was not until our mother returned to teaching that my parents were able to buy their first family car, which happened after I left home.

'Who left these lights on?' Dad would mutter, going from room to room flicking switches. I inherited a similar compulsion. Half a lifetime later, when my friend and colleague Kath was a resident in Nazareth Nursing Home, I used to look in the bedrooms I passed and see lights and air conditioners left on. Knowing that the residents were spending hours in the lounge room, I would creep in and turn them off.

The week before my mother died in 1995, at the age of 86, I was in New Zealand teaching at a missionary orientation course. Late one night the phone rang.

'Is that you, Ruth?' came my mother's voice over the line. 'I wanted to tell you we had the missionary prayer meeting tonight. The people have just gone. Before we had the prayer time I talked to them from Ephesians chapter one.' She shared the main points of her talk. Her voice was excited and happy. 'We had a lovely time!' she said before hanging up.

A few days later she suffered a heart attack after minor surgery and died. But she waited until Kath and I arrived back from New Zealand. 'Here are the girls!' she smiled as we rushed into the intensive care ward. She was gone the next morning.

Those two incidents are typical of Belle Myors. She was an extrovert who enjoyed nothing more than time with family or friends. Although she was a brittle diabetic with several other significant health problems, she characteristically made light of them. Her stoicism in the face of poor health was an example to us all. Above all, she loved teaching.

'You mother instilled in me a love of learning,' one grateful former pupil, now a teacher herself, told me with tears in her eyes. After Mum died former colleagues described her acceptance of problem children being pushed into her class when others found them too difficult.

Being a teacher meant not only teaching other people's children but a tendency to organise all of us. One day when she was giving me some advice I said, 'Mum, I am 60 years old now. I have learned some things.' Her response was, 'I am still your mother. I still know best!' Dad received similar treatment. Often when he sank into a recliner to watch TV after lunch Mum would say, 'Don't you think you should be doing that weeding?' More often than not he would sigh and then go. In spite of it all, he loved her very much. He had seven years as a widower and we could all see the light had gone out of his life.

Two-and-a-half years after I was born, my brother Peter arrived. Perhaps God knew one of my type was enough for any family because Peter is the exact opposite. Where I am a fairly brash extrovert, he is reserved. He is a conformer with a perfectionistic streak. I am slapdash. A graphic example of our differences is to observe our desks. Peter's is immaculate with every paper put neatly away. Mine is buried under a mountain of papers arranged in a manner resembling the aftermath of a tornado. Peter trained as an accountant and worked as the purchasing officer at Newcastle University for 38 years. When he announced his retirement, the university's staff hosted a farewell dinner and the staff choir sung a special song they had composed for him. Peter's meticulous application to his work had made their work so much less stressful. While Peter admitted his work was routine and boring, there was no adventurous streak summoning him to launch out into something more risky.

With sport it was different. Peter was a champion tennis player. He won local championships and was described in one local paper as the best player in a period of fifteen years. He later enjoyed golf, lawn bowls and even tenpin bowling.

While still a teenager Peter met beautiful, blonde Betty Anderson. She was a Novocastrian from a large extended family. Betty stepped outside family tradition by finishing high school, choosing a tertiary education, training as a teacher and marrying an outsider. Fortunately, Peter was accepted into the tribe and learned to appreciate its unique humour and blunt comments. Unfortunately, he never became acclimatised to the family love of camping. I visited them once as they were packing up after a week in a tent. I think it was their last time ever. My brother's facial expression and overall body language spoke of abject misery.

Tragically, Betty lost her father when he was only 49. Her mother was her constant support. Until they went to school, Betty and Peter's two sons, who both grew up to be engineers, were under the care of their beloved 'Ninny'. They both wept as they spoke of their love for her at her funeral.

Because it had always been geographically impossible for us to be close to our uncles, aunties and cousins, it was an education for us to see the relationships in these salt-of-the-earth, mainly mining-related families. In her latter teaching years, Betty worked as a school librarian imparting to generation after generation of primary school children her own love of reading.

My sister Rhonda is six years younger than I am. Married early, she had two sons before being abandoned, not because she wasn't loved but because her husband wasn't coping with his own inadequacies and the responsibilities of a family. This occurred in 1960 just as I was preparing to leave for Africa the first time. In the midst of her grief, Rhonda reached out to the Lord and her life was transformed. God has used her to bless and challenge hundreds of women. She has been a wounded healer, her pain a catalyst to bring comfort to others.

Six years later, with her first marriage annulled, she married Ted Rugendyke and bore two more boys. Together, Ted and Rhonda planted Baptist churches in Cooma and Narromine. Ted, a high school maths teacher, retired after some years as principal of Narromine High. He then spent ten years as a hobby farmer on 100 acres of land bordering the Macquarie River outside Narromine, raising beef cattle, the fulfilment of a lifelong dream. While on the farm he was diagnosed with Alzheimer's, which led to his death eight years later. Rhonda was indefatigable in caring for him, a wonderful example to us all.

Last in the family is Jeff, ten years younger than I am. He is a Baby Boomer. In significant ways he portrayed a different generation from the rest of us. He was Mum's baby, prompting the three older siblings to describe him as over-mothered. After secondary school he trained as a teacher, becoming a Christian at teachers' college. He married Frances and then studied to become a Baptist minister. He and Frances joined a Christian community where everything was shared, even the children, of which Jeff and Frances had three. They moved within the community from ordained ministry to building and then market gardening. Later on Jeff and Frances ran a camp centre with a motel, built a mudbrick house and worked at a series of jobs managing motels. During his time in ministry Jeff trained as a marriage counsellor. It is an understatement to call him multi-skilled. He seems to be good at everything he turns his hand to, and with his counselling background is empathic and caring. In spite of being 'mother's baby' as a child, he grew into a competent and caring man.

After the breakup of her parents' marriage, Frances, with her three siblings, was raised by a childless aunt and uncle. They lived in Walla

Walla, a small town near Albury, characterised by a large number of German-background people. Frances was a gifted singer but turned her back on a musical career to serve with Jeff in ministry and his latter occupations. Their two sons and one daughter have followed them in being hard workers.

Peter took 20 years longer than the rest of us to make a commitment to Christ. We prayed for him all that time. The breakthrough came after he and Betty saw *Jesus Christ Superstar*. When our mother heard his description of the musical, she responded by offering to lend him the book *The Late Great Planet Earth* by Hal Lindsey. Not long after that I received an aerogramme from him.

'As I read that book,' he wrote, 'I realised I was on the losing side and I decided then and there that I didn't want to be there any longer.' He then related the details of this life-changing decision. It is hard to describe what it was like for me, 12,000 kilometres away, living in isolation in the Ogaden Desert, to receive that news.

Soon after reading and weeping with joy over the letter I found myself awake in the middle of the night with a strong urge to pray for Peter. I had no details, just a clear message to pray. When I came home a year later I heard the story.

'Betty and I started going to that church you visited not far from here,' Peter said.

On my last leave I had gone to see the minister of that church to tell him about my brother, who lived nearby, in the hope that he might visit. It was an American missionary church plant, very similar to Australian Baptists in doctrine. The day I went, the minister's father met me at the front door of the manse. 'My son's on holidays,' he explained. 'But I am an ordained minister in our denomination in America and I am filling in for him.' I explained why I'd come and heard later that he and his son faithfully visited.

'So that's the church Betty and I decided to go to,' Peter continued. 'We went to the evening service, and after the sermon the regular minister gave an invitation for anyone who wanted to accept Jesus as Saviour to come out the front. I immediately stood up and went forward. The preacher told me later that he never failed to give an altar call at the evening service and I was the first person who had ever responded!'

The small group of believers became their caring church family. Then a crisis arose after the pastor attended a charismatic convention and returned to his flock, on fire with the teaching he had heard. He excitedly shared what he had learned concerning the baptism of the Spirit. This caused concern to the conservative denominational leaders in Sydney. The result was that the moderator came, dismantled the demountable building that had functioned as their church building, loaded it on a truck and drove off, with pastor, Peter and another good friend watching in horror. The pastor was sent home to America while Peter, his family and the friend, sad and shocked, found another place for regular worship. As I listened to this story, I understood why I had been prompted to pray. I marvelled as I realised afresh that the 12,000 kilometres separating us were immaterial to the Heavenly Father who was closer than breathing to us both.

In spite of the close relationship I enjoyed with my siblings, in many ways I was the odd one out. Firstly, they were all good at sport. I was clumsy and uncoordinated. It was probably due to being forced to change from being left-handed in kindergarten, after losing the sight of my left eye at the age of three.

Peter and Dad were tennis champions. For many years their families managed without them at weekends while they pursued their passion. Rhonda and Jeff were more average but streets ahead of me. Because my father shared so much in their sporting interests, I believed that I was a disappointment, outside the circle of family priorities.

The second difference was that all three married young and raised families while I stayed single. Every time we had a family gathering, even though I experienced their love I was also very aware of the lack of a partner.

Perhaps feeling different made it easier for me to leave home at 17, train as a nurse and eventually travel to and work in Africa. I had heard about missionaries when I was only 12 and always dreamed of joining them. Such decisions are complex. Family background is a significant element in the story.

Figure 2.1 – The 'leader of the pack', Ruth, with Peter, Rhonda and Jeff, 1945.

Figure 2.2 – The 'parents of the pack': Belle and Jack Myors, 1945.

3

SCHOOLDAYS

'Ruth, you were a wretch at school! No one wanted you in their class,' said the woman in the bed as she enjoyed me rubbing her back. She was a patient in the Women's Ward at Albury Base Hospital where I was a second-year trainee. The tables were turned: my fourth-class teacher was now submitting to my care as she recovered from an appendectomy.

I knew she was right. Even now, in my 80s, I think back with sadness on my behaviour at school. While Mrs Hutchinson had been one of my favourite teachers, I was clearly not a favourite pupil. What a contrast it was communicating adult to adult. Her memory of me as a non-compliant class distractor was now challenged by the experience of relating to me as a caring nurse. Roles were exchanged. I accepted the rare opportunity to atone for past delinquency with gratitude.

I realise now that my fragile ego thrived on making other students laugh. I had no interest in learning. Throughout most of high school I watched the clock, waiting impatiently for each 40-minute period to be over. School was boring.

My unhappy relationship with school was spawned when, approaching my fifth birthday, I was enrolled in kindergarten at Drummoyne Public School in Sydney. Nobody at that stage realised that a year before I had lost the sight in my left eye. Although my mother had seen a cat scratch me, a scar on the cornea was only found 12 months later. She and my father had only noticed that I had changed from being a secure and happy child to being miserable and clingy. That much was obvious.

I cried and baulked at going to school. My father was on shift work. Having to take a fractious child to school before he could go to bed made him decidedly irascible.

'I can't go,' I'd cry. 'I want to go to the toilet.'

'Jack, she wants to go to the toilet. There might be something wrong with her,' Mum would say.

'I'll show her what's wrong with her,' Dad would answer and then administer a sharp slap on my bottom. Mum was clearly anxious but could not leave the younger children.

Worse was waiting within the four walls of the kindergarten room. I remember a huge woman in a brown dress, with horn-rimmed glasses and short grey hair. Miss Caldwell seemed obsessed by the need to force me to hold the pencil in my right hand instead of the left.

'You're a naughty girl!' she would exclaim when I used my left hand. 'I told you the pencil goes in the other hand.'

Besides the verbal haranguing I would be sent out of the room for crying. Often when Dad came to pick me up I would be sitting on the floor outside the kindergarten door in disgrace. A pattern was set that lasted for a significant part of my school days. In later years, I progressed from outside the classroom door to the mat in front of the principal's desk. I could write a whole chapter on principals' offices.

So began my formal education. The year after I left kindergarten, an education magazine proclaimed: 'Don't change children from left to right hand! If they naturally pick things up with the left hand, that's how it's meant to be. Leave them alone! Research has shown that forcing a child to change natural laterality can be psychologically disastrous.' My mother, a devoted teacher herself, read the article. 'If only we'd known,' she groaned. It was too late to do anything. They could only watch and wait to see how the psychological disaster developed.

King George VI was forced to use his right hand and ended up with the stammer. That is the basis of the film *The King's Speech*. I certainly did not end up with a stammer. I went the other way, always ready to say something inappropriate that disrupted the smooth running of the class. The tampering with my innate left-handedness, along with my injured left eye, resulted in a lack of coordination for sport and a lack of commitment to learning. In contrast to school examinations, I always scored well in routine IQ tests.

As Dad's career in the Postmaster-General's Department required moves for promotion, I attended eight new schools. I hated being a new girl. My siblings say they didn't mind. I have a theory it is more difficult for the firstborn, who must accept the pioneering role. My strategy for becoming accepted in the new school was to make people laugh. I settled in to each new place by again becoming the class clown.

My secondary education commenced in Albury. My claim to fame there was that my mother had been the girl captain of Albury High. Her name was on the honour roll. Isobel Williams had been a shining light. What a contrast I was! We moved again halfway through my second year and I am sure the teachers were glad to see me go. I arrived at Coffs Harbour the day before the mid-year exams. I didn't pass one subject.

'Are you sure you studied Latin in Albury?' the language teacher asked. I assured her I had as she scratched her head, staring at my score of 3%. For some reason they let me stay in second year despite my disastrous results. The shock and embarrassment had the impetus of an electric shock. With hitherto unknown motivation, I determined to catch up to the class. By the end of the year I passed everything while still managing to spend some time waiting to see the principal because of disruptive talking.

The next year I passed the Intermediate Examination in Coffs Harbour before moving to Newcastle with my parents. I completed Fourth Year at Newcastle Girls' High School, topping the class in French and excelling in creative writing. Little did I dream of the change that loomed.

4

PEGS IN HOLES

The year I turned 16 was 1951. I had just completed my penultimate year of high school and had been anticipating undertaking the Leaving Certificate the next year. But now instead I was sitting in the Central Telephone Exchange in Mayfield, Newcastle, experiencing the darkness of despair.

All around me were telephonists sitting at switchboards busily connecting people to people. Listening through earphones and speaking into microphones attached to their headsets, they endlessly and methodically enabled the people of Newcastle and further afield to talk to one another. There was a low, constant buzz of 'Number please' and other routine, prescribed messages. It was a scene of competence and order.

My father had returned home one day from his work at Belmont Post Office with a devastating message. 'I have made an appointment for you to do an examination to become a telephonist,' he said. By then I was at last enjoying school. I had begun applying myself to my studies and was achieving well in French and English.

'I'm not doing that,' I exploded.

'You need to start earning a living and paying board,' Dad responded. In his family, formal education was viewed as a low priority. As the fifth of nine children he had left school very early. Having worked hard and gained regular promotions, he could see no reason why his eldest child should not follow the same pattern. Remaining at school instead of earning a wage and helping the family finances was pointless. Arguments and tears achieved nothing; the decision had been made.

The day for the post office entrance examination arrived. My friends were at school studying for the Leaving Certificate while I was given a spelling and mental arithmetic test. I passed with flying colours. Why didn't I purposely fail? I would have been rejected for a job. At the time that way of escape didn't dawn on me.

Before I could become part of the system, three weeks' training at the main telephone exchange was required. I remembered a recent IQ test at school. The careers' advisor had told me I could successfully pursue the profession of my choice. What was I doing learning to be a telephonist? The training involved being seated at a switchboard with a supervisor showing me what to do. I faced a board covered with shutters and sockets. The shutters constantly rattled down to reveal a number. Numbers were connected to other numbers by cords attached to metal pegs inserted into holes. Success enabled two humans to talk to one another over the miles. The genius of Alexander Graham Bell! I enjoyed taking advantage of Bell's brilliance, but I didn't want to be a cog in the system.

Verbal communication is a passion of mine. I enjoy being original and creative in what I say. I love helping others to do it better, but here I was locked into a job that required me to recite the following patter.

'Number please.'

'I am sorry, that number is engaged. Please try again later.'

'I am sorry, that number, Belmont 144, is out of order.'

'Please insert two pennies in the slot and press button A.'

Worse was to come. I chose to work at the Belmont exchange, close to home. Belmont was also the office where my father worked. I knew the staff. I had worked as a telegram girl in the school Christmas holidays.

The girls in the exchange welcomed me. They were competent at their job and seemed quite happy. How does anyone enjoy, hour after hour, constantly pushing pegs into holes? All I knew was that I was a square peg being told to fit into a round hole. The year was a disaster. While the others efficiently kept their boards in perfect order, mine exhibited endless chaos.

'How are you going?' the friendly, red-haired postman would ask me when he poked his head in the door at lunchtime. I did not need to answer. Alone while my co-worker was out having lunch, chaos reigned. My rescuer would take one look at the knotted cords, rattling shutters and my face and quickly sit down in the vacant seat.

'Here, let me give you a hand.'

With alacrity he would restore order and keep me company until my partner returned. Without training he could do better than me just by watching the others in his spare time. That was the pattern for the entire 12 months. Everyone was kind and helped me. They could not understand why I found it so difficult, but they were accepting of my inefficiency. The bosses saw it differently. If I had not left when the year was over, I would have been dismissed.

I gladly shook the post office dust off my feet and applied to do general nursing training at the Albury Base Hospital. I was 17 years old and had gradually warmed to the idea of caring for people as a nurse. Having attended so many different schools and knowing my parents were soon moving from Newcastle to Lismore, I sought some stability by spending four years in Albury. It had been the scene of my primary schooling and early high school years. Many of my maternal relatives lived in the area, including my grandparents.

5

ALBURY BASE HOSPITAL

After six weeks in Preliminary Training School I was appointed to work in the Women's Ward.

'Nurses! 5.30 am!' The loud cheery voice of the night sister shattered the silence and interrupted the dreams of dozens of student nurses. I was facing my first early morning shift. Outside, crackling on the grass and glittering in the moonlight, was the first frost of the year. The air was clear and bitterly cold.

Our beds were in line, military style, along a screened-in verandah. The first challenge of the day was to throw back the blankets, step onto the cement floor and leap through the door beside the bed into the room occupied by a roommate. Accommodation in the Nurses' Home at Albury Base Hospital in the early 1950s involved rooms allocated to two, with one sleeping in the verandah and one in the room.

The second challenge was climbing out of warm pyjamas, in an unheated room, into a starched, short-sleeved uniform. Lisle stockings left a naked space between stocking top and suspender belt. The crowning glory was a starched white cap skewered with bobby pins, and most importantly, a red cape pulled around the shoulders and across the chest.

The third challenge was opening the door of the Nurses' Home and plunging into pre-dawn darkness for the 100-yard walk to the hospital. With our breath rising in visible puffs, chattering teeth and involuntary groans, we presented for duty sharp at six o'clock.

The first task was bed baths for the bedridden. Each first-year nurse was given a list of patients to fully sponge. In those days there were no nursing homes for the chronically ill aged. Iron beds stood in an orderly line on the three-sided, louvred verandah. Each one was occupied by an aged, fragile woman who had nowhere else to go. Some of them were there when I began as a nervous 17-year-old and still there when I left four years later. These were our victims on those cold winter mornings.

'Nurse, I won't have a wash this morning, thank you.'

'But you're on my list.'

'It's so cold. Start with someone else.'

'No. You're first.'

Queen of the long-term patients was Miss Edie Lloyd. Joints crippled by rheumatoid arthritis, propped high on her pillows, demanding and imperious, she terrorised the inexperienced. Edie's name on the list of baths assigned to me caused a certain amount of gut wrenching in the early days. Friends who had graduated from looking after her shared helpful hints, but most of us were traumatised by her acerbic tongue.

In retrospect, when I remember those patients, I feel sad. I don't remember quality of life being a factor in our lectures. The outstanding goal was to get the jobs done. Bathing, feeding, panning, dusting and back rubs were all attended to. There was little time for quality communication. Most of those women never had a visitor. It's no wonder people like Miss Lloyd fussed about tiny details.

Post-meal panning for the ward was a cross between comedy and nightmare. Once the dirty dishes were sent back to the kitchen, every bedridden patient was provided with a stainless steel bedpan, toilet paper and pan cover. Most had to be lifted on and off. After a reasonable interval the pans were collected. Becoming accustomed to using the paper for those who couldn't manage was all part of the steep learning curve.

Transforming the collection of the full vessels from an unpleasant chore to an exciting challenge was for me a coping strategy. I made it a goal to be able to carry five full pans piled on top of one another. With my head well back I would make a successful journey into the pan room and the sluice that received all the contents. Every pan had to be washed and scrubbed with a brush by hand. This was all part of a first-year trainee nurse's day in the 1950s. Leaving the sluice and the pans shining gave one an amazing sense of achievement.

Our matron was a former army nurse, a colonel: Charlotte McCallister OBE. She was probably in her 60s. On ward rounds she walked with a military stature; her arms swung slightly out from her sides with fists clenched. Her veil seemed to have as many wings as the Sydney Opera House and swung behind her in starched splendour. Her red cape enhanced the stark whiteness of her veil and uniform. The ward staff always knew when she was coming. Every bedspread was pulled tight up to the patient's chin, with the corners at the foot of the bed neatly mitred. The only sounds were Matron's firm tread and her murmured comments to the sister in charge. The moment she departed the clattering and hubbub resumed.

Each Saturday afternoon during the winter months, Matron McCallister would allocate four trainees to accompany her and a board member to the football (Aussie Rules). The sportsground was on the opposite corner to the hospital. Matron and the board member would lead the procession. Crimson with embarrassment, the trainees would follow through the rows of onlookers, each armed with a wooden collection box to shake and poke at people. Totally unawed by our matron's splendour and ready to joke and tease us, the football crowd dropped their coins into our boxes with cryptic comments or invitations to go to the pictures. 'I might as well be in the Salvation Army,' I used to mutter to myself. It was useless to try to avoid going. Like a bloodhound, Matron ferreted out slackers and announced the dreaded 'Be ready for the football at 2.00 pm, nurse.'

Because I had been so inept as a telephonist, I approached the mandatory three months in the operating theatre with trepidation. I was sure that slapping the appropriate instrument into the surgeon's hand at the right time required the dexterity level of a switchboard. Here I would be another square peg in a round hole. I would be useless.

The dreaded day arrived. The sister in charge in the theatre was tall, slim and clinical, and managed the theatre with terrifying efficiency. She treated me with icy disdain. Together we mentally counted the days until we could say goodbye to each other.

During one operation, when handing the surgeon a pair of scissors, my thumb became lodged in the scissor handle hole. With an irritable expletive he yanked the instrument off the offending digit.

'You nearly broke nurse's thumb,' the sister murmured. For one strange moment she seemed to care about me.

'It's her own fault!' was the answer. 'She shouldn't be so clumsy.' And here was a man I had always enjoyed doing rounds with in the wards.

The operating theatre was definitely not my scene. When I finished the three months, I called my friends together and we had a party.

Many of the patients and ward workers at Albury Base Hospital had arrived as migrants from Eastern Europe and spent time in Bonegilla migrant camp. Highly professional people had fled communism and were making a new life for themselves. We were enriched by our relationship with them.

I remember a wiry older man, with a shock of white hair, who was responsible for using a large wooden barrow to take soiled linen to the boiler room attached to the laundry. Although it was heavy work, he used to almost run with that lumbering machine. He rarely spoke, but still I would hear our wardsman say, 'These bloody new Australians! If it's good enough for them to live here why isn't our language good enough for them?' I knew this particular man had been a professor in a university. I grieved for him as he handled foul-smelling sheets, remembering what he had come from.

For the first time I was relating to people who spoke languages other than English. Fascinated, I was soon picking up greetings and key words needed in the doctors' rounds. Sometimes I was called to interpret and loved it. Once a joker taught me an inappropriate phrase, which I innocently used in the presence of the doctor, causing the patient being questioned to almost burst his stitches as he shot up in bed, exploding, 'Never say that again!'

And so I progressed through the required stages until by the end of four years I could run a ward on evening or night duty, perform all the other necessary duties and pass the final examination.

Coming from a long family history of Presbyterianism, through those years I regularly attended church and Presbyterian Fellowship. I had had Christian friends at Newcastle Girls' High and had learned from them, but I had no one like them in Albury. I was keen to learn, but in those years many of the Presbyterian churches were liberal and lifeless. There was no clear presentation of the gospel, and people like me who were hungering for the truth felt starved.

When visiting an aunt in Melbourne at the age of 12, I had heard a foreign missionary speak about his work. Ever since then I had had a dream of following in his steps. With that in mind, and with my General Nursing Certificate in my bag, I applied to study midwifery at Sydney's King George V Memorial Hospital for Mothers and Babies (KGV) in Camperdown.

6

A CLOSER WALK WITH GOD

'Mum!' I wailed over the phone. 'I can't stay here. I hate it. I'm going to leave.'

'Try a bit longer,' she answered. 'Don't give up yet. You'll settle down.'

There I was in Sydney, with the family living in Lismore. Dad was in the post office, Mum was teaching at the high school, and Rhonda and Jeff were still at school. Peter had left school and was training as an accountant while working in the bank. A week before this conversation I had begun midwifery training. It was mid-1952.

'Why did I decide to come here?' I continued to my poor mother. 'Do you know there are more than a thousand people living in the Nurses' Home? Every time I turn around I get lost.'

She continued to listen and encourage but eventually hung up, leaving me to try to find my way back to my room in that huge rabbit warren. The public phones were in the foyer on the ground floor while my room was several flights of stairs away.

What a transition for a country girl! I had just finished at Albury Base Hospital with 80 trainees. Now I was plunged into the culture of the Royal Prince Alfred (RPA) and KGV community, not knowing one person.

An initial test was the uniform, which consisted of a blue dress with a separate white starched collar. We were supplied with two studs, one to connect the back of the collar to the dress and the other designed to bring together the two front neck edges with the two front edges of the collar. I managed the back but the front was way beyond my limited dexterity. When the whole combination was a crushed, mangled mess, I surrendered and used a gold safety pin to pull the four edges together, discarding the stud.

The Tutor Sister assigned to welcome the new pupil midwives was a stiff, typical RPA veteran who regarded people from other hospitals as a lower species of animal. She had eyes like an eagle.

Immediately focussing on my neck arrangement, she put her thumb under the pin. As she pulled it forward, I heard her mutter, 'Disgusting!'

What an introduction to my fellow students! I don't remember how the problem was solved. Perhaps one of the others gave me some advice. The collar does not feature in subsequent memories, but the sense of being alone continued for a few more weeks.

From time to time I noticed a group of nurses from both KGV and RPA who didn't wear make-up, often sat together at meal times and bowed their heads before eating. I asked one of the more lively girls in my group who they were.

'We call them the pale-faces,' she said. 'And when they get together we say the pale-faces are having a powwow.'

When I started work with some of the pale-faces, I found they were committed Christians who as a group avoided lipstick. This was 1956 when bright shades of lipstick were popular. These nurses, affiliated with the Australian Nurses Christian Movement, had decided that it was more in line with Christian belief not to paint the lips red. Longing for a deeper knowledge of God, I was immediately interested to become better acquainted with these people who were obviously serious about their faith.

'Would you like to come out tonight?' a pale-face, Elaine, asked me one Saturday. Her invitation was to a Christian youth meeting called 'This Is Your Life' in the Assembly Hall near Wynyard Station. I jumped at the opportunity to go, not realising that I was headed for a life-changing event.

The hall was spacious and crowded with young people. They sang Christian songs with joy and vigour. Just being part of the crowd was an exhilarating experience. Then the Reverend Geoffrey Bingham, an Anglican minister from the Garrison Church at Millers Point, just down the road, rose to speak.

'My wife Laurel and I are about to move to Pakistan with our five children,' he said by way of introduction. Then he began to talk from John 7:38, where Jesus said, 'Whoever believes in me … rivers of living water will flow from within them.'

I sat there in that auditorium challenged and moved. The depth and implication of the message reached places in my heart that had yet to be enlightened.

Then Geoff Bingham invited people who realised they needed to make a commitment to come to the front.

'If I go out there these people I've come with will think I'm a heathen,' I reasoned silently. 'I've always been a churchgoer. I've even thought of being a missionary. There's no way I'm going to expose myself like that. Besides, it's not a Presbyterian thing to do.'

Evangelical witness was not new to me. There had been a very special time during the year I had spent at Newcastle Girls' High when my close friends had been fellow-students Jan and Val Foster (twins) and Annette Sutherland. They, as committed Christians, had helped me in my Christian experience. Sadly, during the four years in Albury, attending a liberal church, I had become stunted in my growth and needed to take a new step of faith. However, to stand up and walk down the front of that great hall in front of the people I had come with was too hard.

So I stayed in my seat, and when the meeting was over returned to the Nurses' Home with the others. I avoided the chatter on the train, my mind spinning with what I had heard.

Back in my lonely room, I fell on my knees beside the bed. 'Lord, forgive me,' I prayed. 'I didn't fully understand. Please help me to live for you and experience those rivers of living water coming from my life.'

When I stood up, the world had changed. I felt freer than I ever had before. A miserable situation had been transformed. Forever after I loved midwifery.

The Christian nurses were wonderful mentors. From them I learned to have regular Bible reading and prayer. I faithfully attended their meetings and listened to a variety of speakers. Sixty years later some of them are still friends. The church I attended was St Barnabas, Broadway, where Howard Guinness was the minister. The preaching was first class.

'I must go home and tell my family what has happened,' I announced one night to Margaret Graham (later Gordon), a special friend and prayer partner. 'I need to tell them face to face.'

I was not due for time off. The best I could do was travel all night on the train to Lismore on Christmas Eve and all the way back to Sydney Christmas night. During the journey I decided how to tell my news. My plan was to reverently thank the Lord for the Christmas dinner. I was sure that was a suitable first step. So when the meal was ready and served and the six of us were seated around the table, I announced, 'I am going to say grace!' They looked surprised but bowed their heads obediently. This was my cue. But I blew it. I had a slip of the tongue. 'For what we are about to relieve,' I prayed in reverent tones, and everyone including me burst out laughing. Here we were sitting in front of plates loaded with food and a table groaning with extra Christmas specials. Was this a Freudian slip? It was a family joke for years. My younger brother, Jeff, loved teasing me by saying, 'For what we are about to palliate.'

That night I returned to Sydney with the sum total of my witness to what had happened to me being my botched grace. My family all eventually came to the Lord, but I am not sure my initial effort to testify had anything to do with it.

I look back on my time at KGV as a wonderful year. As it came to an end, after five long years of separation, I looked forward to returning home to the family. Unbidden, a rogue thought insisted on intruding: 'Don't you think you should go back to Albury and tell them at the church and fellowship what has happened to you?'

'No, I don't! I have been away from the family long enough.'

But the conviction that God was telling me to work in Albury for a few months would not go away. My new experience with the Lord needed to be shared with my friends and fellow worshippers at Albury Presbyterian Church.

It was painful to write to my mother, who like me had been eagerly anticipating my spending some time at home. But true to the wonderful person she was, she reacted with understanding and encouragement. 'Of course you must go back to Albury if that is where God is calling you,' she wrote.

With my shiny new midwifery certificate in my possession I took my place in the maternity ward at Albury Base Hospital. Although a graduate, I was inexperienced. The older midwives raised their eyebrows at times as my greenness became evident. They persevered and continued my education. If they breathed a sigh of relief when I left after six months they did not show it.

As soon as possible after my arrival I made an appointment to see the Presbyterian minister. His name was Reverend Norwood and he had come to the church while I had been away.

'That is wonderful,' he said when he heard my story. 'I want you to tell the whole church what you have just told me.' He immediately made a date for me to have the sermon time on a Sunday night. What an opportunity! The minister's daughter made a commitment for Christ. Many people told me how moved they were. I knew without a doubt that the Lord had opened a door of witness for me. What if I had ignored the prompting of the Holy Spirit to return to Albury?

During the six months I stayed I was mentored by a servant of God, Miss Nell McDonald (Miss Mack), who taught me so much and challenged me with her deep love for him. She was renting a dress shop which was part of the property owned by my grandparents and inherited by my Auntie Jessie. Miss Mack was also instrumental in the life of Dick McLellan, who was by then working with the Sudan Interior Mission (SIM) in Ethiopia. Auntie Jessie came to the Lord eventually as well. How high above ours are the ways of the Lord (Isaiah 55:9).

My plans to go and work in Lismore were thwarted again after the six months in Albury. I heard from Miss Mack that prospective missionaries were expected to spend time in Bible college. So there and then, even though the term had already commenced, I applied to the Sydney Missionary and Bible College (SMBC) and was accepted. Once more an unsuspecting institution was to be disrupted by a well-meaning but ill-prepared, extroverted non-conformer.

7

SYDNEY MISSIONARY AND
BIBLE COLLEGE

'You women are training for the mission field,' the old lady at the head of the table declared. 'You must be able to control yourselves. If something like this happened in Africa you could end up being eaten by cannibals.'

The speaker was Mrs Lawlor. She was over 80 years old, long since retired, but called back to fill in as dean of women at SMBC, Badminton Road, Croydon, while a new dean was being appointed.

The dire prediction so solemnly pronounced was in response to me not only laughing inappropriately but also causing others to do so. It was during the evening meal, a formal occasion. Around 40 female students shared three immaculately set tables. A senior person sat at the head of each. On this particular evening I was at Mrs Lawlor's table. The mealtime etiquette was Victorian.

As we commenced eating, three students entered through a side door in going-out clothes. They approached Mrs Lawlor and one by one seemed to bob a semi-curtsey and asked permission to attend a pre-arranged prayer meeting. Mrs Lawlor responded to the obeisance with a nod of her head and granted her permission. The drama of these 20-something-year-old women asking leave so humbly was too much for me.

This lack of self-control was deeply distressing to our dean. That comment about the cannibals made stemming the giggles impossible.

'Oh I wish you had known Mary Bradford,' the old lady continued. 'She was like an angel. She was senior student here when I was the dean. She never raised her voice. She was always self-controlled. Mary Bradford was an example to everyone of how a Christian woman should behave.'

Some people wondered what had hit them when I arrived four

weeks late. I battled with a similar reaction as I sought to adapt to the culture of the institution. My jokes were deemed inappropriate. After telling one, which I thought really funny and quite clean, I was told that if I continued along those lines I would be asked to leave.

On top of that, we were assigned detailed housekeeping chores. Having been away from home and living in nurses' homes for over five years, I was disastrous at housework. One memorable day Mrs Lawlor's successor, Miss Jean Foote, inspected the bedrooms. She found numerous balls of fluff under my bed. Her response was a cryptic note. I couldn't see why it was such a big deal. The bedspread reached the ground. No one could see the fluff without kneeling on the floor and looking under.

To my way of thinking the rules were archaic. We had to wear closed-in shoes and stockings every day, even on Saturdays. Dresses had to have sleeves halfway to the elbow on all occasions, even when gardening. Hats had to be worn to all public meetings. The limit of time in the shower was seven minutes. All lights had to be turned off at 9.00 pm. We were not allowed to talk to male students. The lecture hall was set up as gender apartheid.

At the table, we were not allowed to pass anything across. It had to be passed right around. People who used sugar in hot beverages were only allowed one-and-a-half stirs. Bread could only be buttered and have jam applied in bite-size pieces. When I protested, asking the reason for such rules, I was told that Miss Foote had worked in Egypt with some elegant English lady missionaries and had decided it was important to know the right way to do things. When I later came home on leave from Somalia I resisted the urge to tell her that I never met any finicky English ladies in Somalia. Instead I was surrounded by North Americans who stabbed their meat, cut the whole lot up and then ate it with a fork. At breakfast they plastered their bread roll completely with butter and jam, then held it aloft while eating alternating bites with their eggs.

I had been running my life for the last six years. I had graduated with two nursing certificates and had been in charge of wards on evening and night duty. Now I was being told not only to eat everything on my plate, which was no trouble, but to stay at the table and wait while all the picky eaters had to painstakingly eat their pumpkin! I used to feel like saying, 'Hand it over to me. I'll eat it for you.'

On one occasion I was asked to speak at a Christian Nurses Fellowship rally. I approached Miss Foote and begged not to have to wear a hat.

'These are not old women in the audience. They are young nurses. There will not be another person wearing a hat in the hall,' I said.

'Well, you will be wearing one,' she responded.

'But they'll roll in the aisles when I walk in.'

'Let them roll. The rule is "hats at meetings".'

None of my pleading or arguing changed her mind one iota. My one and only summer hat was hot pink satin with a rosette over one ear. It was an astonishing piece of apparel to wear at a youth meeting. I compensated by acting out the above conversation as part of my talk and having the audience in fits of laughter.

Thirty years later I had the privilege of lecturing at the college in pastoral care. I watched the girls sitting with the boys in lectures and in the dining room, often dressed in jeans or even shorts with sandals on their feet. Instead of the mandatory eating of 'everything on your plate', they served themselves from a buffet and ate what they wanted. The lights in the library were still on at midnight.

In spite of my grumbles concerning the rules, my time as a Bible college student was an appropriate preparation for what lay ahead of me. In a variety of situations in Africa I was thankful that I was used to eating whatever was put in front of me, even though I learned that at home. At college I saw the discomfort experienced by picky eaters. Even the drama with the hat had value. In Somalia, whenever in public, we women wore head scarves since adult women did not show their hair. I didn't like it because chiffon or nylon scarves caused perspiration to run down into my eyes, but I had learned to obey.

Best of all, I learned my way around the Bible. I sat under godly and competent lecturers headed by our principal, Reverend J.T.H. Kerr, who was a wonderful teacher. I will never forget him. Fellow students became lifelong friends.

One outstanding experience during those years was the 1958 Billy Graham Evangelistic Crusade. In response to a relatively simple gospel message presented in the power of the Holy Spirit given by the gifted evangelist, hundreds of hearts were turned to the Lord every night. A team from the college trained as counsellors. Each meeting I counselled people who had responded to the appeal. The memory of the crusade reignites for me the wonder and awe I felt at the time.

8

EFFIE VARLEY

Every Thursday morning at the college we listened to a missionary guest speaker. It was one of my favourite hours of the week. On one occasion the guest's posture vividly demonstrated impatience as she waited for Mr Kerr to introduce her. She had a message to impart and no time for niceties. Her program for the day was packed and her body language communicated her desire to get on with the business at hand.

Her name was Effie Varley. She was 58 and home on leave from Nigeria. She was wiry and worn. Her dress was faded and her shoes were for running. Everything about her spoke of 'no frills'.

It was 3 March 1958. My friend Jan Frisken (now Collins) and I were always interested to see if lady missionaries, home on leave after four years or more in a developing country, had caught up with the current fashions. I nudged Jan and raised an eyebrow. Here was someone not at all interested in modish dress. She strode onto the dais carrying a string bag holding some apples and a squashed hat. We heard later that if she faced an audience with women wearing hats she donned hers. The apples were probably for sustenance between meetings because she rarely stayed long enough to eat a meal or even a snack after a meeting.

Reactions to Effie's appearance were swept away by the impact of her message. She told of how, as a pharmacist, she had travelled in 1923 to Miango in Nigeria to work among the Iregwe people. We, who were struggling to learn the Greek alphabet, heard how she had her regular devotions from her Greek New Testament. In her ministry she broke down barriers by learning the local language and treating the sick in her bush dispensary. Then she branched out into the surrounding countryside. She was famous for trekking 20 to 30 miles a day, knitting. Her goal was to teach those who were interested, encourage the lonely, alleviate the sufferings of the ill and help local churches.

As she concluded her address she spoke of the need in Africa for more workers. She looked at us, students in a missionary training college, with a steady gaze. She read from John 10:16, 'And other sheep I have, which are not of this fold: them also I must bring, and they shall hear my voice; and there shall be one fold, and one shepherd' (KJV).

'Friends,' she said, 'Jesus Christ is the one true missionary. Unless he brings the sheep into the fold, none will come.' Slamming the Bible down she thundered, 'And we don't want you unless you can't stay away!'

Effie made such a stir we hardly noticed a second person slip in behind her like a shadow and sit down on an empty seat at the side of the hall. We found out later, when she was given a few minutes to share her testimony, that she was Joy Newcombe and was preparing to work as a nurse in Somalia.

In those days a fledgling missionary was often sent to meetings with a veteran who was home on leave. This meant exposure to audiences who were interested in supporting and praying for missionaries. Being attached to a dynamo like Effie was a daunting experience. She demanded the mission administration organise at least seven meetings daily for her to address. Those responsible for her program on leave began to dread her time at home. Failure to arrange enough meetings aroused Effie's ire. For Joy it was like trailing behind a whirlwind. She appreciated meeting the interested people Effie addressed, but she soon found the pace exhausting. She decided that even though she was still in her 20s she lacked the vigour of this weather-beaten, intense warrior in her late 50s. Effie carefully metered out the time Joy was allowed to speak.

That Thursday, which began as an ordinary day of lectures in the Bible college routine, is indelibly imprinted on my memory. The challenge of Effie's message went straight to my heart, while hearing about Somalia from Joy turned on a green light that never changed colour. When I met her, I had no idea that this auburn-haired, softly spoken person, overshadowed by the dynamism of Effie Varley, would become my valued co-worker and a close friend for well over 50 years.

Through the impact of Effie's message and hearing about Somalia from Joy, the path ahead became clear. Two years later, as I settled down to learn the language in Somalia, East Africa, I wrote to tell Effie, now back in West Africa, what her message had meant to me.

'Thank you for writing and telling me,' she wrote back after some time, wishing me well in my work. Before the letter reached me I had heard by radio that she had died in hospital after a heart attack, propped up on pillows as she encouraged an aged African pastor. She had passed away with him holding her hand.

9

COUNCIL INTERVIEWS

Some weeks after I heard Joy and Effie speak, I wrote to the secretary of SIM asking for application papers to join the mission. The process moved slowly. Through each tedious requirement, including filling in reams of questionnaires, medicals, asking people for references and raising support, I became increasingly convinced that the desire to work with this particular mission in Somalia was from God. The last hurdle to jump was to be interviewed by the state council.

'You may come in now, Ruth,' said a man in a suit, welcoming me into a room holding about ten other men resplendent in business attire, with a sole woman acting as scribe. The venue was an office in the middle of Sydney owned by the honorary mission accountant and a member of the board.

It was a February evening in 1960. The members of the New South Wales council of SIM were all city men. I was the target for these strangers to aim their questions at. Armed with that information, they would make a decision about my life.

I had come from Lismore to Sydney on an all-night train. My outfit bordered on glorious. An apricot cloche with exactly matching apricot gloves set off a brand new autumn-toned floral dress. Shiny, tan high-heeled shoes with a handbag to match were the finishing touches.

I was ready for the inquisition. I had been told by previous candidates that I would be asked if I had read the Bible from cover to cover. My answer would be a resounding 'Yes'. I had done it in preparation. But I wasn't asked.

'Can you tell us why you believe God is calling you to Somalia?' asked the chairman, Mr R.H. Gordon. For the next ten minutes I held the floor. After a few less comprehensive questions and a prayer, I was thanked for coming and told I could go.

'I have never interviewed another candidate with so many Bible verses,' I heard Mr Gordon say while I was still within earshot. His tone of voice conveyed approval. With this comment ringing in my ears I returned to Lismore, glad it was over. Soon afterwards I heard that I had been accepted and could make plans to sail to Somalia.

Twenty-five years later, permanently settled back in Australia, I was invited to become a member of that same council. Times had changed and there were nearly as many women as men on the council, instead of a token woman as secretary. The men who had interviewed me were all either retired or dead.

It was my turn to take part in firing the questions. There was scant similarity to the night I was interviewed. The candidates were Baby Boomers instead of my generation (people born before World War 2). Now there were no hats, gloves or high heels for the women or suits for the male candidates.

At my first meeting the first couple of interviewees ambled in casually dressed in faded jeans, bulky sweaters and joggers, with the wife carrying a baby. They sat down. The questions, however, had not changed.

'Can you tell us why you believe God is directing you to Africa?' asked the chairman.

'You go first,' suggested the husband, nudging his wife.

That was fine. She had just commenced explaining why they believed it was right for them to go when the baby started to wriggle and grumble. Without missing a word, and with only a slight adjustment of the sweater, the baby was put in contact with the breast and the meeting continued accompanied by sucking and swallowing sounds from a contented child.

The childless chairman's Adam's apple went up and down a couple of times as he swallowed nervously. Others maintained fixed expressions as though nothing unusual was happening. I had been in Africa for many years and I was well accustomed to public suckling. For many in that gathering, however, it was a new experience and composure was maintained with admirable control.

The couple were accepted without a long list of Bible verses. I had a lot to learn. The new breed of candidates were more highly professional and demanded more say in their postings. They were definitely not the 'Yes sir!', salute-the-leader generation.

Conventional missions like SIM had to accept that a new day had dawned. Gone were the pioneer couples who worked for years in isolated settings, often only leaving their work for furlough and an annual holiday. The Baby Boomers had arrived. Born between 1946 and 1964, they had developed in a world with free university education and multiple protests. Women's liberation was an issue, along with civil rights, anti-discrimination and the environment.

During my years in Somalia many of these developments had passed me by. At one stage I wrote to our director because I needed to order some new bras from the United States.

'Why don't you join the women's libbers?' he jokingly responded. 'They burn their bras.'

Momentarily I considered it and then remembered the bumpy roads we constantly travelled and rejected the thought.

We now had to learn that, for the Baby Boomers, and even more for the Generation X-ers who followed them, commitment to an organisation was much less important than seeing their profession and experience used in the best way possible. My generation and those before me submitted to their children being sent to boarding school at the age of six years even though it broke their hearts, and many regretted the outcome. The Baby Boomers bravely said, 'No, we will decide how our children will be educated.' For many this has meant early departure when children reached the latter years of secondary education. The day of long missionary careers has almost disappeared.

10

LEAVING HOME

My departure day, 15 November 1960, was at hand. I was 26 years old. I stood on the deck of the P&O boat *Orsova* almost incoherent with excitement. Here I was, ready to leave Australia for the first time. I was at the doorway to an adventure I had dreamed of for so long.

The fear of the unknown was diminished because I was not going alone. My travel companions, Dick and Vida McLellan, were returning to Africa after home leave. They had already worked in Ethiopia for five years. Because Dick and I had both grown up in Albury, I felt I was not completely cutting ties with home. The icing on the cake was having the three McLellan children, John (four years old), Jane (two) and Miriam (eight months), to become acquainted with.

Before the ship sailed, the family and friends who had gathered to say goodbye formed a circle around us on the deck. A time-honoured custom in farewelling missionaries then was for someone to pray for the travellers, followed by everyone singing 'God be with you till we meet again'. This was the cue for the weepers to weep. My euphoric state of mind was somewhat dinted when I saw big strong Dick in tears as he kissed his mother. I kept on smiling as I hugged my loved ones and watched the boat pull out from the wharf and the streamers break.

I remember my demeanour with amazement now. I was naïve and ignorant of what lay ahead. I could not envisage what four years in a foreign land involved. My inner child was excitedly facing an adventure. Today I fight tears even when I see strangers saying goodbye in a film or at the airport. I hate goodbyes. There have been so many in the last 50 years and they grow progressively more painful. When I left my mother that first time, she was characteristically brave and I did not even try to enter into her pain. I was taken up with what I wanted to do and oblivious to the feelings of others. But before I reached my destination I came down to earth with a thud.

The days on the boat were marred only by slight seasickness when sailing around the Bight, and a feisty cabin-mate who complained about my flowers. 'Take them out!' she shouted. 'You can't have them in the cabin. They're giving me a headache.' The blooms, given by my friends as a farewell gift, spent the journey outside the cabin door.

I love sea journeys. I love the meals, the happy people in holiday mood, the rocking to sleep at night, the gazing out to the far horizon, the foaming wake coming behind, the sitting on deck reading: they are all among my favourite things. A godly Salvation Army officer who led us in a Bible study every day added to the richness of the whole experience.

Reality hit when we reached Aden in Yemen. An American missionary, Jack Maxson, met us with a broad smile of welcome. He graciously handled the hordes of coolies, who terrified me when they dived on our luggage. What would we have done without Jack, whose smile never faded and whose knowledge of Arabic brought a modicum of order?

Leaving the luxury of the *Orsova*, with its Western dining and entertainment, to drive through the streets of Aden left me speechless. Flat-roofed buildings, markets and dwellings were sandwiched between the harbour, with it fishing boats, tugs and the occasional liner, and a ghostly stone mountain range that acted as the city's backdrop. I smelled the aroma of Eastern spices and heard not only the honking of a thousand horns but also the loud, compelling prayer calls from a multitude of minarets.

Turbaned Arab men with wraparound skirts instead of trousers and burqa-shrouded women with little children hanging on to their skirts filled the streets. The seething mass of people indelibly impressed on me the enormity of the task to take the gospel to a lost world. The mission headquarters, a gloomy, square, plain two-storey building, did nothing to alleviate the strangeness I was feeling.

Another shock was finding that my accommodation was in the apartment of the esteemed Mary Bradford. Her surname was now Pascoe. She and her husband Reg were the parents of three little girls.

'Mary Bradford!' I exclaimed. 'Not *the* Mary Bradford, Mrs Lawlor's white-haired girl?' As I told her the story of my misbehaviour at the Bible college dining room table, she just smiled. She was as lovely as Mrs Lawlor described.

She put me in a little sitting room with Reg while she made lunch. Reg was reading the paper, and apart from a grunt to acknowledge our introduction he never spoke another word. The only sound was the rustle of newsprint. He, a former Queensland farmer, could not or did not try to have any conversation with a gobsmacked newcomer. Yet I was told by someone who knew that Reg was a valued member of their team, fluent in Arabic and disarming to the locals. Years later, after the Pascoes moved to Somalia, we became good friends. I realised that his shyness with a strange young woman was the inhibiting factor and not disinterest.

As my first day in Aden began to wane, Mary informed me apologetically, 'Our only spare bed is in the kitchen. The bed is comfortable, but you had better be up and dressed by 6.00 am because that's when the houseboy arrives.' She was right. The bed was all right, but the thought of the kitchenhand finding me asleep in his domain was enough to dispel the thought of sleep.

I might not have slept anyway because there was a demonic yodelling noise outside. The window was small and high, but when I managed to look out all I could see was a huge, bearded billygoat foraging in the street's rubbish.

The next morning the McLellans' plane left for Ethiopia. I dreaded that separation. They had been wonderful travelling companions. With a sinking heart I accompanied them to the airport. As I watched Dick and Vida and their children cross the tarmac and returned their wave before the plane swallowed them, the last dregs of the euphoria I experienced leaving Sydney drained away. I realised how alone I was. All ties with home were cut.

I had two more days in Aden before I caught a plane to Mogadishu. In spite of the relief of being able to vacate the Pascoes' kitchen and take over the McLellans' room, the feeling of homesickness was paramount.

'Can you buy mothballs in Aden?' I asked Jack Maxson at breakfast the next morning. I was thinking of the clothes I wouldn't need in the heat of Somalia. He answered in the affirmative. 'Can you buy just a few? I don't think I'd need a whole box?' I continued.

'You could ask for a few,' said Jack 'but I don't think they'll split the balls.' I loved that man with his wonderful smile and his drawling wit.

Opposite to Jack with his kindness and humour was a glamorous, single American missionary called Gretta, still in her 20s. My response to her confident elegance and American accent was to feel awkward. I hardly spoke at the meal table when she was there and was aware that I was not making a good impression. The worst moment was when she saw my pith helmet.

'Who on earth owns that?' she asked, pointing to the side-table where I had placed it.

'It's mine,' I confessed. 'It was on the mission outfit list.'

'What rubbish!' she scoffed. 'No one wears those anymore.'

She was right; I never saw a pith helmet worn in Somalia. But at that precise moment I wanted to crawl through a crack and hide. I didn't tell her that the outfit list also told us to bring $60 for a mule saddle. I was never required to ride a mule either.

My remaining time in Aden crawled by, miserable except for one bright spot. Ruth May, an Australian midwife, soon to become Ruth Twidale, had a ministry delivering babies in the homes of the women of Aden.

'Do you want to come visiting with me?' she asked on the Saturday afternoon.

'Yes, please!'

Together we walked the streets. Each door we knocked on belonged to a woman whose baby Ruth had recently delivered. There was always a great welcome, followed by an oohing and aahing over the baby and a mandatory bottle of Fanta to consume. I loved it. This was what I would be doing myself in Somalia in a year's time. Seven visits and seven bottles of Fanta meant a hasty walk home. I could also see why Ruth was chubbier than when I had last seen her in Australia. I was yet to learn that most Arabs and Somalis like their women fat.

On Monday morning I was driven to Aden airport to catch the plane to Somalia. I sat in the departure lounge and read from the Bible: 'And thou shalt remember all the way which the Lord thy God led thee … to humble thee, and to prove thee, to know what was in thine heart' (Deuteronomy 8:2 KJV) – words to ponder as I faced the last lap of the journey.

That Aden Airways plane was very old. 'Quite tatty!' I heard one Englishman say on another trip. On this day there was only one other white person on board, an English hunter with a huge walrus moustache and a rifle between his knees. We two were completely surrounded by Arabs and Africans. The plane rattled along the runway and, with many groans and creaks, managed to become airborne. I sat there in the uncomfortable, unpressurised cabin wondering what on earth lay ahead.

Five hours later I staggered down the steps of the plane in Mogadishu, a pathetic sight. My ears were completely blocked by the inadequately pressurised plane. I was almost deaf and nearly bowled over by the waves of heat that hit me. Hugh and Ada Street, the Australian missionaries in Somalia who met me, must have wondered what had struck them, but they were very kind, making polite conversation as we drove through the city.

I stared silently at the white, flat-roofed Italian architecture, the palm-tree lined streets and the slim, graceful figures of Somalis going about their business, and in my foggy mind, super-saturated with new impressions, the message rang loud and clear: 'You are here. You have arrived!'

11

BEGINNINGS

'Please send Miss Myors to Somalia as soon as possible' was the message received by the SIM Sydney office as they were processing my application to be accepted for service in Somalia. It was from Mr Warren Modricker, the SIM director in the Somali Republic. He had received word that I was to go to the Summer Institute of Linguistics (SIL) in Victoria, run by Wycliffe Bible Translators, before I left for Somalia. He did not agree with that plan. He wrote, 'She has studied Greek, French, German and Latin so does not need further preparation by spending three months at SIL before commencing her Somali language studies.'

I had listed those languages in answer to the question on my mission application form, 'What languages have you studied previously?' If the truth was known, I only had a smattering of each. However, Warren and I were in total agreement. He was passionate about getting as many missionaries into Somalia as quickly as possible and I couldn't wait to be on my way. Even now I believe that my method of learning a new language would not have improved from undertaking a linguistics course.

This letter to the Sydney office was my introduction to the vision and drive of Warren and Dorothy Modricker. Once acquainted with their story, the urgency they expressed in all they did and said was easy to understand.

Natives of Boston, married in 1933, they both experienced a clear call to be missionaries to the Somali people. They set sail from the United States in 1934.

'We arrived by boat at the port of Hargeisa in British Somaliland, where we hoped to work,' Warren told me. 'We had legal visas to disembark and enter the country, but the British army stood in our way. "You are forbidden to disembark," the immigration officer informed us while we were still trying to organise our luggage to leave the boat.'

'Who said?' I asked.

"'These are the governor's orders,' replied the officer. "You are not to land." The governor claimed he had enough problems without missionaries coming and causing more trouble. The Somali tribes in British Somaliland claimed to be 100 per cent Muslim and the British administrators were determined not to add to the unrest they were currently dealing with.

'I returned to my cabin and wept,' continued Warren. 'I cried out to the Lord. I could not understand why Dorothy and I both had a strong and certain call and were being obstructed in this way. Everything seemed dark to me. "Why, Lord? Why? Why did you bring us this far to stop us now?" I asked.'

They could do nothing but remain on the boat and disembark in Aden, where there was a large Somali population. They presented themselves at the Danish Mission and were welcomed with open arms. For the next 21 years they worked there. They learned the Somali language, taught English, witnessed to the Somalis, saw some converted and had six children, all the time continuing to pray for an entrance into Somalia.

In 1954 their prayers were answered. This time the door opened, not to British Somaliland, but to Italian Somaliland. It had become the Trust Territory of Somaliland under United Nations trusteeship in 1950 until full independence was to be gained in 1960. Westerners were given entry visas. The leaders of SIM asked the Modrickers to lead this new work. Joyfully Warren and Dorothy found a suitable property for a headquarters in Mogadishu. Their youngest children, two-year-old twins John and Joy, were with them. The older four were being educated in the United States.

Warren Modricker was granted official permission to identify five different places in which missionaries could work. The Mennonite Mission had also commenced work in the Trust Territory. The charter of the United Nations guaranteed religious freedom. During the ten-year period of the trusteeship (1950–1960) the people of the former Italian Somaliland would be trained to take over the governing of their own land. A prime reason for Westerners being welcomed was the need for the local people to be educated in English. Previously all government business was carried out in Italian.

To know Warren and Dorothy Modricker was a unique experience. The tenacity that enabled them to work in Aden all those years, waiting to move to Somalia, was evident in everything they did. In many ways they were larger than life. Warren was the extrovert. He prayed and preached with gusto. His body language, speech volume and illustrations were unique. He used manipulation, strong persuasion, Scripture and appropriate anecdotes to reach his goals. He was a very gifted evangelist who continually modelled perseverance and enthusiasm.

Dorothy was an academic. She was an introvert who must have found the constant contact with people and the hospitality required in her role wearing. Warren exaggerated for effect when telling a story. Dorothy stuck to the facts and never raised her voice. She had a keen sense of humour, enjoying amusing situations, but was more a foil for her husband's life-of-the-party personality than someone who ever sought the limelight for herself. As a linguist she was painstaking and patient. The 40 years it took for her to translate the Bible into Somali were fraught with interruptions, but through her commitment to the task, a trustworthy translation was produced.

Once I sat outside her office waiting to speak to her while she argued with her husband and the language helper. The Scripture in question was Jesus talking about people straining at gnats and swallowing camels. 'Camel' was easy; they were everywhere. But there was no specific word for 'gnat'. Dorothy wanted to use the word for 'mosquito' but the other two wouldn't have it, even though they could offer no suitable alternative. The debate went on interminably. I don't know how she coped – I was exhausted listening. Such energy spent over one tiny word. She ended up using 'mosquito' but, oh, what a cost!

Twice during the years in Somalia, Warren was voted out of leadership by the missionaries on the team. Although they appreciated his gifts and his pioneer role, his indirect way of communicating and his propensity to manipulate tended to create a discontented team. It was embarrassing and humbling for him. In spite of the rejection of his leadership, I never sensed any hint of bitterness or any lessening of his enthusiasm in reaching out to the Somalis for Christ. His passion was for the spread of the gospel. A lasting memory for me comes from when we had all moved to Kenya in the late 1970s, when I saw him, at the age of 76, in a slum area of Nairobi, handing out Scripture portions to street waifs, shop owners or anyone who would accept one. That was his retirement ministry, and he never missed an opportunity to fill his basket with literature and walk his beat.

One day out on the streets of Eastleigh, the suburb of Nairobi where we lived, Warren was knocked over by a car, resulting in him being hospitalised for several days. I offered to drive Dorothy across the city to visit him. They had been married 50 years. There had been many ups and downs. I used to wonder sometimes how Dorothy felt about this man who was one-eyed, pushy and, at times, the centre of controversy. I wasn't left in doubt long. As soon as she saw her husband, pale and obviously ill in his hospital bed, this reserved, often tight-lipped septuagenarian fell on him and kissed him repeatedly. It was a moving display of enduring love.

This was the couple who guided my early days in Somalia. When I arrived they were on a rare holiday, so I began the study of the Somali language under the direction of Anne Ahern, a softly spoken, 35-year-old American teacher who was a passionate animal lover. She had been with the Modrickers since 1954 and was fluent in the language. Tina and Albert Erion, Canadian missionaries and radiantly happy newly-weds, had arrived in Somalia a few weeks ahead of me, so my first task was to catch up with what they had already learned.

Anne was tentative and gentle. When Dorothy Modricker arrived back to take over the class, the atmosphere became electric. We sat up straighter, listened more intently and never dared to neglect our homework. We had the privilege of being taught by a brilliant linguist. No other foreigner knew Somali like Hadiyo (Dorothy's Somali name).

I was in my element. I cannot think of another learning situation that I responded to so readily. Never in my life did I work so diligently or find myself so at ease with the subject matter. I, the distracted student at school who hardly ever applied herself to learning, now looked forward to each lesson eagerly and gave my very best to the task at hand.

After our lesson we engaged in an hour of conversation practice with a Somali helper. Mine was a young, handsome university student called Noor.

'Ruth, I have been watching you and you are prone to be too familiar with your tutor,' Dorothy warned me one day. 'If you keep on like that you are going to give him the wrong impression. Keep your distance. Concentrate on the lesson material only.'

'She's not friendly enough,' I thought privately. 'I certainly don't want to come across like that.' I was tempted to ignore the warning. Then I had to think again. The next morning Noor handed me a folded paper.

'Where are you with your gay green eyes?' I read. 'You are my friend. I love teaching you.' I read on and realised my teacher was right. I had been too friendly. Also I had been swift to judge older and wiser people. They were there to teach me. I realised that the time taken to learn a new language was also a valuable time for learning the culture and appropriate ways of relating.

I didn't mention the note to Noor or to my teacher. Soon after he amicably left for another job and I was able to start again with another language helper, Daud, in a more appropriate student/teacher relationship.

In the 1960s Somali was not a written language. There were no Somali books or newspapers. The grammar book we used was written in the Latin script for the convenience of English-speaking students. The author, Colonel Barry, was a British soldier who years before had worked in Northern Somaliland. His explanations of the irregular, fiendishly difficult grammar were excellent. Not so good was his choice of 'useful phrases' written at the end of each lesson. We went about practising 'jump on the horse' (I never saw a horse), 'aim the gun' and 'call the syce'. The words I needed for future medical work I learnt through painful experience later. (I don't know what 'syce' means either.)

Spoken Somali is rather harsh. There are different sounds to learn such as rolled *r*'s and *ain*'s and aspirated *h*'s. I found it helpful to practise rolling *r*'s in the shower. The word for 'rain' was *roob*. To start a word with a rolled *r* is difficult. It is much easier in the middle of a word such as *warren*, meaning spear.

As already implied, learning a language is difficult. The slow process is beneficial because there is so much more to it than words and meanings. For example, I learnt the words for 'do you want a cup of tea?' without any trouble, but it was not a good thing to say. The cultural response to a visitor is to immediately put the kettle on, make a cup of tea and present it. To ask if it is wanted is to infer it is why the person came and the answer will always be negative and often accompanied by hurt feelings. Hospitality took on a whole new meaning. The poorest Somali householder would always have something to offer a visitor, often at a sacrifice to the family. We learned so much about generosity from the Somalis.

Another day, when out walking and showing off my ability to count, I numbered out loud the cows in a woman's animal enclosure. She was furious and went to hit me. Reeling with surprise, I was told that counting animals lets the devil know how many there are and gives him opportunity to kill some. It could be the same with children. Many people would not say how many children they had.

When at long last I became involved in the medical work, I was dramatically confronted with how little medical language I knew.

'*Hagee lagaa haaya* (where is it [the sickness] holding you)?' was the routine question to ask a new patient. So '*Hagee lagaa hayaa?*' I would ask confidently with a friendly smile.

Boom! It was like pressing a button and being hit in the face with an avalanche as the sick person rattled off a list of symptoms. I knew the question but couldn't understand the answer. Standing dazed and confused, I would hear the other patients muttering to one another, 'This new one doesn't know anything!' They all wanted to talk to Maryan (Joy Newcombe), who had been their beloved nurse for several years. Anatomy and the names of diseases and symptoms had to be learned word by word, often with laughter, sometimes with frustration, but gradually with success.

Some words sounded the same to me but had very different meanings. The most dangerous was the word for 'back tooth' versus the name for a man's penis. I tried very hard to differentiate but several times found myself in delicate situations.

'Come in here behind the curtain,' I would say if I thought the problem was the lower region.

'Now show me.' There would be loud guffaws as the patient opened his mouth wide and revealed a decayed back tooth. Better that way than say 'Show me' in public when it wasn't the tooth.

In reality, the outcome was more difficult when it was a tooth because that usually meant pulling it out. We couldn't do fillings; we had only learned to extract. The other often only involved a dab of gentian violet.

Perhaps I unconsciously misunderstood 'back tooth' on purpose because pulling teeth was not easy if the patient was a big man who had had a lifelong diet of camel's milk. The teeth had long roots and needed a lot of rocking to and fro before they would give up the fight and agree to be extracted. We didn't have a dentist's chair, so to support the head I would hold it firmly with my right arm wrapped around it and clamp the extraction forceps onto the offending tooth with my left hand. This was after injecting the patient with local anaesthetic. A difficult tooth could take an hour or more. Meanwhile the number of people waiting for treatment increased and many became impatient.

Learning a language is a matter of survival as well as an essential part of a satisfactory ministry. As I progressed, I often found myself able to quench the fires of anger by using a Somali proverb in the appropriate place or using humour to deal with ticklish situations. For example, a favourite proverb was: 'A man who boasts is like a she-goat who sucks her own milk.' I used it often and found it worked wonders if a difficult man was sounding off in anger in the clinic. The audience would roar laughing at the appropriateness of the maxim and very often the troublemaker would subside with a wry grin.

I learned to love communicating with the people and became increasingly familiar with their colourful idioms and metaphors. It was a positive and productive time of my life. But, of course, I am an extrovert. Extroverts have to talk or bust.

12

DAUD (HIS STORY)

I knew from the beginning of our relationship that God had provided a special person to be my second language helper. The more time I spent with Daud, the more my appreciation of his intelligence, sense of humour and growth as a Christian brother increased. The following is his story.

Forty-eight years after I first met Daud, when I was back home in Australia permanently, I answered the phone to hear this tragic message.

'They are all dead,' said Pat Warner, one of my former Somali co-workers.

'Who are dead?'

'Daud and his colleagues,' she answered.

The night before, members of Al-Shabaab, an Islamic terrorist group, had shot our friend and his fellow teachers. It was news I found almost impossible to absorb. One of the brightest lights I had known in Somalia had been snuffed out. Daud had achieved so much. His goal of bringing to his hometown and to the children of the area the education he himself valued so much was coming to fruition, and now he was gone. I thought of his family and all those who loved and supported him.

In my grief I thought back to when I first met him. He was my second informant for conversation practice. He was about eighteen, tall and thin, and as keen to improve his English as I was to learn Somali.

An immediate rapport grew between us. It was the beginning of a life-long friendship. We used to sit on two straight-backed chairs in the yard under a tree. It was hot and humid, but occasionally a breeze direct from the Indian Ocean delivered a moment's relief. The stark white of the flat-roofed Italian-style houses around us dazzled in the midday sun. The scent of frangipani blossoms filling the air mingled with the spicy fragrance of African cooking. The hour we had together was a highlight of my day.

We usually commenced with the greetings in Somali.

'Is it peace with you?' I would ask

'Yes, it is peace. How are you?' he would answer.

'Were you kept safe in the night?'

'Yes, I was kept safe in the night.'

'Is the family well?'

'Yes, they are well, praise God. Is your family well?'

And so it continued. The greetings may seem tedious but they were an essential element of daily interaction. One morning in the hospital in Bulo Burti, before any patients had come into the clinic, I was working alongside one of the male workers when he said, 'Did we sleep together last night?' He was a quiet, polite person, not at all confrontational.

Surprised, I asked, 'Why did you say that?'

'Well, you didn't ask me how I am; you didn't ask if I was kept safe in the night. How would you know these things if you didn't sleep in my house?'

I got the message. In my Western, task-oriented busyness I had probably grunted a monosyllabic acknowledgment of his presence and got down to business. For Somalis the minimal requirement in a morning greeting was: 'Is it peace with you? Were you kept safe in the night? How are you?'

One repeated pitfall for foreigners was when there was loud knocking at the door of the house, often out of clinic hours, after a busy morning or at some other inconvenient time. It was so easy to open the door and say, 'What do you want?' Very, very bad manners! I know I failed often. No matter how inconvenient the situation, it could always be mollified a little by polite greetings.

After the greetings with Daud I would practise a Bible verse and then we would progress to some of the complex grammar constructions of the Somali language. Somali was a challenge to learn, firstly because it was not a written language, and secondly because there were many irregularities. Then we would chat together so he could correct my pronunciation.

One day I was counting in Somali. I intoned '*kow, laba, saddex, afar, shoon—*'

Daud had been sitting with his chin on his chest in a semi-dozing posture. He suddenly shot up straight. 'Never say that again!' he exclaimed. 'The word for "five" is *shun*.'

'What did I say?' I asked.

His chin returned to his chest and he started chortling. 'Don't you worry about what it means. Just never say it.'

As soon as he left I found the Somali girl who worked in our house 'What does *shoon* mean?' I asked. She roared laughing when I told her I had said it to Daud. '*Shoon* means pubic hair,' she giggled. I never forgot how to pronounce the word for 'five'.

As I progressed we had time for extra conversation, and Daud and I explored our individual, vastly different backgrounds.

'Did your family live in a village?' I asked.

'Some time was spent in a village but other times we travelled around with our flocks. I remember being very small and being put into a frame on the camel's back. I remember falling out of that once. But I was all right.'

It was hard for me to imagine Daud as a boy from the bush. When I met him he was impeccably groomed. His trousers and shirt were as dazzlingly white as the Italian houses. They were also beautifully ironed. He was a student and invariably arrived for our appointment carrying a book.

'Were you from a large family?' I asked.

'I was. My mother had three sons and one daughter who lived to adulthood. I don't know how many died as children. But during his life my father married nine different women. As a Muslim he was allowed three at a time. So I shared many other brothers and sisters who had the same father and different mothers. My father died when I was three so I don't remember him very much. I was the youngest of his children when he died.'

I later met some of his brothers. Although there was little family likeness because of different mothers, there was obviously a strong brotherly bond.

'What about school?'

'When I was eight, I went to live with a married sister in town to start primary school. Before that I attended a Qur'anic school in the village. I will never forget my sister saving up to buy me my first trousers. Before that I only had a loincloth.'

Daud had recently become a Christian through reading John's Gospel as well as completing some accompanying lessons. He never deviated from this faith.

'I've got another job!' Daud told me with a smile one morning when he arrived to have his hour with me.

When I asked him what it was, he told me he was teaching the Somali language to some American Embassy wives. Then he laughed and said, 'It is very different from teaching missionaries. The missionaries are very serious. They act as if learning Somali is a life and death affair. The American women laugh at each other and engage in much social chitchat. They only want to learn greetings so they can relate socially to employees and their neighbours.'

'We've had it drummed into us that we will never succeed here without a good grasp of the language,' I explained.

'They not only pay more but they also teach me different kinds of English,' Daud continued. 'For example, they talked about someone having an affair and then explained what that meant. I can see why I never learned that from the missionaries!' We both had a good laugh and then continued my lesson.

The next step for Daud, after being a language student informant, was to be employed as an Arabic teacher in a mission boarding school for girls. These primary school students were nearly all daughters of wealthy families. They were bright and beautiful and full of fun. They loved ribbing their serious male teacher.

'You look like an ostrich,' I heard some of the girls say to him one day when I was visiting. I looked at his tall thin body and long neck and could see why they said it. Everyone laughed, including Daud. The convivial atmosphere in the school was apparent for all to see. The principal was gentle, loving Anne Ahern, who had introduced me to my language study. Sadly, this happy situation was short-lived. A 1963 government decree stating that it was mandatory for all schools to employ a Muslim sheikh to teach the Qur'an caused the school to be closed.

Daud lost a job he loved, but unknown to him, significant changes were on the horizon.

A Christian group, knowing of Daud's Christian commitment, arranged for him to gain a scholarship to study in a Bible college in Lebanon. He accepted the offer with alacrity. The desire for a foreign tertiary education was rampant among the young Somali men who had completed secondary school. All needed to be granted passports and to pass other requirements of government red tape. Repeatedly

Daud negotiated what seemed to be impenetrable barriers by bumping into someone he knew in a key position. He was determined to go. His persistence, plus the fact that his journey had been planned from above, meant that permission to travel abroad was granted. After negotiating the hurdles required for a passport, he arrived in Beirut to commence the course.

At the Lebanon Bible Institute (LBI) the students were drawn from a variety of Middle Eastern countries while the lecturers were mainly Westerners teaching the Bible in Arabic.

'An early realisation that was rather shocking,' Daud admitted later, 'was that I had an exaggerated self-esteem because of the nurture and attention I had received from the missionaries in Somalia. They made me feel special. Mixing with these other students, I realised I was only ordinary.' He was also disappointed in the curriculum. A simple Bible college course was not going to result in the tertiary education he dreamed of.

Daud was aware that there had been sacrifices made to send him to Lebanon so he made up his mind to press on and finish the course. Unexpectedly, the 1967 Six-Day War and other political unrest meant he gained his qualification earlier than he expected. Armed with his LBI diploma, he began the search to find the kind of education he envisaged when he left Somalia. His passion to gain a tertiary education in English kept him pressing on in spite of repeated roadblocks.

'I was not distracted from my goal, nor had I forgotten the grinding poverty at home,' he later confided. 'It was as though I was on a self-imposed leash all the time. Nothing was going to get in the way of opportunity through education with an eventual escape from poverty.' And he succeeded. He gained a scholarship to a three-year teacher training course at a college in England.

At one stage during his studies, he found work in a residential college. With the job he gained accommodation and food, but the work included peeling vegetables and washing saucepans. Daud, as a proud Somali male, had never before descended to such women's work, but the money was worth it. He was further mollified by meeting many college graduates, more highly qualified than he was, doing similar work.

During this time the people who had sent Daud to Lebanon were disappointed. Their plan had been for him to be trained as a leader in the Somali church. They concluded that he had accepted their generosity and then deviated on to a selfish path to follow his own plans. To a certain extent they were correct. But Daud was sincerely God's child, and in spite of a certain immaturity, step by step he was led into a place of significant usefulness in the Father's overall plan. Isaiah 55:8–9 is pertinent: ' "For my thoughts are not your thoughts, neither are your ways my ways," declares the LORD. "As the heavens are higher than the earth, so are my ways higher than your ways and my thoughts than your thoughts.' What happened to Daud as his life continued could well be the higher way that God had chosen.

In the course of preparing for teacher training, Daud was introduced by an Englishman who had been a mentor and friend to an English girl named Margaret. He described her as well-educated and beautiful. She was also deeply interested in the Somali people. Although there was a time of separation, during which Margaret went to work among the Somalis in the Ogaden, the relationship continued. When she returned to England after a year away, they were married.

It was September 1971. Daud was in his second year of teacher training. Margaret, already a graduate, found employment as a secondary teacher.

Eventually Daud graduated and taught primary and later secondary school. Then, after 16 years of teaching and the birth of two sons, he studied psychology and eventually gained a Master's degree in education. Much of his time in later years was given to guiding immigrant children in the United Kingdom through the transition process. His wisdom and experience made him a valuable and widely respected educational psychologist. Somali visitors were always welcome in their home. In a place where there was neither the restriction nor the danger in Christian witness that there was in Somalia, relatives and friends were exposed to hospitality, love and Christian testimony.

Whenever I had the opportunity, I visited the family in the UK. I was blessed to know them. The boy from the bush, who had exchanged a loincloth for a pair of shorts to go to primary school, spoke perfect English with an educated English accent and was always impeccably dressed.

As he grew older, however, a new dream was born. His burning passion now was to return to his hometown and give something back. As he had fought so hard to be educated himself, he now wanted to help children in his hometown achieve.

Figure 12.1 – Ruth with Daud and his family in the UK in 1982.
Left to right: Ruth, Robleh, Margaret, Kenadeed and Daud.

On retirement, in 2004, Daud returned to the area where he had been reared. With his own finance plus gifts from interested friends, he rented rooms for classrooms and had a library built. During term time he taught in Somalia. In the holidays he returned to his family in the UK. While teaching fulltime, he negotiated the purchase of land on the outskirts of the town. There he oversaw the construction of classrooms and ancillary accommodation to replace the school's temporary home in a rented house in the centre of the city. There were 110 children in four daytime classes and 60 adults in the evening English proficiency classes. In all of Somalia it was unique.

I had only recently received pictures of the beautiful new buildings, not yet occupied, when the phone rang.

Receiving the news that Daud and his staff of committed Christian teachers were dead, killed by terrorists, was very hard to accept. That school and the library were rare bright spots on the Somali horizon. All the money had been donated by friends outside the country. The dream of returning to his home community some of the blessing he had received was destroyed by blind, mindless hatred. We can only pray for those who are so misled and be thankful that, through another school and reading room in a safer area, Daud's dream is now being kept alive.

13

MOGADISHU HOUSEKEEPER

I'd finished my first six months in Somalia and was on a high. It was June 1961. Learning Somali had been a challenge but I had loved it. I was now looking forward to leaving Mogadishu and beginning the rest of my life as a missionary nurse in the hospital at Bulo Burti.

With a picture in my mind of earlier missionaries, Mary Slessor and Amy Carmichael rolled up into one, I was ready to go. I had passed the first language exam so there was nothing to hold me back, I thought. Even when I was told that the East African field director, who was visiting Somalia from Ethiopia, wanted to see me, I wasn't worried. I thought he was going to congratulate me and wish me well.

The interview proceeded along these lines: 'Now, Miss Myors, you've finished your language study.'

'Yes, I have.' I smiled and waited for some measured adulation.

'Well, we have decided that for the next six months you are to manage the Mogadishu HQ Guesthouse.'

'What! I can't do that.'

'Why not?'

'I'm a nurse. I can't cook. My mother never taught me.' I could have gone on to tell him that my mother was not a very good cook herself and that I had left home when I was 17, but I didn't think he would have been interested and I was choking on my words.

'You won't be doing the cooking; you will be managing the Somali workers.' His tone was matter of fact. He was spelling out a plan of action that had already been decided.

'I can't do it!' I repeated.

'In SIM the custom is to do what the leaders decide. After six months, if you still feel it is not what God wants, we will pray and reconsider.'

With those words the interview was over. I was told the reason for my appointment was that the present manager/hostess, Dorothy Modricker, our language teacher, needed time to finish translating the

Bible. I agreed that she should be relieved, but not by me!

The 1960s were not an era when people in missions argued with the leaders. The practice was, as I had just been told, to obey by accepting directives as if they had come from the Lord. Complaining would be seen as a low level of spirituality.

The next morning, rising with a deep foreboding, I knelt beside the bed to pray prior to going to the kitchen to help with breakfast. After sobbing for a while with my face buried in the bedclothes, I reluctantly rose to my feet and began the first day of my life as a guesthouse manager. Manager! What a misnomer. There were two Somalis working in the kitchen. They knew what they were doing and I didn't have a clue. I immediately got in their way. Their response to me, after polite greetings, was '*Ka tag!*' Translated it meant 'get out of the way!' It wasn't rude. In Somali it was logical common sense.

The 'kitchen', besides being the place where food was cooked and dishes were washed, was also the sole entrance to the area where everyone ate and guests were accommodated. It was in the shape of a hallway, about five feet across and ten feet in length. Along one side was a stone sink with a cold-water tap and a stone drainage board next to a charcoal stove. The opposite wall had a serving bench and some cupboards. Tea towels hung on a line down the middle. Due to constant contact with cooking pots blackened by charcoal, the towels' original whiteness was gone forever. Because of the room's size and shape, visitors entering the guesthouse were forced to walk in single file in order to avoid unpleasant interactions with the tea towels and, at meal times, the workers.

That first day for me was every bit as bad as I expected, or even worse. I felt redundant, ignorant and rebellious. I kept up a 'this is not why I came to Africa' chorus in my mind. I could not think of one good reason why I should be delegated to work in a guesthouse. This was a bad decision.

However, the feeling of redundancy was to be transitory. Mrs Modricker's cook was a gem called Haawa. Probably still in her 20s, tall, slim and attractive, she was pregnant with her fourth baby. Her children's father was a Muslim sheikh. Sadly, she wasn't with me long. Soon after my appointment to the guesthouse we noticed that her feet were swollen, and after a visit to the doctor, it was decided she should stop work until after the baby's birth, followed by the mandatory 40 days of postnatal seclusion at home.

Now there was no cook! The other worker was trained to set the table, wash the dishes and do the floors and other cleaning. He could also go to the market and do the shopping, but he was not used to choosing meat and vegetables the way Haawa could. The support we thought I would have was gone.

The first problem was that my cooking experience was limited. The second was that I had been a language student and had heard other students' comments about the meals. Dorothy Modricker had trained Haawa to follow four main meal recipes and they were a continuous cycle. There was lamb's (or rather goat's) fry and onions in gravy, spaghetti bolognaise, meat loaf and vegetables, and meatballs and vegetables. Haawa cooked these beautifully and they were always tasty. However, a cycle of four tended to become monotonous for people who were captive devourers for at least six months. Breakfast was always fried eggs, rolls and fruit and the evening meal was either tinned soup or tuna in white sauce. While there was plenty to eat, the missing ingredient was variety, and people studying language all day tended to dream about all the food that was unavailable. I had often listened to complaints about the same old meals and heard conversations commencing with the words, 'When I get home, the first thing I am going to eat is …'

Dorothy Modricker was a linguist, a translator of the Bible, a language teacher, a wife and a mother. She was a thinker and an academic. Variety in the menu for her students was not a priority. What she had set up was nutritious and plentiful. I don't know if she ever knew that people were groaning and moaning about the monotony of the menu. But I did know she had put a program in place that she believed was adequate. She trusted Haawa to implement it and that was that.

But Haawa was gone. I would have to manage.

First I faced the daily trip to the market. Because there was no freezer, everything was bought on the day. Transport was by *dugdugleh*. These three-wheeled, scooter-like vehicles with a little cabin were plentiful on our street. The owners were always on the lookout for passengers and their vehicle went 'dug-dug-dug' all the way. The ride was fun. The drivers were good for banter as well as learning new words. A typical conversation with me went like this:

Driver: Are you married?

Me: No.

Driver: Do you want to marry a Somali man?

Me: No

Driver: *Mahaa jiraa* (why not)?

Me (quoting a Somali proverb): Every bird flies with its own kind.

Driver: *Waa run* (that's true)!

No one needed to tell me when we were nearing the meat market. A blind man could easily find it by following the pungent smell of blood and offal. The sighted would smell but also see dozens of carcasses impaled on huge hooks, the remains of old camels or cattle. Many animals would have had their throats cut as they were about to breathe their last elderly breath. An experienced friend had said to me, 'Go by the colour of the fat. The yellower, the older.' Choosing my animal I would point and say, 'I'll have a kilo of that one.' Immediately, the owner would slash a mound of meat from the carcass, plop it onto a questionable piece of newspaper, wrap it up and mutter the price.

Beside the hanging carcasses were tables of goat pieces, varieties of offal and multitudinous bones. On goat's-fry day the carcasses were passed by in favour of the liver. I ignored the buzzing blowflies and ubiquitous skinny dogs. No point in giving mind space to the inevitable.

Sounding from the nearby vegetable market were calls of '*Kali, kali* (come, come)!' Women of all shapes and sizes sat on the ground with little piles of cherry tomatoes, chillies, root ginger and garlic. Varied Eastern spices abounded, wrapped in tiny newspaper funnels. I would choose something from as many little piles as I could and talk and joke with the cheerful vendors, laughing at comments about the shape of my legs or any other part of me on which they chose to comment.

There were no salad vegetables. Our usual greens were tinned peas or beans, which we grew to loathe. Potatoes were a luxury usually found in the Italian shops. The good news was the delicious fruit. There were stacks of paw paws, mangos, bananas and limes, all very cheap. Paw paws and bananas in Australia never taste as good as the Somali ones.

Because I had heard so many remarks about the limited menu, I decided to try some new recipes. Eagerly I leafed through an interesting cookbook someone had left in a cupboard. There were limits, however, to what I could try – the meat, to be chewable, had to be minced or pressure-cooked. But within the limits I exercised my creativity. One day I ventured a concoction called Devilled Steak. I presented it with a measure of excitement, announcing the name of the dish only to hear one of the younger male diners mutter, 'Looks though the devil's still in it and he's bleeding to death.' Because I had no illusions about my cooking ability, I thought that was very funny. Dorothy Modricker, who was present, told me later she would have cried. I didn't mind, but I also thought the meat tasted delicious and the 'bleeding to death' was really tomato sauce. Everyone ate it.

Every now and then, on red-letter days, there would be a loud '*Hodi!*' at the kitchen door. Then:

'*Malai ma rabtaa* (do you want fish)?'

'Yes! Yes! We want it.'

The vendor was a bearded Somali fisherman who caught the fish in the Indian Ocean and hawked it from door to door. We were good customers and often given the first offer. The basket would be full of fillets of a breed of fish I never knew the name of but which was always delicious. Everyone enjoyed a welcome break in the regular menu schedule.

Other backdoor salespeople were wizened old ladies with woven baskets of little eggs. They would shout, '*Ukun ma rabtaa* (do you want eggs)?'

'Yes, yes, we do!' The drill then was to take a bowl of water out to the lady to immerse the eggs. It was only safe to buy those that stayed on the bottom of the bowl.

As I returned the floaters to her basket, she would mutter, 'Buy them all. Why are you returning these?'

'Because they are not fresh. If they float they are no good.'

'They are fresh. Allah knows they were laid this morning. Would I lie to you?'

We all knew they were probably weeks old, but that was the story and it never changed. In a few weeks that egg lady would be back. We were always glad to see her along with her friends, but we never could buy all their eggs.

Because the door-to-door salespeople came with wares we needed, I was pleased to see them. There was just one pitfall. They came at meal times. After the sale was complete and the money paid, I would rush back to what I had been doing and say to myself, 'I'll write that money up later!' Foolish woman! It was the last I thought of it.

'What happened to the household books? There is a huge discrepancy,' the mission accountant said to me the day my time as housekeeper ended. I knew, but there was nothing I could do about it, so I forked out the difference. I didn't mind. Now in my 80s I don't think I'm any different. I still have trouble balancing books, and I don't have nearly as good an excuse.

When Haawa left, her assistant Mahamuud quickly learned many of her responsibilities, including some cooking and marketing. But that left some of his jobs undone. We needed another worker.

Mahamuud said, 'My brother has just come from the bush. He wants a job. He is very honest.'

'Just come from the bush' should have been an orange light but I did not know how to find a new worker. 'Mahamuud will teach him,' I said to myself in an effort to quell niggling doubts. 'Besides they will get on well together.'

The brother, named Robleh, arrived the next day. Perhaps he and Mahamuud had the same father. They had the same surname. But they must have had different mothers because there was no family likeness. Mahamuud was slim and neat with finely chiselled features. Robleh was big-boned and angular with huge feet in heavy homemade leather sandals. He was eager to learn but totally new to town ways, and very clumsy. He had been herding camels in the bush for years.

Figure 13.1 – Camels, with houses on their back, being prepared to move to greener pastures.

One of the first jobs was to teach Robleh to set the table. He had never been in a building before. He had always lived in nomadic bush huts that were transportable by camel. He had never had any experience of a knife and fork. The Somalis eat by scooping the food to the mouth with the right hand. To set a table for 12 or more people was an utter mystery. The first lesson was to find the cutlery stored in a drawer in the dining room cupboard. I said to Robleh, 'See that little iron ring? Pull on that.' Wrong command! Robleh grabbed the handle with his big calloused hand and yanked with gusto. The drawer flew out, crashing to the floor.

'*Bismilaahay* (Oh my God)!' Robleh grunted in amazement as cutlery scattered everywhere. He looked at me as if to say, 'Why did you tell me to do that?'

Waiting at the table was another challenge. I tried to explain the protocol for being present in the dining room while people ate and politely removing the finished dishes. Robleh began by leaning over the diner's shoulder, breathing down the diner's neck, grabbing the plate as the last morsel was removed from them. One mission official asked, 'Could you please ask your man not to stand so close?' With difficulty I stifled my mirth. The assembled diners did not know we were trying to create a butler from a camel herder.

Robleh was not the only one who had much to learn. One day I decided to make a raspberry coconut rough slice for afternoon tea. It turned out beautifully. I cut it into squares, arranged it on a platter, placed it in the fridge and went to have a siesta before people gathered for their afternoon tea. I was anticipating the excitement when they saw and tasted the slice. A disappointment was ahead. During the early afternoon, Mr Modricker, seeking a cold drink, had tipped the water container all over the slice. My creation was a soggy heap.

'It was going to be a treat!' I whimpered.

'Well, what do you expect when you put an uncovered plate in the fridge like that?' was the only response.

No one realised I was close to tears. I'd never made slice before and had never been told that it needs to be in a container in the fridge. I had many lessons, some painful, to learn.

Before my six months as guesthouse manager were over, there was a radical change in my outlook. As I grew into the role, I was increasingly aware that I was enjoying myself. I loved working with the Somalis.

I loved greeting the tired, dusty missionaries as they arrived from their workplaces to spend some time in Mogadishu. I loved offering hospitality. As an extrovert, constantly being with people who looked to me for care and encouragement was deeply satisfying.

This set a pattern of life that has never left me. After initially rebelling against a task I was appointed to, it became, to my amazement, the beginning of a ministry of which I have never tired. I realised that often, when I think a mistake is being made, the Lord has something wonderful in mind. F.B. Meyer wrote, 'Your disappointment can be God's appointment.' Amen.

14

MORE ABOUT HAAWA

One day, while I was still working in the guesthouse, I was returning to my room after the midday meal. Postprandial somnolence, intensified by the humid heat of Mogadishu, inevitably convinced nearly all of us to have a rest. Suddenly I heard Haawa, an unusually pleasant and cooperative employee, recently returned from maternity leave, screaming abuse and saw her throw herself onto Mahamuud, her kitchen assistant, like a frenzied cat. Cursing and threatening, she scratched his face, bit him and pulled his hair. As the taller of the two, her fury gave her superior strength. Pinned to a wall, Mahamuud seemed either helpless to defend himself or determined not to engage in a physical struggle with a woman. Had we not rushed to his aid, his injuries would have been worse. Even so, he had deep scratches on his cheeks.

We were stunned. These were our employees who had worked harmoniously together for as long as many of us had been in Somalia. It was such a relief to have Haawa back from maternity leave. We had missed her so much. What could have triggered such a display of fury?

'He is an infidel!' screamed Haawa. 'He has betrayed our prophet!'

Light broke. Mahamuud had been a regular attender at a meeting run by Warren Modricker called the Bible Information Class. Recently he had confided in some of the missionaries that he had become convinced, through Warren's teaching and reading the New Testament, that Jesus was the Messiah and had decided to become a follower. Haawa, hearing talk of this, challenged him. On receiving an affirmative reply, she, as the wife of a Muslim sheikh, responded with a venom that was totally out of keeping with the woman we knew.

After telling Haawa to go home, we took Mahamuud inside and bathed his scratched cheeks. He was very quiet. He uttered no invectives against his attacker. Thanking us for helping him, he simply said he would have a rest and come back to work tomorrow.

When Haawa returned later in the day to prepare the evening meal, the incident was not mentioned. She never referred to Mahamuud's conversion to Christianity again. If she apologised to him we never heard of it. Their previous good working relationship resumed as if nothing had happened.

Haawa's sheikh husband was a gentle man. Whenever we met him he was polite and friendly. He appreciated the income from Haawa's job with the mission, and, even more, that Haawa was the mother of four sons, an impressive contribution. Possessed of beauty and intelligence, she was a wife to be cherished.

Most Somalis saw Westerners as *gaals*, infidels. When we walked the streets of Mogadishu or in villages where we were not known, we would hear the children calling '*Gaal!*' after us. Once, on a narrow bridge, I met a man walking to the mosque to pray having already washed himself in preparation. He nearly fell into the river below in his efforts to avoid letting his clothes touch mine. 'Dirty infidel,' I heard him mutter as he walked on.

So for Haawa, Mahamuud's conversion was a capitulation to the enemy. It was contrary to all she had ever known. Turning from Islam was worthy of death. Contamination by the infidels was her greatest fear about working for us.

Since I had been overseeing the guesthouse, Dorothy Modricker had been translating the Bible into Somali in a room next to the dining room. She heard everything I said to the staff and often called out corrections. For me it was an opportunity to learn humility. It was also excellent for my acquisition of a difficult language. I never met another foreigner as proficient in the Somali language.

'Ruth, could you come here for a moment,' she called from her room one day. I responded, expecting another explanation relevant to my errors in using Somali prepositions. Dorothy sat at a little table that held an old-fashioned typewriter, in a room that served as office as well as bedroom. Leaning against the foot of the marital bed were spare Land Rover tyres. Piles of books and heaps of papers covered every available surface.

Trying not to stare, I waited to hear what she had to say.

'I have come across a roll of pictures,' she said. 'They are all from the Old Testament. I wondered if you would like to tell the kitchen staff a story after breakfast each day. It will be good for your language and it will expose them to some Bible teaching.'

'Do you think they will agree to listen?' I asked. 'Don't forget how Haawa attacked Mahamuud.'

'Ask them and see what they say.'

The next morning I put some chairs in a circle, hung the scroll of pictures on a hook on the wall and told the workers I was going to tell them a story from the Bible. There was no hesitation whatsoever. They all sat down and listened with great interest. I watched Haawa's face.

'*Waa wax yaableh, Anab* (it is amazing, Anab)!' she said from time to time with her hands clasped together. Anab was my Somali name. I could hardly believe what was happening. I still look back on that time, half a century ago now, with the joyful surprise I felt when morning after morning, in very simple language, I told a Bible story to the obvious interest of the listeners.

After six months, as my time of being guesthouse manager ended, I left to join the medical staff at Bulo Burti. Haawa and I separated as old friends.

Haawa continued to work as chief cook at the mission HQ. She welcomed new missionaries when they arrived knowing not a word of the Somali language, and patiently encouraged their early faltering efforts. She greeted the veterans when they returned from leave or visited Mogadishu for a rest. All were blessed by her smiling welcome and enjoyed her delicious cooking. A number of young men followed Mahamuud in accepting Jesus as the Messiah. Never again was one abused as was Mahamuud.

Then, one day, Haawa admitted that she believed. She was our first Somali sister in the Lord. She openly confessed as she attended Bible studies. We did not hear that her husband had reacted negatively. He never seemed to interfere. She was the beloved mother of his boys. He was an unusual Muslim sheikh, perhaps with questions himself.

When I left for Bulo Burti I missed the time I spent with Haawa. We were separated by 110 kilometres of bumpy road, both busy in our separate spheres, she with her family and employment and I in the hospital. Only on my rare visits to Mogadishu did I see her.

15

JOY'S STORY

'Maryan! Maryan!' the children cried, running after the white woman as she made her way through the village of Bulo Burti. They dogged her heels until she turned into a gateway and then ran off because they knew that pestering Maryan would earn them a rebuke from those she was visiting.

Maryan was the Somali name given to Joy Newcombe, who had first told me about Somalia. She had become a well-known figure, walking with a firm tread along the dusty village streets, visiting women whose babies she had recently delivered. These were early days in our work in Somalia. It was 1959, the year before I arrived. The hospital was only half built and the babies had to be delivered in the homes. Never before had the village women had the comfort of a professional midwife to look after them. And never had they experienced the care and expertise Joy showed. Soon Maryan was known all over town.

When Joy was not delivering babies in the houses or visiting the mothers, she was treating outpatients in a house on the mission compound. Two years before the hospital was finished, Joy had established a popular and widespread medical practice. Late at night she sterilised her instruments in a pressure cooker on a kerosene burner in preparation for the next day. Indefatigable, she had come with a vision and was determined to do all she could to see it fulfilled. If she was up all night delivering a baby in the village, she still opened the clinic in the morning.

In a culture where men had a low view of women Joy had gained wide respect, with the odd exception. One morning, when the clinic was buzzing with patients and a crowd was waiting outside, the watchman who directed people into the treatment room came wide-eyed to Joy.

'Haji Guleid is outside, wanting to come in immediately,' he said.

'Tell him he has to wait his turn,' said Joy.

'You tell him,' said the watchman, making a hasty retreat.

There was no need for anyone to tell him. The irate Haji, who was the local MP, barged in with his walking stick raised ready to beat down any opposition. Joy stared at him without blinking. After a few tense moments the big man lowered his stick and walked out. If they had been brave enough, the onlookers would have cheered. Instead the story went around the village in hushed tones.

For two years before our doctor, Jo Anne Ader, and I arrived to make up the team, Joy worked alone. The medical work was thriving long before the hospital was finished. I was broken in by accompanying Joy for home deliveries before I had my own list of patients. Not only did I need to earn trust from the women, but delivering a baby in a mud-thatched house, with an audience plus the complication of female genital mutilation (FGM), was a daunting prospect.

'We know Maryan, but we don't know Anab,' I would hear them say to one another. 'Perhaps she's a learner.'

Joy had graduated as a midwife from South Sydney Women's Hospital in Newtown. Originally called 'The Home of Hope for Friendless and Fallen Women', it had been established in 1905 by George and Louisa Ardill for women who had nowhere else to go to have their babies. An offshoot was excellent training for midwives. Joy delivered over 100 babies during her time there. People like me who went to the big hospitals were lucky to do 20 to 30 deliveries, always with tutors hovering.

Joy's dream of successful medical work, with an efficient well-run hospital as the hub, bordered on a passion that had a ripple effect on all of us. What was it that energised her and enabled her to persevere when others trembled with exhaustion?

Her father was a farmer. She was the eldest of five. Running the farm filled Joy's father's horizon. It was all he had ever known. Working hard, he progressed from share farming in the early days to owning a property raising beef cattle in the hills of Dungowan outside Tamworth. He had grown up in a family where hard work was the norm and expressing affection non-existent. He followed that tradition, and Joy had inherited this model of single-minded commitment to the task at hand.

'I was 15 when I passed the Intermediate Certificate,' Joy told me. 'Afterwards the teacher sent me home with a letter: "Dear Mr and Mrs Newcombe, I am writing to ask you to please let Joy continue at school until she does the Leaving Certificate. Her ability is obvious. She has already won a prize for her art and performed with excellence in all other subjects." '

Waiting anxiously to hear her father's response, Joy was disappointed but not surprised when she heard the weather-beaten farmer, toughened by hard work, say, 'Girls just get married and have children. Keeping them at school is a waste of money. There's plenty of work here on the farm.' Knowing it was useless to argue, Joy hoped, by submitting, it would be easier for the brothers and sisters following her.

Leaving school was a disappointment but not a disaster. Joy never saw those years as wasted. Her mother was small and gentle but also a resourceful farmer's wife and a positive role model for her daughter. The high jinks and adventures of farm children were now replaced by hard work and a different kind of education.

'Do you want to cook the dinner or make the cakes for smoko?' her mother asked her on mornings when there were shearers to feed. So Joy, still in her teens, learned to cook for a crowd of hungry men, to make light, fluffy scones when visitors arrived without warning and to sew her own clothes. Her mother was not only a wonderful cook but also a trained seamstress. Driving the tractor and working with the cattle were all part of the program. God was giving Joy an opportunity to learn a resourcefulness that would be invaluable in Somalia.

'Then one day I opened the paper,' said Joy, 'and saw an advertisement for nurse training. "There you go," I told myself, "I don't have to stay on the farm forever." The door to high school matriculation had closed but the door to nurse training opened wide.' And so began Nurse Newcombe's four-year general nursing training at Tamworth Base Hospital. I heard from others who had been there about her reputation as a skilled theatre sister.

Joy's introduction to finding the Lord Jesus as her Saviour began at a holiday camp held at Tahlee, a Christian centre built on the shores of Port Stephens. With other young people, she heard the gospel explained. Later at Tamworth Baptist Church she made a full commitment to follow Christ.

All of Joy's siblings eventually became Christians and developed wonderful Christian families. Both parents also made a Christian commitment, her father just before he died.

Joy sailed for Somalia in April 1959. Her first task on arrival was the inevitable study of the Somali language. Four young people from New Zealand joined the class before she finished.

Dorothy Modricker was their teacher. For Joy, formal classes and exams were not the optimal way to make a language her own. She was tone deaf and very shy practising in front of the others. Just as she was beginning to feel discouraged, the unexpected happened. She was summoned to talk with the director.

'Come in, Joy, and sit down,' said Warren Modricker when she knocked at his door. 'We have had bad news from Bulo Burti.'

Joy's interest was immediately roused. Bulo Burti was where the hospital was being built. That was where she would work once she had negotiated the language-learning hurdle. She waited to hear more.

'Both our builders, Hugh Street and Gordon Helyar, are ill with severe cases of hepatitis, and now Ada, Hugh's wife, has the symptoms,' the director continued. 'Could you postpone your language study and go and nurse them?'

For Joy this was a welcome interruption to the continual study. She viewed caring for the three needing her nursing experience as a privilege and a break from the pressure of trying to become familiar with a very difficult language. The three patients were extremely ill; at one stage Joy felt they could even lose Ada. But with skilful nursing and constant prayer, all three pulled through.

Back in Mogadishu once the patients had convalesced, Joy continued her course. Plodding along on leaden feet, determined to persevere, she completed the study requirements. One benefit from the break away was the realisation that using the language day by day in the village situation she had experienced in Bulo Burti suited her better than the classroom.

'Well done, Joy,' said Dorothy. 'You made it. You have passed your first language exam.'

So began the story of Maryan the nurse/midwife, who pioneered in showing a village the love and care that is the practical outworking of the gospel. The farmer's daughter from Dungowan, thwarted in finishing school the conventional way, had not deviated from doing what she believed was God's will. With Joy, no effort was spared in giving 100 per cent, whatever the task.

A hilarious situation in Bulo Burti occurred when Joy gathered together a group of traditional birth attendants to give them basic lectures on hygiene. We knew their practice was to arrive for deliveries equipped only with a sharp cutting instrument (razor or knife) carried under their left armpit in a fold of their wrap-around sarong. If the knife needed sharpening, any old rock or other surface would do as a honing instrument. The blade was used for the inevitable incision to allow the baby to be born as well as for the umbilical cord. If washed in between, it would be with water out of the clay pot standing near the door. Wounds were closed with thorns. No cloth was bought for the baby until it was safely born. Then a family member would be sent to buy a yard of material for a wrap. No point in buying ahead when the outcome was unsure.

The traditional birth attendants listened to the training talks with some scepticism. Those who completed the course were presented with a basic midwifery kit which they probably never used. All they were taught was taken with a grain of salt. We interpreted their body language as suggesting that white women younger than themselves were green and inexperienced. Only good manners stopped them saying as much.

It was completely different with the nurses we trained in the hospital. They were required to pass an official government examination. When we left them, they were competent and committed to maintaining the standard they had learned. These nurses worked with us for years, whereas the traditional birth attendants' training was only three weeks.

Joy was a nurse to the backbone. Night and day she worked to the point of exhaustion, longing to see the hospital fulfil her dream. Every patient she cared for received the best treatment available within the limitations of an African village. Any stress she experienced came when she was unable to replicate what she had been able to accomplish at home as far as hospital discipline and treatment of patients was concerned. Through it all she was totally dedicated, painstaking and thorough.

There was constant frustration for a person with Joy's standards. Patients used to mud-plastered homes had no qualms about wiping greasy palms on the green paint of the hospital walls, or, even worse, wiping their noses with their fingers and plastering the wall with that unsightly glob. During Ramadan, when swallowing saliva during daylight hours would break the fast, we tried to point to spittoons to avoid the floor being splattered, often without success. One morning in the middle of a delivery the patient's mother experienced an urgent need to spit. She bustled over to the window of the labour ward, cleared her throat and let go. How amazed she was when the frothy result ran down the window glass! 'Oh my God,' she gasped. 'I thought there was nothing there.'

I was not such a dedicated nurse as Joy. I wanted people to get better but I was more relaxed. I often laughed at things that upset her, such as the bubbles on the window. God brought Joy and me together to make a balanced team. It would have been disastrous if we had both been like me and very serious if both like Joy.

'I was a pain in the neck for you, Joy, wasn't I?' I said to her recently.

'No,' she answered, 'I only remember how funny you were and how well you got on with the people.'

Our combination was an effective demonstration of synergy. We both learned and were enriched by our differences.

Upon returning to Australia, Joy trained as an orthopaedic nurse specialist and was in charge of the orthopaedic ward at the Tamworth Base Hospital. She became a nurse consultant, on call throughout New England. Her standard was excellence, her contribution of inestimable value. We enjoyed a holiday together every year with other friends – all former missionaries.

Joy died on 21 May 2015 after a painful battle with bowel cancer. An example to us all, she faced death with joy as she contemplated meeting the Lord face to face. It is still unreal for me to believe she has gone. There was so much I learned from her, above all her deep appreciation of every expression of love and friendship. In the front row of mourners at Joy's funeral sat three nurse midwives: Pat Warner, Anne Donaldson and I. We had all gone to work in Somalia after hearing about it from the one whose life we were celebrating that day.

Figure 15.1
Joy Newcombe,
c. 1977.

16

O HOLY NIGHT

I sat alone on the cement verandah step, still warm from the heat of the day. It was Christmas Eve, my first Christmas in Bulo Burti. The evening air was balmy. The stars in their myriads seemed to be close enough for me to reach up and pluck one. The Milky Way was a radiant display. The beauty of the night sky amply compensated for the day's dusty, arid desert landscape.

Far from home and loved ones, adjusting to a new culture, language, people and work, I thought back to the last Christmas before I left Australia. One day, sitting on a bus travelling through Broadway, Sydney, my attention was caught by the billboard outside St Barnabas Church: 'Don't mistake the wrapping for the Gift!' It spoke to me that Christmas, as it has each succeeding one.

In Bulo Burti the advice was hardly necessary. The village shops sold the bare necessities. The food available in the market was not the stuff of banquets. We did not need Christmas gift lists as there was nothing appropriate to buy. There was no concern about overindulgence in eating in those early days. We were free to meditate on the 'unspeakable Gift'.

As I sat on the step I thought on the message of John 1:14, 'The Word became flesh and made his dwelling among us. We have seen his glory, the glory of the one and only Son, who came from the Father, full of grace and truth.' The words lit up my mind as the stars were lighting the sky. I enjoyed a sense of worship that was beyond my normal experience. With deep gratitude I thanked God for the Gift of his Son to the world, and I also thanked him for bringing me to this desert place and for what he was teaching me.

Subsequent Christmases brought other rich experiences. The first time we had Somali believers to celebrate with was a special joy. Two young men had come to faith in Jesus earlier that year. I have never forgotten the wonder on their faces as they heard the story of the nativity with the message of the angels and their realisation of God's Gift to the world. There was a heart-piercing significance in the words of the carols as we sang them with our newborn brothers.

Then there was the time when the first child of Albert and Tina Erion, Alan, was old enough to experience Christmas. Two years after my first Christmas in Bulo Burti, what was available in the shops was still underwhelming, but I remember Alan with his Christmas presents. He had a small plastic truck, a few blocks and a wooden clock with a hand that could be manually manipulated. Placed on top of one another it was a tiny, pathetic heap. But not to Alan. His little hands straightened the pile and he beamed as though he had been given a million dollars. Over and over he caressed each item. These were his treasures, and his joy infected us all.

As the years passed Christmas became more lavish. Parcels from home arrived and there were gifts to share and food more fitted to the occasion. But as I look back, I remember how, in those early years without the wrappings, the Gift was worshipped with an incomparable clarity.

17

THE CRUEL CUT

'Anab, tomorrow my daughter is going to be circumcised,' the woman, holding her eight-year-old daughter by the hand, told me. 'Could you do me a favour?'

'No. You know I won't do that.'

'I beg you, I entreat you – in Allah's name I ask you to be merciful to my little girl.' The begging body language involved stroking my chin. The frightened brown eyes of the child were fixed on me. It was an unbearable situation. 'If you won't do the operation, will you sell us some local anaesthetic?'

Again I refused. As they walked away disconsolate, I fought back the tears and tried to block from my mind the dreadful thing that was to happen early the next morning.

As a missionary team we had agreed we would never take part in female circumcision. Our hope was that the government would intervene and make the procedure illegal as had happened with foot-binding in China. Since 2013, 18 African countries have legislated against the practice, including Egypt. Thus far Somalia is not one of them.

No one told me about female circumcision before I left Australia. Three days after I arrived in Mogadishu, one of the missionaries, a New Zealand mother with her first baby, said to me, 'Did you know they circumcise the women here?'

'What? How can a girl be circumcised?' I asked. I listened in horror to her description. Here I was with two nursing certificates, hearing from a non-medical person about a practice I had never dreamed of.

What my new friend, Pattie, called female circumcision is now known as FGM in Western countries. In Somalia it is an integral part of a woman's life, a rite of passage that is universally practised. It was to have massive implications for our medical work. The World Health Organization (WHO) defines FGM as 'all procedures involving partial or total removal of the external female genitalia or other injury to the female genital organs for non-medical reasons'.[4] What we observed in the Somali women is described as 'infibulation', meaning that the inner and outer labia are incised and fused, with a small hole left for the passage of urine and menstrual blood. During this procedure, all or part of the clitoris is also removed.

As nurse midwives we learned the fine, gory details by painful experience. Every new piece of information was difficult to digest. In the villages, FGM was (and still is) usually carried out by traditional female practitioners on girls ranging from six to ten years old. There was no anaesthesia and the instruments were usually knives sharpened on a rock or a razor blade that may have been used and re-used multiple times. The labia were joined together with long, sharp acacia thorns crisscrossed over the incision and kept firm with thread wound around them. The girl's head was shaved as a routine preparation, and after the operation her legs were tied together at the knees to keep the wound intact. From then she could only hop around with the aid of a pole until healing took place.

The traditional operation was extremely painful with frequent complications such as haemorrhage, infection, urinary retention, urinary tract infection and tetanus. At puberty menstruation could be complicated by painful periods or even retention of menstrual blood. In many villages or rural situations, medical help was, and probably still is, unavailable. Wealthier city families sometimes sought safer medical environments.

The operation was a vital part of raising a daughter. One of our unmarried clinic workers, a Christian who had been educated, approached his mother and grandmother with the suggestion that they not arrange to have his little sisters circumcised. His argument was that the procedure was medically unsafe and extremely painful, as well as unnecessary. The response from his mother was to tell him to mind his own business. His grandmother slapped his face.

How could we, with our Western mindset, begin to understand such a practice? Cultural norms are deeply embedded and not easily explained by the locals. 'You are objecting to something our people have been doing for thousands of years,' one of our Somali nurses

---

4. World Health Organization, *Eliminating Female Genital Mutilation: An Interagency Statement*, WHO, 2008, p. 1.

pointed out. 'How can you expect us to stop just because you tell us it's wrong? It's set in our minds like cement.'

Recently I was sitting in a coffee shop here in Newcastle wondering why a young woman had a ring in her nose, studs under her eyebrows and bright-orange dyed hair. Did she think this was beautiful? What was the deeper meaning? She was from my own country and yet there was a wide gulf in our thinking. How much more difficult is it in a strange land with a strange language to begin to understand what is considered beautiful and acceptable?

Over the years I listened and related to women as they told me that circumcision was seen as preparation for womanhood and marriage. They said that after circumcision they believed they were more attractive. They also believed that circumcision helped preserve their marriage because the results of the operation increased their husband's sexual pleasure. Another important function was to keep young girls virgins until their wedding night.

There was also the mistaken idea that female circumcision was related to the teachings of Islam, which I have been told is not true.

A WHO report adds:

> In every society in which it is practised, female genital mutilation is a manifestation of gender inequality that is deeply entrenched in social, economic and political structures. Like the now-abandoned foot-binding in China and the practice of dowry and child marriage, female genital mutilation represents society's control over women. Such practices have the effect of perpetuating normative gender roles that are unequal and harm women.[5]

As medical people, my friends and I were forced to decide how we would respond to a centuries-old practice that we were impotent to change. As a group we were determined never to be involved in the actual operation on little girls. We did, however, agree that we would treat postoperative complications. We also decided that after childbirth we would re-suture the labia that needed to be cut for the delivery. Healing would be quicker and less open to infection by bringing the edges back together. The alternative was traditional birth attendants

---

5. *Eliminating Female Genital Mutilation*, p. 5.

being called in with their unwashed hands and barbaric equipment. Over a period spanning 18 years of medical work, I did not meet one Somali woman who had escaped FGM.

Delivering babies in the homes, before the hospital was finished, involved us in a variety of challenging situations. At first I delivered babies for multiparous women while Joy, the more experienced midwife, looked after the first babies. However, I was knocked out of my comfort zone one night when she was sick. Breaking the silence of the night there was a sudden loud knocking and shouting at our door. I opened it to find a young man I had never seen before standing there. He begged me to go with him straight away.

'Who are you?' I asked after an appropriate greeting.

'My name is Salah,' he answered. 'I am travelling on the back of a truck with my wife to Mogadishu. She is pregnant with the first baby. We were going to her parents. But labour has commenced. Please come. Hurry!'

I argued for a while. I didn't want to go. I was apprehensive. Usually we knew the families we delivered babies for. We would have done antenatal checks and become familiar with the home situation. I knew nothing about this couple or what the house would be like. Eventually, convinced that there was no option but to comply, I nervously gathered the necessary supplies and went with him.

After a short walk Salah led me to a group of houses. Stopping at the door of a hut he had rented, he grunted, 'This is it.' Bending down, I squeezed through the narrow opening. It was the kind of home that bush Somalis use, made of sticks planted close together into the ground to make walls then curved into an igloo shape. The sticks were bound together with twine then covered with waterproof thatch.

I could just see Salah's wife, Nuurto, lying on a woven grass mat on the ground. There was no furniture except a small stool about six inches high.

'What will we do for light?' I queried, squinting in the semi-darkness.

Pointing to a hurricane lantern flickering through a blackened glass, Salah announced that he was leaving us to it. 'Allah be with you,' he said as he crawled through the hut opening. No caress for his frightened wife or word of encouragement for the terrified midwife.

Somali husbands do not have anything to do with babies being born. It would be shameful for a man to be present at a delivery. Sometimes with first babies I even wondered how much they had to do with the conception. It seemed to be mechanically impossible.

When Salah left, after greetings and initial icebreaking, I said to Nuurto, 'I need to examine you to see if the birth is close.' I put a clean cloth under her buttocks and washed my hands with water out of a clay pot in the corner. I donned surgical gloves, swabbed her and attempted to do a vaginal examination. To my horror I could not even insert my little finger. How on earth did the baby get in there? And how on earth was it going to get out?

The foetal heartbeat was strong and regular, the baby's head was engaged and there were regular contractions. Nuurto groaned softly with each pain.

Prepared for a long wait, I sat on the low stool beside her and thought about KGV in Camperdown, Sydney. Instead of a brilliantly lit labour ward, stainless steel fittings, sterile cleanliness and midwife tutors hovering, I sat alone in the gathering darkness. The delivery table was a mat on the dirt floor, the light was a dim lantern and there was no one to help. I had very little experience of solo performance and no idea how I would manage. I knew I would have to cut, but would I know when?

The long hours of the night dragged on. Myriads of insects gathered around the lantern and stuck on to the exposed parts of my anatomy. My back ached from my hunched-up posture on the low, backless stool. Hyenas giggled in the dark night outside while I sat and prayed and wondered what lay ahead before we saw daylight again.

Although I would have loved a helper, there was one advantage of Nuurto and Salah's being strangers in town. We were spared the bevy of female relatives and neighbours who usually gathered for a delivery. These 'helpers' invariably touched the sterile equipment, gave conflicting advice and interfered in ways that intensified the stress of the midwife. Instead of that commotion, Nuurto and I were alone with God.

Towards dawn I could hear Nuurto's groans changing into the typical low grunting sound of pushing. It was almost time for the baby to be born. Murmuring words of encouragement, I prepared for delivery. Fortunately Nuurto was a very good patient. As I knelt over her, a tiny tuft of black hair could be seen in the stretching black hole, enabling me to inject some local anaesthetic into the join of the labia and successfully snip between the head and the stretching flesh. It happened 50 years ago, but as I write I can feel again the fear, the prayer and the joy when the baby was safely born. There was no damage to the mother except for the need to suture where I had snipped.

Eventually Salah returned. The placenta was out, the suturing complete and the baby bathed. I greeted him joyfully, 'You have a beautiful daughter!' He did not smile. I am sure Salah loved his daughter in time, but I rarely met a Somali man who was pleased when the baby was a girl.

After the time of recovery I never saw Nuurto and Salah again. They continued their journey. I was left to pack my stuff, go home, put calamine on my bites, start work in the clinic and thank God for a good outcome.

18

MURDER IN MOGADISHU

'Come on, Anab! What's the matter? Hurry up!' This was the regular call from patients as morning after morning I walked towards the outpatients' clinic. Eight o'clock was our opening time. I was always there on time, but our clientele were not governed by clocks. They went by the sun, often arriving at daybreak.

Most days a mixture of people who lived in the town and those who had trudged long distances from the bush was waiting. The women from the town were decked out in brightly coloured, loose, ground-length dresses or wrap-around sarongs with gaudy shawls around their shoulders and chiffon headscarves tightly covering their shiny black hair. They called out to the people they knew and shared the details of why they had come. In contrast, the nomads stood apart, quietly waiting. Their clothes, originally plain white fabric, had inevitably adopted the colour of the muddy water used for laundering. The women's head covering was typically heavier material.

The townspeople tended to look down on *dad baadiya* (bush people). There was a wide disparity in lifestyle and priorities. Conversation between the two groups was limited. The nomads' lives were a daily struggle for survival. Usually they did not come for medicine until a person was gravely ill. Sometimes a patient with advanced tuberculosis would be brought in on the back of a camel, the accompanying relatives helplessly begging for one injection to restore health. Sadly we would say there was no such injection and they would walk away back to the bush and wait for their loved one to die.

I used to look with wonder at the younger rural women. With the simplest of dress and minimal adornment, they walked with the bearing of royalty. Daily required to carry water from the nearest well or river or loads of wood for the fire, their backs were straight and their heads held high. No model strutting the catwalk in a fashion show in Australia could ever have moved me to the admiration I felt as I spent

Figure 18.1 – A typical Somali bushman.

time with some of the Somali bush women. With finely structured facial features and flashing dark eyes, they could match many a Western beauty queen. But physical beauty was far from their minds. The decision to come for medicine was a costly one involving long distances and a significant break with their traditional lifestyle. Would the sick person be helped? We needed special patience and empathy to enter their world.

Our challenge in running the clinic was maintaining a semblance of order. Somali men had never before been told by women to sit down and wait their turn. One strategy was hiring Hassen, a crippled man who 'walked' by pulling himself on his hands in a kind of frog jump. Hassen would come early and record the names as people arrived. From time to time an official would appear and refuse to wait with ordinary mortals. These men were prone to shout, threaten and force their way into the clinic treatment area. One memorable morning I gave in to the demands of one pompous gentleman, letting him in ahead of his turn. Hassan was so angry at being overridden he threw his book at me. I didn't do it again.

Most days, for an extrovert like me, running the clinic was stimulating. I enjoyed the variety, the banter, the encouragement of seeing people respond to often very simple treatments and the challenge of the repartee. The Somali sense of humour was infectious. On good mornings the treatment area would reverberate with laughter.

But on 17 July 1962, I dragged my feet wearily and groaned as I heard the usual loud voices of the waiting crowd. I had delivered a baby in the village at midnight. A joyful night for the family, with a boy born after four daughters, meant an exhausting morning for me in the clinic after minimal sleep. 'Keep going,' I kept saying to myself. 'It will soon be over.' I tried not to snap at people as I fixed my thoughts on rest hour, that wonderful practice in sub-Saharan Africa when most folk enjoyed a siesta. When there was no medical emergency, it was bliss to stretch out with a book and drop off into oblivion.

At last the final patient was treated. Hooray! At 1.00 pm I returned home with a grateful heart, ate lunch then lay down and went *biduq* (Somali for deep sleep).

Peace was shattered by a loud knocking at the door. I opened it to find Brian Maret, an American co-worker, who, with his wife Jenny, ran the boys' boarding school that was still functioning at that time. A boyish, handsome father of three, Brian was pale and close to tears.

'Merlin Groves is dead!' he blurted out. 'He was murdered by a Muslim sheikh yesterday.'

Filled with horror, we called the rest of the team. Soon the eight of us were together in my lounge room. We tried to digest the shocking truth that a fellow missionary, the head of a boarding school just like ours and a good friend, had been stabbed to death while he registered new students. His wife, Dorothy, who had rushed into the room

Figure 18.2 – In Somalia, women typically bear the heavy loads.

when she heard the screaming of the bystanders, was also stabbed by the assailant as he ran out. Her wounds were not thought to be life-threatening.

We sat praying for Dorothy and their three children as well as Merlin's co-workers.

'I have to go,' I said, looking at my watch. 'I have to visit the lady who delivered last night.'

'Be careful,' Brian cautioned. 'People in the village may well have heard the news.'

Believing it was right to go as I had promised, I set out with medical case in hand. Immediately on the road I was confronted by hostile men, all strangers. Their first words were: 'Don't you know one of you infidels has been killed in Mogadishu? We want you all dead. We don't want you here. You will be dead yourself soon.'

Usually my walk to the village was marked by friendly greetings and smiles and children running along beside me. Not that day. There were curses and stones and threats. In retrospect, I don't know why I didn't turn around and go home. But I doggedly kept going.

After a 15-minute walk I arrived at the house where the mother, Mahuubo, was waiting. I didn't tell her what had happened. I was too upset to talk about it. Instead I bathed the baby and gave him a cuddle. Mahuubo had tea made. We drank a cup together. It was just like any other companionable visit. Then I set out for home. The return journey was the same. Angry faces, jeers and hostility. None of my usual friends were to be seen.

Arriving back at my house distraught, I did not want to see anyone. In my bedroom I sat on the edge of the bed and, Job-like, confronted God. Job had said, 'Does it please you to make me your target, you watcher of men?' (see Job 7:20). My question was along the lines: 'Why did you bring us to this place where they hate us? They don't want us here. They have killed Merlin and they won't rest until they kill all of us.' Into my turmoil I heard Jesus say, 'They don't hate you. They hate me. You are here as my servant and that is why you are being rejected.' Opening my Bible, I traced with my finger the words of Psalm 69:7–9, 'For I endure scorn for your sake … and the insults of those who insult you fall on me.'

We were not there as preachers. We were there to help sick people and to demonstrate the love of Christ by caring for them. We were there in his name. There and then I was able to accept the cost and to pray, 'If it is for your sake I am willing.' I was calm again and able to face whatever lay ahead.

Merlin Groves, his wife and their three children were Canadians and had come to Somalia in 1960, the same year I arrived. They were members of the Mennonite Mission, the only other evangelical group working with us in Somalia in the 1960s. Combined, our two organisations may have been about 40 adults. We worked well together, meeting for worship and Bible study on Sunday nights when in Mogadishu and studying the language together. The Groves loved the work at the boys' school. The reason missionaries were given visas into Somalia was because of a felt need for English teachers. With many of the students being the sons of high profile officials, the school had been welcomed as a valuable contribution to young people's education.

Now Merlin was dead, having been stabbed over 14 times. His abdomen had been slashed open. Dorothy recovered, taking the three children back to Canada. She testified that, as she was attacked, she was aware of a wonderful love for the Somali people. Years later she returned to Somalia and for a time engaged in relief work.

19

BUILDINGS AND BOMBSHELLS

'They rushed me here to run a hospital and what did I find when I arrived? A roofless, floorless hull with grass growing up in the middle!' exclaimed Jo Anne Ader in exasperation. 'And on top of that, no one is doing anything about it. I'm ready to get going, but I am a doctor without a hospital.'

I had met Jo Anne the day I arrived in Mogadishu. She was on the verge of completing six months of Somali language study as I was about to begin. Two days before my unheralded arrival, she had taken the bus to Bulo Burti to view the embryo of the hospital and to see the house destined to be her home.

'I sat on the front step, looked across at where the hospital was to be and felt utter despair,' she told me later. 'No building was taking place, and I'd just been told there was no one to share the house with me. Joy Newcombe, the nurse already working there, shared a house with Pearl Thomsen, a New Zealand school teacher. As an introspective melancholic, I knew it would be a disaster for me to live here alone.'

Jo Anne arrived back in Mogadishu from her trip to Bulo Burti as I was sitting in the dining room at HQ in my non-communicative, new-girl, self-conscious mode.

Figure 19.1 – The shell of the hospital at Bulo Burti, 1961.

'I had been praying for someone to share my house as I travelled on the bus. I thought that perhaps this was the answer,' she told me. 'Then I saw you. Sitting there tongue-tied, obviously ill at ease, giving no evidence of being someone who would ease my loneliness. My heart sank.'

Fortunately, that first impression was momentary. After I'd thawed, we found we were kindred spirits. We decided God had brought us together to be friends and co-workers. We were to share a home for 13 years, very grateful for each other.

While Jo Anne waited for a hospital, those in authority in the mission had an idea. She was equipped with the language and had no hospital, whereas in Kelafo, a town in the Ogaden in Ethiopia, there was a doctor who had not had time for adequate language study. 'Are you willing to go and relieve Dr Dick Scheel so he can come and study Somali until your hospital is finished?' they asked her. Jo Anne agreed. It was an appropriate solution all around. Dick and his family moved to Mogadishu for intensive language study and Jo Anne filled the post in Kelafo.

But who was going to finish the hospital in Bulo Burti? Two brave young Australian tradesmen had been the first builders for SIM in Somalia. Hugh Street was a plumber, Gordon Helyar a farmer. Hugh, whose parents were missionaries among Aboriginal people in Australia, was a studious introvert while Gordon was an outgoing people person, emotionally volatile. With minimal language and huge difficulties getting supplies, they had trained Somali labourers in the burning desert heat and built three cement-brick houses in Bulo Burti, two in Belet Weyn, a school in each place and a clinic in Belet Weyn, as well as beginning the hospital in Bulo Burti. Galvanised iron roofs had to be raised at night because the reflection of the sun on the metal was blinding during the day. None of the workers knew English. The difficulties they faced and the fine calibre of buildings they produced challenge description.

Both Hugh and Gordon were engaged. The mission had a rule that new missionaries who had plans to marry had to pass their first language exam before the knot could be tied. In order to make life more bearable, it was decided that the two fiancées, Ada for Hugh and Pauline for Gordon, both still at home in Australia, could proceed to Somalia and marry before their own language study was finished in order to be there with their men. In the 1950s, when rules were tightly adhered to, this was a rare concession. But it happened. A double wedding was celebrated, providing the comfort of wives for our intrepid builders. It also meant that a single nurse could open a clinic at Belet Weyn because there would be a couple there instead of an unmarried builder.

Ada and Pauline arrived with their beautiful wedding dresses in their luggage. The guests at the wedding were mainly other missionaries. The long boat journey from Australia deterred family members from attending. The brides also brought their wedding cakes with them. Pauline's cake was sealed in a tin and packed in a barrel with her linen. A friend in Mogadishu, who just happened to have locally unavailable icing sugar, decorated it. It had pride of place at the wedding feast; but alas, when it was cut, expectant eaters grimaced or even spat into their handkerchiefs because of a dreadful mothball taste. The deterrent to stop silver fish or moths destroying the sheets and towels invaded the cake tin with disastrous results. The Streets' cake was not contaminated and it sufficed.

The building continued with the now married builders. When the so-called hull of the hospital was beginning to take shape, however, both Hugh and Gordon became ill with hepatitis. At that time Pauline was in Mogadishu having had their first baby and Ada was cooking and washing for the men. Soon the care became nursing. Both men developed jaundice, followed by the nausea and debilitation of the disease. It was not long before Ada realised she was also suffering the symptoms and, as already described, Joy Newcombe interrupted her language study to go and nurse the three of them.

Illness took the builders, then thieves stole valuable building material. New builders and new supplies had to be found. Eventually Albert Erion took on the project and the hospital began to take shape. Then again illness threatened the progress: Albert was often unable to work because of malaria and amoebic dysentery. Finally Charlie Bonk, another Canadian, arrived, and with his help the hospital was finished.

A shining white cement building with wards, outpatients' clinic, delivery room, operating theatre, kitchen and laundry had risen out of the desert sand. The inside walls were painted a soft green and the floors were white tiles. The devil had fought the building every step of the way, but we who had watched and prayed believed that this hospital

Figure 19.2 – Side view of the completed hospital at Bulo Burti, 1963.

was standing there as evidence of God's faithfulness and a fulfilment of promises he had given.

Triumphantly, the hospital was officially opened in April 1963. Town officials and leaders from SIM all took part. Our first two Somali girls had been employed to begin training. The beds were made, the cupboards stocked. At last Jo Anne was a doctor with a hospital, supported by Joy Newcombe and me as her trained nurses and a growing staff of excellent Somali trainees. Over the years Jo Anne was often heard saying, 'Give me Aussie nurses every day.' Both the products of rural hospital training, Joy and I were used to hard work and taking responsibility.

Soon after, though, a bombshell was dropped. In June, a new law prohibiting the propagation of any religion other than Islam came into effect, even though under the United Nations trusteeship religious freedom had been guaranteed. Not only was that freedom now taken away but in August 1963 it was decreed that the Qur'an be taught in mission boarding schools with a Muslim sheikh as the teacher. For us that resulted in the closure of the SIM schools except for adult night classes held mainly in Mogadishu. Disappointing as it was to close institutions so valuable to the community and with such potential for relationship with families, compromise with the government requirement was against all we stood for. Seeing it in a different light, the Mennonite Mission kept their schools open.

'Do you see any point in staying here in Somalia when you have no freedom to preach the gospel?' one of our East African mission leaders asked me. 'Would your friends at home, who are supporting you financially, agree with your staying here when you are being muzzled? Ethiopia needs workers. There is complete freedom for preaching the gospel there. Why stay here when you would be gladly welcomed there?'

We were all challenged to consider our future. We didn't hesitate. God had brought us to Somalia. The hospital was finished. The human cost had been heavy. The battle had been won in answer to prayer. We had perfect peace about staying. We were called to work with Somalis, not Ethiopians. Like the modern TV program, we all answered with a loud voice, 'No Deal!'

Darkness threatened, but the light shone through it. The veto against propagation of the gospel left one loophole. If an adult was willing to sign a request for Bible teaching we were free to go ahead. The newspapers had published details of new laws against Christian ministry, and literate adults, mostly men, wanted to know what was being forbidden them. As a result, many came and asked to be taught the Christian religion. What had seemed so dark to us now turned to be our first real breakthrough as a number of the people seeking teaching from the Bible made a Christian commitment.

In an almost universally Muslim country it is easy to give in to discouragement. Right next to us was Ethiopia where there was amazing growth of the church. We heard that in some areas there were hundreds of baptisms a month. Although we rejoiced in seeing some people turning to the Lord in Somalia, it was very slow, with much opposition. The law prohibited preaching of the gospel. People who did accept Jesus faced serious family ostracism.

Discouragement at times was a tool the devil used. At one such time I wrote the following:

QUEST

Lord, I believe; help thou my unbelief.
The way is dark ahead; I cannot see.
When service has not brought
The fruit for which I've sought,
Dear Lord, I pray renew your word to me.

Lord, I am willing; help my unwillingness.
You know I long to serve you as you choose,
But heart and flesh are faint
And sad is my complaint.
O strengthen me, lest I your blessing lose.

Lord, I would love; help my unlovingness.
Pour your strong love once more within my heart,
The love that knows no end,
The love that made you send
Your Son to die, salvation to impart.

Lord, I would see; O heal my blindness now,
Open the eyes of faith that I may see
The harvest you will reap,
The saved ones you will keep,
Proving your grace through all eternity.

Lord, I would praise; help now my lack of praise.
Open my lips and I will seek to sing.
The sacrifice of praise
To your dear name I'll raise
Till joy engulfs my soul: my Lord and King!

20

DOCTOR IN SOMALIA

'The blood pressure is 50/0!' I announced. 'And I can hardly feel the pulse it is so weak.'

'Give her some ephedrine,' the doctor, Jo Anne Ader, ordered with a tremble in her voice. The situation was descending into a nightmare. The patient was in the operating theatre ready for surgery. Although she was rapidly losing strength, the operation that was needed to save her life and the life of her baby could not proceed because her relatives refused to give the necessary permission.

It was 4.00 pm. The family had brought her to the hospital at midday as an obstetric emergency. With her haemorrhaging freely because the placenta was lying in front of the baby's head, a caesarean section was her only hope. The operating room and the doctor were all prepared, but the moment surgery was mentioned there was an immediate eruption of shouting and weeping.

'*Maya! Maya! Maya!* (No! No! No!),' they shouted. 'Just give her an injection to stop the bleeding. You cannot cut her open!'

Never in our years at Bulo Burti hospital was major surgery agreed to without drama. Islamic fatalism decreed that life and death were in Allah's hands and the surgeon's knife was interfering with the will of God. If the patient died of the disease then it was accepted. If the patient died on the operating table then the surgeon was responsible and would forever after be labelled a murderer.

'There is no injection that will stop the bleeding,' we insisted.

'Well, try one anyway!'

'I'd rather die than be cut open,' said the patient.

The hours ticked by as precious blood continued to flow out. Then, just as it seemed as though her life was ebbing away, without any obvious change in her relatives' body language, permission was given. Thumbs were jabbed from the stamp pad to the permission slip, and surgery was commenced on an almost moribund patient.

To our relief the operation was successful. The mother pulled through and the baby was fine. The relatives acted as though it was all their idea. They were as loud in their praise as they had been in their objections.

We, the staff, were relieved but also exhausted. The hours of tension beforehand, plus the grave condition of the patient as surgery commenced, had drained our emotional and physical energy. It was always the same. Operations were invariably complicated by the arguing and subsequent deterioration in the patient's condition. Not a single one ever went ahead smoothly, yet we never lost a patient due to surgery.

'Come and let me get you a drink,' I said to Jo Anne, leading her away from the hubbub of the rejoicing crowd. Surgery was a strain because we didn't perform enough operations for us to develop into a smooth, well-oiled team. Jo Anne was the only doctor and her anaesthetist, me, was still on her learner's licence. Added to that was the knowledge that if we lost the patient we would be blamed.

Jo Anne was a Texan, five foot tall, olive skinned, in her mid-30s and an introvert. If given her choice, she would have opted for a quiet life with books and a few friends to share ideas with. While she enjoyed the Somalis' sense of humour and the challenge of working with them, the arguments and loudness were exhausting. I looked at her as she sipped her drink. She was pale and the hand that held the glass was shaky. Without the strong conviction that she was here because God had led her, she would have returned home long ago.

When Jo Anne willingly offered her medical training to the Lord to be used wherever he led her, she didn't anticipate the frustration of working in a fanatical Muslim community. Hopeless despair often gnawed away at her. She would remember the nine long years of training and preparation. Because there were no family finances to pay for medical school, she initially trained as a nurse and then worked at night to finance gaining a medical degree. Working with the surgeons as a scrub nurse in the operating theatre, she delighted in their meticulous skill. Her orderly mind was stimulated by their expertise and discipline. When she responded to what she believed was God's call to go to a country where medical help was pitifully scarce, she dreamed of replicating what she had experienced with the surgeons in Texas.

Nothing could have prepared her for the reality she faced. Women were not respected. Patients were often removed from the hospital in the middle of treatment, and in the 1960s in Somalia there was no way of conferring with medical colleagues. Repeatedly she found herself in scenarios with the qualities of a nightmare. But it was not all bad news. The hospital did make a difference, and many people who would have died were saved because we were there. The bulk of the work was performed by the nurses, however, and it was easy for Jo Anne to feel that all that medical training was being wasted.

One day the mail brought news that a fellow graduate from medical school, Dr Ardell Vietti, had disappeared in Vietnam. She and other colleagues working in a leprosarium had been kidnapped by the Viet Cong and were never seen again. This news helped climax a thought that had been simmering for some time.

'What does God see as waste?' Jo Anne asked. 'Is it too much for me to give back to God my years of training and preparation? It may not be as I imagined, but I know he brought me here.'

Figure 20.1 – Ruth and Jo Anne in uniform, 1973.

She thought of the woman with the alabaster box of precious ointment pouring it out on Jesus' feet. 'Why this waste?' asked Judas. Jesus did not see it as a waste. That woman was the only one who had the privilege of embalming his body while he was alive. The women who visited the tomb took their precious ointments home again.

'It is not for nothing,' Jo Anne decided. 'Nothing is wasted if freely given back to God.' She learned that he has many ways of showing his love, often when it means persevering in difficult and disappointing situations.

Even though the medical work did not develop as Jo Anne envisaged, her sacrifice was not in vain. She was our leader. She taught us all so much and took every opportunity to use her training to ease the suffering of those who came seeking help. In the village, 'Dr Amino', as she was known, was a well-known figure, beloved by many.

21

EGYPTIAN SHEIKH

'Anab! Anab! *Daqso kalay* (come quickly)!' our friend Marian Sheik Salim shouted as she pushed her way through the waiting patients into the clinic. She was a large, powerful matriarch. Her word was law. None of our workers would have dared challenge her. She was also one of our best supporters in the village.

Not used to hurrying, she arrived gasping for breath and struggling to speak.

'What's wrong?' I asked.

'Just keep quiet!' she ordered. 'Look who's coming behind me.' I looked and saw another woman, almost completely hidden by the Arab burqa, sobbing as she clung with difficulty to the child in her arms.

'It's the Egyptian sheikh's wife,' Marian whispered in my ear.

The clinic crowd was hushed trying to comprehend the scenario being enacted before them. I led the two newcomers into an inner room to examine the baby. He was deathly pale and unconscious. As I watched, his little body was wracked by a seizure. His mother was wild eyed and hyperventilating, fully aware that her baby, the only son, was close to death. My heart went out to her.

And yet I was also apprehensive. She was the wife of our enemy, the Egyptian sheikh, the greatest opposition to our work in the village. This baby was obviously critically ill. If he died, what would be the ramifications for us? The two women said they had come secretly. The father did not know they had sought help at the despised Christian hospital.

Gamal Nasser, president of Egypt from 1956 to 1970, in reaction to Somalia giving work permits to Christian missionaries, had sent sheikhs (Muslim teachers) to oppose us in every village where we were working. Sheikh Fuad, the sheikh sent to Bulo Burti, demonstrated his bitter animosity towards us regularly and with passion. Every Friday, the Muslim holy day, when the clinic was closed, he preached against us in the mosque, making amazing accusations such as that our injections were designed to make people into Christians and similar absurdities. Every Saturday our outpatient clinic numbers would be significantly depleted. Only the extremely ill would come. Others were either deterred by Sheikh Fuad's propaganda or fearful of reprisal for being associated with us.

'What will we do?' I asked Jo Anne and Joy when I told them what had happened. The baby had a raging fever with a history suggesting cerebral malaria. The medication of choice, chloroquine given by injection, was risky. Sometimes babies died as a reaction. One Somali tribal chief had made murderous threats towards a missionary doctor when his baby boy had died after this treatment. Here we were with a critically ill baby, son of a powerful father who hated us, needing a dangerous medicine capable of curing him but at the risk of fatal side effects.

'We can't waste time,' Jo Anne said, her voice husky with emotion. 'This child is critically ill. If we wait we could lose him.'

Nadia, who had never met us before, came because her friend, Marian, had such confidence in us. She was in an agonising dilemma. If the baby died she would face the wrath of her husband. Our hearts went out to her as we observed her anguish.

'We have an injection we can give your baby,' I said to her through Marian. 'And we need to pray to God that it will help him. Your baby is very sick and cannot get better without this medicine, but sometimes babies still die.'

She was a brave mother. With huge dark eyes full of fear, she searched each one of our faces. Then she nodded. 'Treat my son,' she said. 'I know he will die if you don't.'

Carefully weighing the baby and calculating the appropriate dosage for his size, we prayed as Joy gave the injection. Leaving the little boy in a cot, his mother and Marian watching over him, we tiptoed away and resumed our interrupted schedule. As we worked, our minds were constantly returning to that quiet room where two anxious women sat with a desperately ill baby boy.

To our relief, within two hours there was an obvious improvement. Little Mastaffo was conscious and able to take the breast. Nadia was smiling as she looked down at him. They stayed a few days with us. The father never came. We had no idea what he was thinking.

Life was not easy for Nadia. Far from home, unable to communicate with the locals, desperately homesick and with Marian as her only friend, she daily struggled with loneliness. After she returned home with Mastaffo, she invited us to her house when her husband was preaching in the mosque. She had heard that Westerners like hot chocolate, but she made it so strong it was very difficult to drink. We couldn't converse. We smiled, bravely drank the strong cocoa, played with Mastaffo and the other children, and took our leave.

But that was not the end of the story. One evening at twilight a ghostly figure emerged through the trees in our compound and knocked at the Twidales' door. Like Nicodemus, Sheikh Fuad came at night. He would certainly have been recognised had he come in the daytime. Tall and thin, he wore a full-length grey coat and a dark red fez with a white turban wound around the lower part. Dignified and unsmiling, he waited for the door to be opened.

John Twidale, our station head, seeing who it was, swallowed his surprise, remembered the Arabic greetings he had learned in Aden and welcomed him in.

'I want a Bible,' the sheikh responded in strongly accented English.

Then began a series of weekly meetings when the sheikh came at dusk and read the Bible with John. He never spoke to the hospital staff. When he and his family left a few weeks later, he took a Bible with him. We do not know what happened to Fuad and Nadia and their children. They returned to Egypt and were not replaced. We never heard from them again. Mastaffo would be over 40 now.

Egypt is a troubled nation. We have committed the austere sheikh to God and marvelled at his working. Could it be that an injection of chloroquine given prayerfully to a critically ill baby resulted in his father becoming a Christian? Did his own prophecy come true?

22

AMAZING MILK SUPPLY

The stranger sat with the other people waiting for treatment in our clinic. It was plain to see he had travelled a long way. His thick leather sandals were broken and mended with twine. His clothes were the colour of the muddy water they had been washed in and his posture was one of complete exhaustion.

We managed the outpatients' clinic crowds by calling ten people at a time from the waiting room into the actual clinic. On this particular day nine were either laughing and chatting or telling us to hurry up because they were tired of waiting. But this man just sat. Our trained Somali workers treated return patients who were on a regular course of medicine while I dealt with the newcomers.

I walked over to greet the stranger. Then I saw he had a baby wrapped in a cloth lying across his knees. The baby was awake but lying quiet and still.

The father, who said his name was Ali, looked at me and said, 'His mother has died.' The chitchat ceased. There was a sudden hush in the room as the stranger murmured, 'I have brought you the baby. I don't want him to die too.'

I looked into his grief-filled eyes as people around me expressed their sympathy. I took the baby in my arms. Ali added that he couldn't stay long as he had other children.

My mind was in turmoil. We had agreed as a team not to keep motherless babies. But if I let him go he was going to die. What could I do?

'What is his name?' I asked Ali.

'It is Yuusuf,' he replied.

'OK, Ali, you come back in a few weeks.'

After a long, hard grip of my hand he left for the walk home, far into the bush. My heart ached for him as I watched him go. Yuusuf was bathed and fed before being settled in a hospital cot in the nursery.

Although some of our team reminded me that I had broken a rule, they all grew to love Yuusuf. He had plenty of cuddles. New aunties and uncles took turns to give him his bottle. He soon became chubby, dimpled, smiling and gurgling. He was a delightful baby.

Too soon the time arrived for him to go home. Ali had found a relative who was willing to take him. When she arrived, we all looked at her with doubt and suspicion. Could she be trusted with our beautiful baby? We had no choice. He had to go. We gave her detailed instructions concerning his feeding routine and the importance of cleanliness. She tied him on her back, walking away with him bobbing behind her.

We all missed him. 'I wonder how Yuusuf is?' was a regular refrain.

We wasn't long before we found out. One evening I walked into the hospital and saw sitting on one of the seats another lady from the bush with a moribund baby lying in her lap. It was Yuusuf. He was hollow-eyed and grey. He had had diarrhoea for days. He was a frail shadow of the child we had sent home. We started him on glucose fluids. It was hard to keep the tears back when he tried to smile his recognition, with weak gurgles.

He must have been a strong little fellow because he was soon well again. Once more we said goodbye, with even stricter instructions about hygiene, well aware of the difficulties in bush situations. Water, always scarce, had to be carried long distances in clay pots on women's heads.

This time we didn't see Yuusuf again for a long time. Then one day I saw some women talking outside the hospital. When they noticed me, an older one in the group called out, '*Halkan kalay* (come here)!' I went over feeling curious as they were all strangers. The one who had called me was withered and weather-beaten with a baby tied on her back. That wasn't remarkable because grandmothers often cared for babies.

When I reached her, she pointed to the child. '*Waa Yuusuf* (it is Yuusuf),' she said. I looked in amazement, and although he was longer and somewhat thinner, I could see it was our Yuusuf. He appeared healthy and alert.

Impressed, I exclaimed with joy and congratulated her on the good care she had obviously given him. This grandmother was proving successful in a project where so many failed: raising a motherless child in the Somali bush.

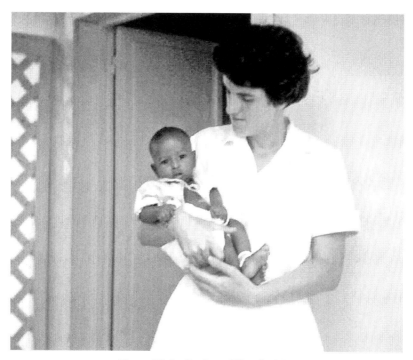

Figure 22.1 – Ruth and Yusuf, 1964.

'What do you feed him?' I asked.

'The breast, of course,' she muttered, scornful at such a silly question.

'The breast!' I repeated in amazement. Between the loose cloth tied over her shoulder I could see two pendulous, leathery bags hanging down below her waist. 'There wouldn't be any milk in those,' I exclaimed.

'Wouldn't there?' she snorted as she picked one up, squeezed the nipple and squirted a stream of milk into my eye and down my cheek.

I wiped my face as the audience enjoyed my astonishment. They were laughing more at my reaction than at the squirting. They all knew that a grandmother could reinvigorate the mammary glands when the need arose. I didn't. They left me standing there still in awe at what I had seen. Probably they were saying to one another, 'Just an ignorant foreigner who knows nothing about what really matters in life.'

That was the last time I saw Yuusuf, the little boy we had grown to love, and his feisty, funny grandmother.

23

MARRIAGE THE SOMALI WAY

'Anab, have you heard the news?' one of our nurses gasped as she rushed into the hospital to commence duty.

'What news?'

'The wife of Asaasi has gone crazy. She went running down the middle of the main road screaming. Her headscarf was off and her hair was standing up and she didn't have her proper clothes on. Everyone was staring at her.'

'Do you know what's wrong?' I asked.

'Yes. She heard that Asaasi had taken a second wife,' she answered. 'She's gone off her head.'

Asaasi was our sergeant of police. He was handsome, well built and somewhat aloof. His predecessor had been like a flash of quicksilver, always on the move and much more approachable. Asaasi walked the streets of the village with a certain presence and people needed to pluck up courage to approach him. His wife was of similar stature and bearing: a stately lady admired by many. She had borne him a fine family and seemed socially and intellectually a good match. Her name was Medina.

The thought of a husband taking a second wife haunted many of our Somali friends. Islam allowed for four wives when resources were sufficient for the husband to provide adequately. Even a happy, compatible relationship with the first wife did not insure against a second being taken. It was a painful situation for both women. The older wife would grieve because her husband was going to be involved with someone else and eventually raise another family, and the younger was vulnerable, not knowing how the older wife would treat her.

When taking a second wife, most men arranged a house for the new spouse in another part of the village. They understood there could easily be conflict. We at the hospital were confronted with a variety of situations. We sometimes had to patch up wounds where there had been biting and scratching.

Over the years we heard of a wide variety of scenarios. Domestic abuse was common. Young wives were often beaten into submission during the week after the wedding. One morning a young bride was brought into the clinic by relatives.

'What's the problem?' I asked, touched by the sad face of a very attractive young woman.

'She was married a few days ago,' the friend who brought her answered. 'She did not cooperate with her husband and he punched her on the side of the head. There is blood coming from her ear and she cries with the pain all the time.'

Examination revealed a ruptured eardrum.

After treatment I shared my shock and sadness with one of the Somali male clinic workers. His response left me lost for words. 'I had trouble with my wife when we got married and to bring her under control I punched her and broke her back tooth,' he said. 'She was good after that.'

Many of the lovely young girls we trained as nurses had marriages arranged by their fathers to men who had other wives. Often it was a business arrangement. The prospective groom asked for the daughter. The culturally appropriate response was for the girl's father to agree, especially if there had been favours done on either side. The daughter would only hear about it when the deal was sealed and the bride price paid. There was no going back.

My feelings towards 'our girls' were strongly maternal. On several occasions I tried to interfere. Horrified that a lovely young woman, a competent nurse in her late teens, was going to be married to a man perhaps 40 years older who had had many wives, I would go to the father and protest. It was a pointless exercise. Even though I knew our girls' families well, my arguments bore no weight.

There were kind husbands who treated their new wives with care. One unusual situation was a wife married to a district commissioner, who said to me, 'I can't wait for my husband to marry a second wife. I don't know why he is taking so long.'

'Why would you want him to take another wife?' I asked. I never expected to hear a first wife express such a desire. I knew her husband had been educated in Italy. Perhaps he was happy the way things were.

'I am tired. I have borne him many sons and daughters. I need a rest,' she answered. 'If there is a young wife she can go to the garden and do the digging. She can help me in the house.' It sounded to me like she was describing house help with some marital privileges thrown in. I never heard the outcome.

Sometimes we were invited to a wedding where it was a first for both husband and wife. Even then the agreement had been made by older relatives. Often the bride and groom had not met before the wedding. However, many of these unions had compatible outcomes. The benefit of an arranged marriage was the support given to the couple by both families. It was a community project. It was not a young husband and wife struggling to solve problems on their own. Both extended families had agreed on the arrangement and both were committed to giving their support.

I knew one family where four older wives of the same man shared a compound with mutual harmony and support. The walls around their plot were made of plaited sticks and were very tall. A rectangular house of mud-plastered sticks stood in each corner. The ground was swept. Everything was clean. There was no sign of garbage anywhere. When I visited, the four of them sat with me on low stools with a kettle boiling in a brazier in the middle. Somali *chai* was made by adding a cup of sugar, a small paper funnel of tea leaves and cinnamon to the boiling water. After a few minutes of further boiling, foaming tea was poured into Pyrex glasses.

At times like this there was joking and teasing, and I was often asked personal questions about my non-marital status: how I coped without a man and who would look after me in my old age if I had no children. This gave me permission to explore their situation.

'You four seem quite happy together.'

'Oh we are. We love each other!'

'Not many women married to the same man can live together like you do.'

'We are married to a good man who looks after us well. Also we are cousins. We have known each other all our lives.'

'How does your husband cope with four of you?'

'He is very happy with four of us. He likes having four.'

'How does he divide his time between you?'

'We take it in turns to cook his evening meal and he spends the night in the house where he eats.'

Figure 23.1 – Somali men of courting age coiffing one another.

'What happens after you eat?' I asked, following their example of asking personal questions.

'Well, first he has to be massaged with oil. Then he might just go to sleep. Perhaps there will be something else.' Loud laughter followed.

'What would happen if he got confused about whose turn it was?'

'That won't happen. Would you forget where you had dinner?' More laughter.

I loved visiting these women. They were unique. I never met another group like them.

I felt very sorry for Medina, Asaasi's first wife. She eventually calmed down and accepted the situation. She had no choice. That was the culture she lived in.

24

GOING SOLO

Around dusk one Monday night in 1964, I was called back to the hospital. One of the wealthy Arab shopkeepers of Bulo Burti had been carried in semi-conscious. What had happened to him was a mystery. He had suddenly collapsed in his shop. His name was Nasser, a strong healthy person in his mid-40s. He was influential in the town and a loyal support to us.

Unable to ascertain any kind of history, I sat with him throughout the night, taking his blood pressure and sponging his sweat-soaked body.

Jo Anne, our doctor, and Joy, our only other nurse at the time, were both home on leave. I was running the hospital with some Somali girls we were training. 'What more can I do?' I wondered. I had no idea what was wrong and his condition was deteriorating.

We had no telephone, no electricity, no pathology department, no Google. However, we did have one source of information. An amazing resource for nurses in isolated situations is a book called *The Merck Manual of Diagnosis and Therapy*. Joy often went to sleep at night or in siesta time with her friend Merck open on her chest. She loved it. I only resorted to it when desperate.

This night I was. As I leafed through, I came to a page on lizard bites. It described a black and white four-inch lizard whose bite was often fatal. I had seen them shimmying up walls and knew Nasser could have easily been bitten by one. His history and symptoms matched the description perfectly. The good news was that the antidote was very simple and available. The treatment recommended was an intramuscular injection of adrenalin. I could do that.

With a fervent prayer I inserted the needle into Nasser's flaccid arm and pushed the plunger. The effect was dramatic, with improvement almost immediate. In a few hours Nasser was able to walk home.

Throughout the long hours of that night, as I sat with Nasser and prayed for wisdom, I had plenty of time for reflection. I felt very much alone as far as human help was concerned. After Joy had returned home to Australia and as Jo Anne was preparing to leave for the States, I had been vociferous in my protests that I was to be left to run the hospital as the only trained nurse.

'This is crazy!' I said to Jo Anne one night. 'We have been busy with the three of us. How can I be the only one?'

'What do you suggest?' she replied. 'We've tried in every way to recruit help and no one has been available.'

'But I'm the worst one. Why me?'

'Well, you're not due for leave yet. Joy was overdue. She was exhausted. And I need to go. I've been here four years.'

As I continued to protest, Jo Anne interrupted by suggesting we pray. I agreed.

'O Lord, you can use the weak and foolish to confound the mighty,' she began in her deep Texan accent. I opened one eye to see if she was smiling, but she was dead serious. She continued praying, asking the Lord to help me. I knew she was reluctant to go and would continue to pray for me. There was nothing else I could do but accept the inevitable and trust God.

As I mulled things over that night, I remembered a conversation with one of the senior sisters at Lismore Base Hospital. 'What do you think you're going to do in Africa?' she asked me. Before I had been sent to her ward I had been told she was an ogre and everything that happened between us made me agree. As a first-year graduate in a new hospital, I had descended into my new girl coping style. My confidence disintegrated like a sandcastle in the path of the incoming tide. No wonder she questioned what value I would be.

'There is no other hospital where I am going to work. I'll be helping to look after the sick people who come to us,' I answered.

She made no comment, but her expression seemed to say, 'Poor people who need you to look after them.'

But she had reckoned without God. Nasser had not died. He had gone home well. I was not alone. I worked in the clinic the next morning with the thought of the divine help I'd experienced buoying my flagging energy.

With the outpatients all treated and lunch eaten I looked forward to an after-lunch nap. Stretching out under the mosquito net was bliss after a sleepless night. Sadly, the comfort was short-lived. Before I was able to close my eyes and surrender to exhaustion, there was an urgent rapping on the window. I looked out to see Albert Erion standing there.

'What's wrong?' I asked, although I knew the answer. His wife was due to have a baby.

'Something's burst on Tina,' said Albert. 'There's water everywhere.'

Albert and Tina Erion were my friends from Canada who had studied the language with me. Afterwards Albert had been involved in completing the building of the hospital and was now our local team leader. The mission directors had suggested the Erions go to Nairobi for the delivery of their second child. 'No,' they said. 'We will stay here with Ruth. We know she has delivered lots of babies.'

Now the membranes had ruptured, and because it was a second baby I did not expect any drama. I had helped Jo Anne deliver their son, Alan. Everything had been straightforward then. Why not now?

However, the hours went by with Tina in strong labour but without the progress I expected. 'What's wrong?' I kept saying to myself. Everything appeared normal. What could be the hold up?

There was no escape. We had to stay where we were in Bulo Burti. The van wasn't working and Mogadishu was a seven-hour drive away. I hid my fears. I tried to check the baby's heartbeat but my own heart was beating too loud for me to hear it.

About midnight I stepped outside. The desert stars were huge. The sky was decked in pristine beauty. I cried out to God in desperation, 'What will I do? What *can* I do?'

Then I heard the sound I longed for – the deep-throated grunting of a woman starting to push. I dashed into the delivery room. Sure enough, the cervix was fully dilated with the baby's black hair beginning to show. As the head was born I saw the problem. The cord was wound tightly around the neck several times. As soon as I clamped, cut and unwound the purplish coil, a beautiful baby girl was born.

Tina was ecstatic. 'A girl! Oh Albert, it's a girl! Tell Ruth the name,' she cried.

Albert was too choked up to talk. He just looked at his wife in speechless relief.

'We're calling her Rhonda,' said Tina.

Rhonda was my sister's name. 'What a pretty name,' Tina had remarked when I first told her. Having never heard it before, they decided that if the baby was a girl they would call her Rhonda and keep it from me as a surprise. The excitement was multiplied as I wrote home to tell my family not only of the birth but also the name.

The busy week continued with me forced to survive on minimal sleep. When I could snatch a spare moment I visited Rhonda, sharing in the joy of the parents. On the Friday night another woman, Habibo, a stranger to the hospital, was brought in in labour.

I examined her to see how the labour was progressing.

'How many babies have you had?' I asked.

'This is my 13th,' she said with obvious pride.

'Did they all come out head first?' I asked because this was a breech presentation.

'Yes, all head first,' she answered. I did not say anything then because the Somalis believe breech births are bad luck. I decided if 12 had been born head first, it would be a breeze for number 13 to come out backwards.

Habibo was accompanied by a hoard of relatives who were noisy and unaccustomed to hospitals. They became increasingly restless as the hours progressed without a baby appearing. One of the older women called me over to where she was sitting.

'It is our custom, if the baby is delayed, to pick the woman up by the feet, with her head on the ground, so we can shake her to loosen the baby from what is obstructing it,' she informed me. 'We want to call someone from the village to do that. We need a strong man.'

'You can't!' I exclaimed in horror. 'This is a hospital. If you try to interfere with the treatment I will send you all home.'

'If we go, Habibo goes with us,' the spokesperson threatened.

I was tired and concerned that they would try some of their outdated practices right under my nose. I left a Somali nurse to guard the patient and went over to where Albert and Tina lived. I brought them up to date with the drama. 'If only we could do an x-ray. Then we could see if all is well,' I said. But we knew the x-ray machine had not been working properly before Jo Anne left and no one had worried because I was not expecting to use it.

Albert, an eternal optimist, was a marvellous person with technology. 'Let's go and see if we can make it work,' he said with a big smile.

We walked back to the hospital, announcing to the milling, increasingly irate relatives that we were going to do an x-ray. I told them I would show them the picture. The effect of this news was electric. They all smiled and agreed it was a good idea. My mind was filled with foreboding, doubting we would succeed. Still, trying would give us a little more time.

We wheeled the portable machine over to the patient, read the instructions and followed them carefully. With the click of a button the exposure was accomplished. Albert took the metal film into our linen cupboard, which served as a dark room, while we all waited. The only light for us was a pressure lantern. There was absolute silence. At last he emerged from the closet with a huge grin on his face. He held the film up to the lamp and showed us a perfectly clear picture. The baby was lying in a good position. The pelvis was adequate and there was no obvious reason to worry.

An excited buzzing of conversation from the relatives signalled a mood change. Not too long after, a beautiful big baby boy was born. What a relief! Was it a miracle to encourage me in my extremity? Although we tried, we were never able to get the x-ray machine to work again.

The sister at Lismore Base had been correct in doubting my suitability. But she didn't know what God could do. I now look back on that year as a year of wonders. I was often stretched to the limit and exhausted, but my overall memory is of an amazing series of events in which I was guided in how to treat difficult cases and saw wonderful answers to prayer.

25

FIRST FURLOUGH

'We're not all deaf, Ruth! You don't need to shout.' Those words from my mother caused me to deflate like a pricked balloon.

I had arrived home after four years in Somalia. My dream of furlough had focussed on joyful reunions with family and friends and eating the food I had been missing, such as crisp apples, green salads and grilled lamb chops. But here I was after a few weeks feeling depressed and wondering what was wrong with me. When I did venture to tell a story, I talked too loudly and received the above response. I was defensive and felt isolated and misunderstood. I was not like the person who had left home four years before.

In Africa I was aware there would be major adjustments. I had read missionary biographies and been exposed to missionary speakers. I had heard that learning a new language and coping with strange ways of thinking and living would be stressful. Because of this preparation and a natural affinity with the Somalis, I felt at home more easily than I expected. But no one had told me that going home on leave after four years away is another emotional adjustment. I developed a serious case of reverse culture shock.

I arrived in Sydney on the P&O boat *Orcades* in February 1965. My family and close friends came to meet me and it was just as I had imagined: a joyous reunion. Mum had sent me a dress to arrive in so I would be up to date. I had lost at least a stone and was looking svelte. The time at sea was restorative. The family even coped with my slight American accent, which was transitory.

But I wasn't prepared for the plethora of changes. Although my mother had written to me faithfully every week, I felt significantly out of touch with life in Australia.

I had a room in my parents' house, but they had moved twice in the four years I had been away. I had left them in Lismore, where I knew people in the church. Now they were in Wellington in western

New South Wales, where I knew no one. My mother was a teacher, and although I was her firstborn, the others were all married and my singleness encouraged her to believe that she still had a child not only to mother but also to organise. She suggested what I should wear, that I needed a haircut, that I should smile at people more and that I should keep my voice down.

She was dying to introduce me to her new friends, but I didn't want to meet them. Conversation was stilted. Strangers didn't know what to talk about with me. Their best effort was often 'What did you eat over in Africa?' I had no energy to make polite conversation.

There was no debriefing in 1965. I had no idea how to process all that had happened in the four years. The loud voice was from habitually having to shout over the crowd in the clinic in order to gain some control. I missed the missionary team, who would have understood what I was feeling.

The negative emotions escalated into my saying to myself that I had been an utter failure as a missionary. Before I had left for Somalia I had a secret belief that I was God's gift to show his love to the Somalis. Now that inner voice had a different message: 'You didn't show God's love at all. Think of all the times you were angry in the clinic. You shouldn't be allowing people to support you financially. If they knew what you were really like, they would drop you like a hot cake.'

I knew that as soon as I had had a reasonable time for a holiday I was expected to visit the churches whose congregations had supported me to report on what had been achieved. I had seen other missionaries do it in the past. 'Dear, that was wonderful! Your mother must be so proud of you,' I had heard people say after a missionary address. I can't do that, I told myself. I wasn't wonderful. I was an abject failure.

One night it all came to a head. I was home alone and determined to spend the evening reading and praying. My passage for the night was Romans 7. I identified completely with Paul's words in verse 19, 'For I do not do the good I want to do, but the evil I do not want to do – this I keep on doing.'

'That's me,' I murmured. 'How can I go to churches and pretend I am OK? No. I will resign from SIM and do something else.'

But I kept on reading and turned the page to Romans 8:1–2, 'Therefore, there is now no condemnation for those who are in Christ Jesus, because through Christ Jesus the law of the Spirit who gives life has set you free from the law of sin and death.'

For me, reading those words was like turning the light on in a dark room. I had read them many times before, but at this point in my life they came with new impact.

You are not condemned. You are disappointed. You did not come up to your own expectations, but you are not condemned. Press on. Keep learning and be honest about your mistakes.

With this message from the Lord I went to the churches and spoke with absolute honesty about my failings.

Did my audiences take in what I said? Were they listening? As they thanked me for coming and pledged continued support, so many said, 'Dear, that was wonderful! Your mother must be so proud of you!'

No other homecoming was as difficult. I was more prepared on subsequent occasions and handled it better. However, the first experience showed me clearly the need for professional debriefing. Years later I was trained in the practice. What a privilege it has been to ease the way for others to help them avoid the painful experience I endured.

Between 1960 and 1983 I travelled to and from Africa many times. The first three crossings were by boat. I had the joy of sailing over the ocean in the P&O boats *Orsova*, *Orcades* and *Canberra*. Subsequently, it was always by plane.

Planes saved time. Boats gave time. The sea journey became a holiday, with space for reflection and clarifying thinking and mental and spiritual preparation for what lay ahead. I revelled in those trips. One of my favourite occupations is still sitting on a boat deck with a book on my knee gazing out to the far horizon and then back to the relentless track of a mighty liner cutting its way through the foaming sea.

The trip on the *Canberra* was in early 1966 after my first home leave. It happened to be a *Women's Weekly* tour. Because of that there were more ports visited and more entertainment. The boat wore a festive air. It took 28 days between Sydney and Aden. I had the joy of two special companions: John Warner from Brisbane and Anne Donaldson from Tamworth, who were both heading for Somalia as brand new missionaries. Both were 'rare finds' destined to have a valuable and lasting impact on the Somali work. I was blessed to have time with them. Another bonus was meeting some of John's and Anne's former Bible college friends in both Singapore and Hong Kong, ports we visited, and being exposed to genuine, grassroots Chinese cuisine, as well as hearing about their work.

As the senior missionary I decided we would do one hour of Somali language study every day of the journey. John and Anne agreed. We had a great time learning greetings, counting and some useful phrases. There was laughing and groaning and enough progress to ensure that they landed in Mogadishu with a few responses to the inevitable bombardment of greetings and questions aimed at them on arrival.

Figure 25.1 – Anne Donaldson teaching a village woman to sew, 1982.

26

THE DAY I RAN AWAY

'Come into my room. I need to tell you something,' Jo Anne said one evening in a tone of voice pregnant with emotion. It was early 1972.

'What is it?'

'I've found a lump in my breast. I'll have to go to Addis Ababa for a biopsy.'

That very week I had finished reading the biography of Isobel Kuhn, a Canadian, who had worked with her husband among the Lisu people in China's Yunnan Province. She, my favourite missionary author, had died of breast cancer in her mid-50s. Consequently my wild imagination leapt to a similar conclusion for Jo Anne, who was only 40.

As soon as we could make a booking for the trip to Ethiopia, I drove Jo Anne to Mogadishu to catch the plane. We traversed the bumpy, washboard dirt road in our hospital van in relative silence. I was battling with my emotions while Jo Anne didn't like chitchat during travel. She was an extreme introvert who at that time was more than ever caught up in deep thought. We arrived safely at the mission headquarters where I stayed for only one night because I was needed back at the hospital. Wondering what the future held, I said goodbye to my friend as I prepared to drive back to Bulo Burti with a Somali worker for company.

With Jo Anne gone we had no doctor. I bore the responsibility of running the hospital with two other missionary nurses and the Somali staff to help me. In the evenings I went home to an empty house, lonely, with no one to rehash the day's events. During all my waking hours, at work or at home, I was conscious of the shadow of the as-yet-unknown biopsy result.

Working in Somalia was hard. Having a friend to share a home and the hospital work with transformed mere survival into a rich and enjoyable experience. Our divergent personalities resulted in a mutually satisfying synergy. Jo Anne was studious, loving nothing more than a couple of free hours to read a book or *Time* magazine. I revelled in filling the house with visitors, experimenting with what we could buy in the market and cooking something special.

'Do we have to have people here every night?' Jo Anne would sometimes murmur.

'Why, we've hardly had anyone this week,' I would answer, wondering why she minded.

In spite of our differences it was a harmonious household, both of us learning from the other and so grateful for a close friendship where we could share our inmost thoughts and know there was a genuine acceptance.

'Is it all going to end?' I asked myself. 'Has it been wrong to be so happy?'

A few days later a cable arrived. 'Tumour benign. Returning to Bulo Burti. Jo Anne.'

For me it was like Abraham having Isaac restored. I waited impatiently for a message to collect her from Mogadishu and bring her home. But that message never came. Instead a second cable followed the first with the message, 'Dr Ader suffered coronary occlusion and is being repatriated to the USA when able to travel.'

With that news I stopped being reasonable, descending into blind panic. I imagined Jo Anne in Addis Ababa, with no close friends, weak and ill. I decided I had no choice but to go and care for her.

SIM had strict rules concerning travel, one being that permission was required before leaving our work. Nevertheless, I asked no one. I packed a bag and the next morning caught the bus back to Mogadishu. All the way over the bumps my mind was in turmoil. No one at HQ knew I was coming. The first they knew was to see me alighting from the three-wheeled taxi that transported me from the bus station.

'I'm going to Addis Ababa on the next plane!' I announced to Albert Erion, now the director in Mogadishu. 'I have to go and look after Jo Anne.'

Albert and his wife, Tina, my good friends, now had a third child, Glenn, also born in the Bulo Burti hospital, this time with the doctor to officiate. They were surprised to see me and hear what I said, but they didn't try to deter me. There was only a murmur about plane bookings. That was all. The plane did not go to Ethiopia every day. I retired that night with no travel plans finalised.

Once in bed I began my evening reading. Suddenly there was an amazing return to logical thinking. It was as though what I read was a mental chiropractic manipulation. A sharp click and balance was restored. Strangely enough, it was all about having our hearts circumcised before the Lord. I read it in *Daily Light*, a regular devotional book of mine consisting entirely of Bible verses arranged in topics.

'What are you doing,' I asked myself. 'You can't run off like this! What do you think is happening at the hospital? Jo Anne certainly wouldn't want you to leave everything and go to her. No. Go back to Bulo Burti and do what you know is your responsibility.'

I turned off the light and instead of stewing was able to sleep. The next morning I caught the bus back to Bulo Burti. The Erions looked so relieved when I said I had decided not to go to Addis Ababa. Again they did not say anything about my unexpected arrival and departure.

When I appeared back at Bulo Burti, I was greeted with joy. 'Thank goodness you came back,' the other nurses said. 'The colonel's wife is in labour and he has been shouting for you.'

I was back in my rightful place. The delivery went well. The colonel, an officer from the Somali military, was happy even though the baby, their first, was a girl. He didn't seem to mind at all, which was unusual. He even rewarded me with a beautiful Somali outfit.

Jo Anne flew home to America, and before she was fit to return to us, we were all evicted from the country by the communist government. She never came back to Somalia.

Many years later, when I was working in Kenya, I was again a co-worker with Albert and Tina Erion. One day Tina and I were sitting in the car reminiscing as we waited for an appointment.

'I always feel guilty about that time in Somalia when I ran away from Bulo Burti so impetuously to go to Jo Anne after the heart attack,' I said. 'Do you remember when I announced I was going to Addis Ababa without asking permission?'

'Is that the time you arrived on the bus and returned the next morning?' Tina asked.

'Yes, that time.'

'Don't you remember what happened?'

'I only know I wasn't thinking straight and was prepared to do a Jonah and leave the others to run the hospital,' I said.

'Ruth, I will never forget that day,' Tina continued. 'Glenn, our youngest son, had been sick for weeks and no doctor in Mogadishu had been able to help us. You arrived out of the blue, looked at him and said, "If Jo Anne were here she would give him full treatment for malaria." We hadn't done that because there was supposed to be no malaria in Mogadishu and the doctor we visited was sure that wasn't the problem. We followed what you told us to do and soon Glenn was well again. I can't believe you don't remember.'

'No, I only remember what a fool I felt thinking I could just down tools and run off.'

'Well.' said Tina, 'on our next trip home in Canada, whenever we were invited to speak in a church, among our other stories we told them how sick Glenn had been and how one of the nurses unexpectedly appeared, told us what to do and then left once more!'

27

GOODBYE, BULO BURTI

Fifty years have passed, yet the memories of my ten years in Bulo Burti are forever etched in my mind. Life was filled with busyness, problem-solving and deep satisfaction. What a privilege to be centre-stage in a drama where the sick found health, babies were born, gifted young people were trained to help others medically, deep friendships were formed and a precious nucleus came to Christ.

Like a flashing thunderstorm out of a clear blue sky, one day in 1969 everything changed. Somalia's ten-year-old democracy was shattered when the president was assassinated by his own bodyguard.

'Somalia is now governed by scientific socialism,' blared Radio Mogadishu. 'The Soviet Union is shoulder to shoulder with us in governing our country. No more Western imperialism.' For us the result was two bullies: the communist regime and the Somali doctor appointed over our area.

The hierarchy decreed that private enterprise was now nationalised. Produce from gardens must be taken to central points where a set price would be paid to all. In our hospital we were forbidden to charge the minimal fee for service that had enabled us to keep going. Government spies haunted the outpatients' clinic. Where once we enjoyed open conversation and light-hearted banter, now there was a constant wariness. A thoughtless comment could lead to arrest and imprisonment. Fear reigned. Work satisfaction among the people plummeted.

Up to this point we had been completely independent. Now we were under the rule of Dr Muhidin, a Russian-trained Somali medico. 'Open your medicine storeroom,' he regularly ordered, proceeding to fill a waiting van with the medicine we imported from America. 'I will be arriving to inspect your wards tomorrow,' he would announce. Then he would parade around criticising imagined specks of dirt.

'What's that on the floor?' he asked me once as I accompanied him on a round.

'A Fanta bottle top,' I answered, retrieving it.

'You should run the hospital properly,' he said. 'You could be arrested for that.'

The months we worked under this regime were filled with stress and uncertainty. Our time in Somalia was almost over. The pressures from the communist government were inexorably closing in. I was glad that Jo Anne, convalescing at home in America, did not have to go through the pain of working under this regime.

At that very time, Haawa, the cook from Mogadishu, was a patient in Bulo Burti. She arrived totally without warning. One morning as I walked to the hospital I saw a tall, slim woman walking slowly towards me. Her shoulders were slightly stooped, her steps were dragging and the whole movement of her body spoke of extreme weariness.

Then she smiled and said, '*Anabay, nabat miya* (Anab, is it peace)?'

'Haawa!' I exclaimed. 'What are you doing here?'

'I've come for medicine,' she answered. 'I've been sick for a long time. My husband told me to come to you.'

I looked hard at my friend. The light had gone out of her eyes. Her face was haggard and the skin hung loosely on her arms and shoulders.

I hugged her, leading her into a ward where there was an empty bed. We were saddened when she tested positive for pulmonary tuberculosis. This is a dreaded diagnosis for the Somalis, often fatal. They seek treatment too late and fail to persevere. The whole family is vulnerable because of their one-roomed houses, with everyone sleeping together, often in the same bed.

'It will be all right,' Haawa said when I broke the news. Her body was weak but her spirit was strong. 'I will stay here as long as you say. I know God will heal me.'

'You must get that woman out of the hospital!' the communist doctor ordered after she had been with us for a few weeks. He had been doing a round with me and asked what was wrong with Haawa. Although we had kept her carefully isolated and she was not coughing, he was adamant she could not stay.

Previously there had been an occasion when he had criticised the hospital for a trivial incident. Haawa, who had heard him, told him in no uncertain terms that it was the best hospital in Somalia. She added that she had heard how filthy the town government hospital was. How dare he talk to me in such a derogatory manner! He did not react then, but perhaps this was his retaliation.

'Haawa, I want you to come and stay with me,' I told her after the doctor had gone. 'I have a spare room now that Dr Amino is not here. It will be quieter for you.'

The next few weeks with Haawa sharing my house were a benediction, a blessed period when I shared deeply with a Somali Christian sister. What a memory to take away with me! I would wake in the morning and look across to her room where she sat in front of a window reading a devotional book. At lunchtime when I came home from the clinic the table would be set and lunch prepared.

Some people murmured that I was foolhardy for having a tuberculosis patient in my house. I took no notice. I was exposed to a wide variety of germs in the clinic every day and I knew that Haawa was scrupulous in washing her hands. By nature my fear of germs is minimal. I have found that the people who are most fanatical at avoiding bacteria are often the ones who succumb most often.

After several weeks of treatment, Haawa returned to her family with a liberal supply of medicine and the strict instruction that she was not to have a baby for at least another year. Both she and her husband agreed that she would faithfully take the contraceptive pill.

Soon after she left, the news we were dreading came. We were to pack our personal belongings and leave. The final week for me was a blur of malarial fever, packing and a constant stream of people coming to say goodbye.

We had delivered eight babies for one young Arab woman, Zeinab, including one set of twins. 'Where will we go now?' she wept. 'Who will look after us?'

Watching her weep, I remembered a nightmarish day when she had rushed into the hospital with her four-year-old boy, Osman, in her arms. He was cyanosed and fitting.

'What happened?'

'He found a bottle of aspirin and swallowed all the tablets.'

We were three Australian nurses. Immediately we looked up our faithful *Merck Manual* for aspirin poisoning. The remedy was an infusion of intravenous dextrose. I knew I would not be able to get a needle into the veins of a four-year-old who was being racked by seizures. 'I can try,' said Pat Warner, who had worked in Gaza with the

Southern Baptists and become proficient with children's veins. She was successful. She said she had learned it from the Arab trainees, who had it down to a fine art.

The result was amazing. As the dextrose flowed in, the fitting stopped. The bluish tinge faded and normal colour returned. Osman was a stocky little fellow who was unusually daring and soon ready to face the world again.

I knew Zeinab was right. Who would help them?

The farewells were heartbreaking. The girls we trained as nurses, our closest friends, came one by one to the house while I was packing to say goodbye. We held each other for a moment and cried, then I watched each one go out the door back to the hospital, now forbidden to us.

In happier times, whenever one of us left Bulo Burti for a holiday or for home leave, a crowd of Somali friends would gather to wish the traveller well. There would be gifts of eggs, cake and the occasional live chicken.

'*Nabadt geliyo* (go in peace)' and '*Safar wanaagsan* (safe journey)' would ring out, and, most importantly, '*Soo noqo* (come back)!'

On the day of our final departure, Christmas Eve 1972, we left in an eerie silence. Not a solitary Somali was to be seen. Howard Borlase,

Figure 27.1 – Noor giving an injection, 1969.

122

Figure 27.2 – Three of the mission's trained Somali nurses, c. 1967.

one of our leaders, had come to take us back to Mogadishu. Our Bulo Burti van had become government property. Six of us climbed into his Range Rover and were driven away.

Were the staff working in the hospital told not to come or were they too sad? We will never know. To the government officials, we had become unwelcome aliens. And for our friends, fear of reprisal reigned.

Except for Noor. He was our most experienced hospital worker, the beloved leader of the Christian group. He had driven to the village for a patient. As he returned he saw our vehicle leave. Over the bumpy road he drove fast enough to overtake us. We opened our doors. Wordlessly he embraced us all. We could feel his body shaking with emotion, but not a word was said. He returned to the van, drove back to the hospital and we continued our journey.

We celebrated our last Christmas in Somalia in Mogadishu, with an abundance of special treats that had arrived in food parcels from families at home. What we didn't eat would be left behind as we were departing for Ethiopia the next day. What irony! Food that was a rare delicacy covered the table, yet we hardly noticed what we were eating.

We arrived in our new homeland, Ethiopia, on Boxing Day. Here was the base of the East African headquarters of SIM. Debriefing was not yet known or understood. There was no counselling or opportunity

Figure 27.3 – The first baptism at Bulo Burti, c.1968.

Figure 27.4 – Our first Christian wedding at Bulo Burti, c.1969.

for us as a group to meet and process our grief. Overhearing comments such as 'How great to have these nurses come from Somalia – they will be wonderful to fill some gaps' merely aggravated our pain.

Because I was sharing a room, the only privacy I had was the bathroom. Periodically I would lock myself in and sob convulsively, then wash my face and emerge feigning normality. With broken nights and emotions out of control, I reached the stage where I needed medical help, which I received. However, the knot of grief deep within did not dissolve for many years.

28

EXIT BELET WEYN

While we faced the sadness of leaving Bulo Burti, John and Kae Thornhill were preparing to leave Belet Weyn, another mission station three hours north. I heard the details from them later and share here what they described.

On the day they were due to leave they had an unexpected visitor. In a cloud of dust the government Land Rover screeched to a stop outside their house. John watched with a sinking heart as the District Commissioner (DC) sprang out of the vehicle and walked towards him. New to the town, this official had been cold and unfriendly towards the foreigners at every encounter. Now he strode inside the house and looked around.

*Figure 28.1 – John and Kay Thornhill with baby Christopher, 1972.
Used with permission.*

In the middle of the lounge room were four 44-gallon drums, sealed and padlocked. 'Unlock those barrels and tip everything out!' he barked.

At this order John gasped in horror. Due to leave Somalia, first for home leave in Australia after four years in the country and then to continue their work in Ethiopia, he and Kae had begun packing in their spare time weeks before. Arriving in Somalia newly married, they had brought precious wedding gifts to brighten their home in a spartan situation and as reminders of the givers. Ample time to pack carefully was mandatory.

'We can't just tip,' said John in response to the demand. 'Many things will break. But we can unpack.' He wondered what the official was looking for. When they had reported to the authorities their plans for departure, they had been told they could take personal possessions.

Although Kae and John had been packing for regular leave, just as they finished they had received the message that all mission personnel were to pack their personal belongings and vacate the properties. The entire Somali team, spread over four different locations, was packing, saying goodbyes and grieving.

The Thornhills had shared the work at Belet Weyn with two nurses. Along with Kae, also a nurse, they had run an outpatients' clinic and a small maternity hospital. John had led the work and also conducted English classes for adults as well as Bible studies for those who were interested.

Belet Weyn, with the Webi Shebelli (Leopard River) snaking through the middle of the town and tall palms towering over mud thatched rooves, was the capital of the Hiran region. One exciting feature was a swinging bridge over the river. The Somalis called it *liqliqety*, mimicking the noise it made as a constant human stream traversed its 100-metre width.

During their time in Somalia the Thornhills' first child, Christopher, now aged 12 months, had been born and Kae was pregnant with their second. The move to Ethiopia was because of Christopher's intolerance to the heat in Somalia.

The DC grunted agreement in response to John's suggestion that he unpack rather than tip. In spite of this concession, undoing several weeks of work was a blow. Packing barrels takes time and skill. It has to be done carefully because, once on the road, the drums, although strong and waterproof, experience many adventures before being reunited with their owners. Some journeys require them to be wrapped in rope hammocks, picked up by huge cranes and dumped on boat decks, or loaded on rickety trucks and driven along bumpy roads – or worst of all, dropped from a height by careless handling. Possibilities like these require breakables to be wrapped and wedged into tight spaces, where no matter how violent the jolt, there will be no movement.

Through many tedious, backbreaking hours John and Kae had packed their treasures. Now John was being forced to undo it all, with the truck they had ordered to transport the barrels to Mogadishu waiting outside. Adding to the nightmare was the lack of information as to why they had to do it. Stoically, John determined to comply, remaining gracious in the face of the unreasonable demand.

After the four barrels were emptied, Kae arrived from the midwifery centre where she had been visiting. She had been prepared by a friend for what she was about to see. With the contents of the four drums spread over the tiled floor, she and John looked at each other and then at the official inquiringly.

'Is that everything?' the DC asked.

'All except my tool box, which is on the verandah,' John answered. The tool box was his pride and joy. He had made it in his spare time while working at Belet Weyn and had surprised even himself by how good it looked.

'Open it!'

In the box were the tools John had brought with him from Australia. He had either bought them himself or they had been given to him as gifts.

'Nationalised!' the DC announced.

'They are my personal property,' explained John.

'Prove it!'

There was no proof. The tools had been bought over the years in a variety of places. Because they were personal property, receipts had not been kept. The DC confiscated them all.

'Can I keep the box?' John asked. 'I will need to put extras in now. We will have to pack in a hurry.'

'No. Everything is nationalised.'

On hearing that, one of the government men who had accompanied the DC, and who had been silently watching the drama, murmured

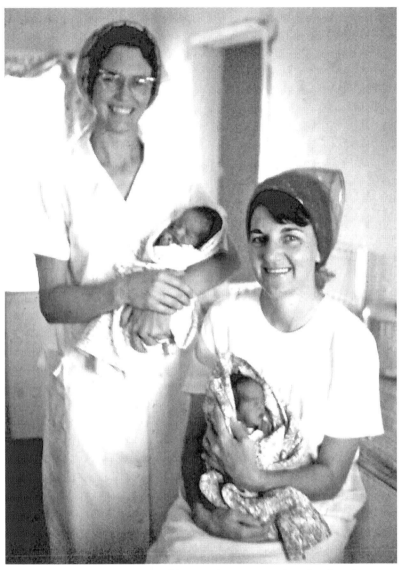

Figure 28.2 – Anne Donaldson and Pat Warner (nee Fordham), midwives at Belet Weyn, 1969.

something quietly to him. 'Keep the box,' the DC said grudgingly in John's direction.

Leaving the Thornhills' home, the official made his way over to the ladies' house to see what could be found there. Lined up on their verandah were 14 barrels, the property of the present nurses plus those people currently on home leave. The sheer volume was too much for him and he returned to his jeep. Perhaps other duty called. The tools were what he wanted and they were safely in the vehicle.

Through it all John had remained courteous and respectful.

'I am sorry we had to do this,' the DC said as he left.

'See it as your good fortune,' John responded politely.

'I don't understand,' the DC muttered as he drove off. Perhaps he couldn't fathom why John didn't fight for what was lawfully his.

It was hard for John to understand too. Had he known that it was the tools being sought he would not be facing repacking four barrels. He then had to endure the long journey on a bumpy road with a one-year-old baby and a wife in early pregnancy.

However, through the entire ordeal, he was aware of the all-sufficient grace of God and the importance of leaving a good testimony. He truly believed that all these unexpected happenings, no matter how stressful, would work out to God's glory. He had prayed that his family would be kept safe. Now he committed the final outcome to the Lord. He hoped that one day he would be able to see the funny side.

29

LEFT IN MOGADISHU

Our Bulo Burti team spent two nights in Mogadishu before flying to Addis Ababa. While there, John Warner, who had been working in Mogadishu, stunned us with an announcement.

'We're not going! We've decided to stay on.'

'How can you do that?' I asked.

'We have not been ordered to leave the country,' he pointed out, 'only to vacate our properties.' He told us that he and his wife, Pat, along with Christel Voll, had decided to remain in Somalia for as long as possible. 'We want to be here for the Christians who will be left and to continue to teach the Bible for those who want to learn.'

Pat and John, in their 30s, had first met in Somalia, fallen in love, married and now had three-year-old Michelle, a loquacious blonde treasure. Pat and John were both the firstborn of large families. Each was used to taking responsibility, leading the way. Pat was from north-western NSW and John from Brisbane. Christel, who was from Germany, came from a small family with only one brother. Her father had been in Christian ministry. She was quiet, precise and passionately committed to the Somali work.

So the rest of us left them there. To stay was a brave decision. Not only would they be bereft of the team and the structure of the regular work they had been involved in, but the country was in turmoil.

'When it hit us that everyone had gone and we were on our own, an indescribable sense of aloneness descended on us,' they said later. 'Although we were convinced that the decision to stay was the right one, we never dreamt how alone we would feel that first day.'

Those in power were suspicious and repressive. As in other countries where communism had taken over, spies for the government were ubiquitous. Local people were arrested for criticising the regime or mentioning their tribal relationship. Tribalism, a defining factor in Somali culture, had been forbidden by the communist government because it was seen as dividing loyalty. Public demonstrations to symbolically bury it had been conducted. From now on, to mention one's tribal origin was a criminal offence. False accusations were rife and innocent people were often punished unjustly.

Where would our friends live? Would they find a landlord willing to rent to Westerners? At last we received news by mail. After trekking around the winding streets of suburban Mogadishu, they had found a duplex whose owner agreed to have them as tenants.

'It's not perfect,' wrote Pat. 'There's a big iron gate making it impossible to see who is knocking. The kitchens are pokey. There's not room for two people to pass each other. The bathrooms are big enough to hold a party but with blue exudate coating over all the fittings from the mineral deposits in the water.'

Still, the geography was good, the place would make it easy for others to find them and the rent was affordable. They did not discover until later that the National Security Services were almost opposite, resulting in them being under constant surveillance.

The ups and downs of finding accommodation and settling in were both challenging and encouraging. Narrow bookcases bought for the school at HQ and never installed were perfect in the tiny kitchens. Little gardens outside the duplex doors proved to be havens for centipedes. Apparently, every time water hit the earth, the centipedes raced for cover. Stomping on them to prevent them going into the houses was nearly as good as going to the gym.

In the early days of this new situation the only regular visitors were a boy who brought fresh bread and a fish vendor. Hundreds of pupils who had previously attended the mission adult English classes avoided them. One old and trusted friend whom John met in the bank told him he knew where they were but could not visit their house. 'Even chatting with you here could invite interrogation,' he said.

There was constant fear of spies in government employ. In such a situation one seen as a best friend could prove to be a Judas. 'How could I know that the other fellow who visited you while I was there wasn't a spy?' a senior believer they had known for years asked John. 'He could easily be an enemy who would report me.'

One woman, whom Pat had been tutoring, arrived in a flustered state.

'Are you OK?' asked Pat.

'I was stopped and asked why I was coming to this house,' she answered. 'I told them you were teaching me the Bible and then the man asked me if there was any political talk. When I said no, he said it was OK.'

Goodwill was still evident in the general community. When a fire destroyed part of the former mission headquarters, locals remarked that it was God's judgment on the authorities for stealing what had been lawfully bought by the missionaries.

The enmity of the ruling party was not only towards Westerners. The Muslim leadership enraged the regime by reacting against atheistic communism. The government tried to appease them by using the title 'scientific socialism'. While appealing to young students, this did not influence the Islamic hierarchy. Why would it when some of the military instructors openly mocked the idea of God and belittled protestors by looking into the sky and saying, 'No, there is no one there'? Eventually the government decreed that seven sheikhs be executed by firing squad because of their continued opposition. On the very day the sheikhs were killed, two MIG army jets collided over the city, one crashing into a populated area. Opinions were divided. Some saw the crash as the judgment of God. Others praised the government for being strong.

The creation of the Green Guards added to the confusion. These were young people, often taken off the streets, who were trained in basic military drills then given an authority superior to the police. They were charged with learning the name of every person in the section of the city allotted to them. Then they were expected to call their constituents out when the country's leaders or other heads of state were visiting to give the impression of cheering, enthusiastic crowds lining the streets.

One night, after banging loudly on the Warner's iron gate and calling for entry, a group of Green Guards barged into their house. 'We're here to inspect your premises,' they announced. They flexed their muscles by rifling through personal effects and asking probing questions. They then left without revealing any reason for the search.

'Perhaps they were just curious about us,' John said later. 'I remember another night when a high-ranking official visited. He took me aside and asked some very strange questions. Again, I was never told the purpose of his visit.'

Officials who came at night inevitably left a sense of eerie uncertainty. There was no way of knowing how the authorities viewed this remnant of former mission activity. Three adults and a child in the middle of a hostile city, where no one trusted anyone else, were in an extremely vulnerable situation. Only the peace that passes all understanding could keep them safe, plus their belief that God had convinced them that staying was the right thing to do.

What could be achieved in such an environment? Only eternity will reveal what it meant to the infant Somali church to know that a small group had stayed on to be there for them.

Somalia in the grip of a communist government was not a happy place. The euphoria of independence only 13 years before completely disappeared.

The Mennonite missionaries had stayed on with a government contract to train some UN personnel until asked abruptly to leave. Their children and other American children were part of a Sunday school the Warners and Christel had taught.

Gradually a stream of men sought Bible instruction and discipleship classes. Special encouragement was experienced when new people came for teaching. John, Pat and Christel were convinced that their decision to stay on had been the right one. In the midst of the tension and danger, they experienced the assurance of God's ever-present care in the knowledge that young Christian believers had been blessed.

A year after the majority of us departed, Pat and John were due for a holiday. They planned to spend it in Ethiopia. To my surprise I was asked by the East African mission director whether I would be willing to return to Mogadishu to keep Christel company for the month the Warners were away. What an opportunity! With my grief still raw I answered 'Yes!' without hesitation.

'Do you think we could go and see Haawa?' I asked Christel soon after I arrived. I longed to see if she had recovered from the tuberculosis and how she was.

'Let's try,' Christel responded.

We set out late one afternoon, giving people time for their afternoon siesta. With a vague idea of the area where her house was, we were able to find her by asking people we met for directions. The streets were dusty. Children were everywhere. Many were playing with balls made of socks and other rags. When we appeared, they left their game to follow us. Westerners were a rare sight in this area.

'Follow the *gaals* (infidels)!' was an automatic response to the appearance of white skins.

It was a crowded suburb. Many small compounds held four mostly one-roomed houses made of thatched walls and iron roofs. Outside each dwelling stood clay charcoal braziers and water barrels, and dotted around were four-legged stools ready for sitting and talking to neighbours or to be used for meal preparation.

'*Hodi!*' I called at the door pointed out to us as Haawa's.

'*Yaaway* (who is it)?' came a scream from inside. Haawa emerged from the house. 'Anab! Sophiyo!' she cried, throwing herself into our arms.

Words are inadequate to describe the next few minutes. The three of us talked at once. We thought we had said goodbye forever and here we were together again. Explanations as to why I was there and amazement at how well Haawa looked were mixed with the usual queries as to the health of husband, children and mutual friends.

'I have something to show you,' Haawa said with a broad smile when the hubbub died down.

'What?' asked Christel and I simultaneously.

'Wait here.' Wonderingly we watched Haawa return into the darkness of her house, emerging a few minutes later with a baby in her arms.

'Whose baby?'

'Mine. It's a girl. Her name is Farhiyo (Happiness).'

'How?' I asked. 'You were told not to.'

A long explanation followed. One of the boys had climbed on the bed and reached the handbag, hanging on a hook, that held the 'pill'. Painstakingly he removed each pill from its packet, tipping them all into a container of water. He told his horrified mother when she returned that he had mixed a cake.

'So,' Haawa continued, 'I threw the lot away.' There was a twinkle in her eye as she cuddled her baby. I don't think she was sorry at all. In fact, I wasn't even sure about the story. I only knew that the baby was beautiful, her first daughter. She seemed to be blooming with joy and well-being. And that was the last time I saw her.

The month flew by. Warners returned from their holiday. I went back to Ethiopia. Soon after, the mission leaders in Addis Ababa, who had requested regular reports, sent word that the group should leave Somalia. After 18 months in their rented accommodation, believing they were right to be there, they were told to pack and leave. This was made even more difficult when they understood that the decision was due to a misunderstanding gained from their own reports. Ironically, they arrived in Ethiopia to work on the eve of a much more violent communist revolution in that country.

Figure 29.1 – Christel Voll (left), with Pat and John Warner and their daughter Michelle, 1973.

30

A YEAR AWAY FROM THE SOMALIS

Nineteen seventy-three was my year away from the Somalis. For the first month I fell to pieces. I did not know how to deal with the grief of leaving the people I loved. Sleep evaded me. I lost weight. I cried a lot. The mission doctor put me on Valium. The result was extreme dizziness and a feeling that the effect of the medication was worse than the disease. In the end, through an Aussie friend, Dawn Bryce, I met a midwife from Guernsey, Margaret Jehan, who was employed by British Aid. Margaret took me to her lovely house where she looked after me. Through her care and time to rest, gradually the pieces came together again.

The SIM leaders then sent me to work in a mission hospital at Dilla, southern Ethiopia, on the main road between Addis Ababa and Nairobi. Our compound was surrounded by ranges of mountains as far as the eye could see. Because of the temperate climate, the gardens were lush, full of tropical plants and coffee bushes. An avocado tree bigger than a house was close by, loaded with fruit. What irony that instead of revelling in it, my heart ached for a flat, dry, desert land. The Dilla people were humble and respectful, but I missed the brash, loud, often demanding Somalis. The spice was gone.

The doctor in charge of the SIM Dilla hospital was an American, Dr Nathan Barlow. He and his wife, Doris, were probably in their late 50s, and both eccentric. Doris habitually jogged every morning at the crack of dawn. She used to call from outside my window for me to join her, and I, 20 years younger, could not keep up with her. Subsequently I hid under the blankets when I heard her voice. She was also a food fanatic. Visitors in Dilla who were billeted with the Barlows were told breakfast was at 6.00 am and spinach was often the main ingredient. No deviation was made for guests. Nathan periodically slipped into my place for a piece of chocolate cake, unavailable at home.

I never saw Nathan lose his cool. But he told me it had not always been that way. As a young man his currently white hair had been red. With a naturally volatile temper, he had learned through self-discipline to control it.

'How did you do that?' I asked. His patience in stressful situations had deeply impressed me.

'One morning I was examining a woman from a rural area who seemed very nervous. Suddenly she grabbed my stethoscope and yanked it out of my ears. It shocked me and was quite painful.'

'What did you do?'

'I almost lashed out at her. Instead, I excused myself to the nurse, telling her how to treat the woman and took some time out. I knew that if I couldn't control my temper I would have no impact among the Africans. I went to my house and prayed, "Lord, help me to learn to control my temper in every circumstance you bring across my path. I can't do it on my own." From then on it was easier. Unexpectedly, that woman really did me a favour.'

It was true that the Ethiopians quickly lost respect for a person with an anger problem.

Nathan's unique adjustment to African thinking periodically left me lost for words. One day an older man walked into the hospital leaning on a stick. During a fight his skull had been cracked open. The brain, visible through large fissures, had been liberally sprinkled with a yellowish powder.

'How can I help you?' I asked. I thought it was a needless question, but as it turned out it wasn't.

'I don't want treatment. I just want a court letter.'

I was about to protest when Nathan walked in and asked me what was happening.

'They don't want treatment; they just want a court letter. But look at his brain!'

'If they just want a court letter we'll give it to them. If they don't want treatment there's nothing we can do.'

This philosophy was made clear another day when I was arguing with a different patient. 'What's the problem?' Nathan asked as he walked past.

'This man signed the form to say he would complete his five-day amoeba treatment as a condition for us treating him. Now he says he's leaving and he hasn't finished,' I said, with obvious pique.

'If he wants to go, he will go, and you getting your blood pressure up isn't going to change a thing,' the doctor said as he walked away.

In spite of shocks like these I loved working with Nathan and was often amazed at what he accomplished.

For the last four months of that year of exile, I left Dilla to study Amharic in the mission language school at Debra Berhan, situated in the scenic highlands. The teacher was excellent and once more I enjoyed language study.

Then word came to pack up and spend the month with Christel in Mogadishu before moving to Kelafo in the Ogaden Desert. This meant that while I would still be in Ethiopia, I would be working with Somalis again. John and Ruth Twidale had returned from leave in Australia and were ready to go with me. I did not hesitate.

31

JO ANNE AND MARRIAGE

'Do you wish you were married?' Jo Anne asked me one night while we still in Bulo Burti.

'Yes,' I answered without hesitation.

'Tell me more.'

'I can think of lots of reasons. I love children. There are so many practical things I can't do that a man could. Most of all, I would like a relationship that was accepted by everyone as permanent. I love living with you, but if the mission leaders decided to send me somewhere else to work, I'd have to go. And your family is in America. You could be called home to look after your mother. There is no possibility of a permanent relationship.'

'I don't feel like that,' said Jo Anne after listening to me. 'I'm quite happy single.'

As I have already said, having a good friend like Jo Anne meant I was never lonely during the Bulo Burti years. In the midst of the stress and exhaustion of the medical work, there was a familiar place where we could both be at peace and minister to one another and to others. Our house was a base from which we extended hospitality to missionaries and Somalis as well as a series of cats and even a tiny dik-dik. Dogs were not possible. Because Muslims believe they are unclean animals, a pet dog would have kept most Somali visitors away.

I was happy and satisfied with the situation, which was just as well – if I had come to Africa hoping to find a suitable husband, disappointment would have been inevitable. I had been shocked when I arrived to read the SIM statistics. Of approximately 1200 missionaries, the majority were family units. The bombshell was that there were 240 single women and eight single men.

'Only a one in 30 chance of getting married!' I said to myself. The reality was even worse. When I saw some of the eight, the odds narrowed dramatically. Eight single men did not mean there were eight who were suitable husband material. Not at all.

The years passed by, and before the communist government took over mission properties in 1973, Jo Anne had left because of ill health. She returned to join the rest of us only after we had settled in Ethiopia.

When I was working at Dilla, to my joy she came and worked there too, giving invaluable help to Nathan Barlow. We had the joy of sharing a house again.

Then there was a strange twist in the life of my friend who had told me she wasn't interested in marriage. In 1970, when I went home on leave for the second time, she had travelled to Australia with me. Because she had been mentioned repeatedly in my letters to family and friends, I thought they would all love to meet each other. I could also show her some of my country. We travelled and visited for two months.

'Can you two have breakfast with us tomorrow morning?' asked Bill Dennett, one of my supporters, when he met us at the Katoomba Easter Convention.

'That'll be fine,'

I might have refused had I known the eventual outcome. But I didn't, and Jo Anne and I enjoyed a 'get to know you' meal with Bill and his wife, Aldwyn, the next morning.

On our return to Somalia the Dennetts wrote to us both. We were shocked to read in one of the letters that Aldwyn had been diagnosed with lung cancer. She died after a relatively short illness. Bill was left devastated, with two teenage boys, Ian and Warwick, grieving for their mother.

We wrote our individual letters of condolence. Then there was a new development. The letters to me petered out while Jo Anne, who had only met Bill once, continued to receive regular communication from him. Not only that, but a romantic flavour emerged.

I didn't worry at first because Jo Anne had told me she wasn't interested in getting married. But then to my amazement Bill came for a visit to Addis Ababa. Jo Anne met him at the airport. Then she accompanied him to his hotel, where he proposed and she immediately accepted.

'You don't even know him,' I marvelled when she told me.

'I have assurance from the Lord that it is the right way to go,' she said.

There was nothing I could say in answer to that. But I harboured some questions in my mind. Jo Anne was a very tidy and organised person, but with nothing at all invested in cooking or other housekeeping skills. She had worked hard to train in medicine and Bill had told me he envisaged her giving up work completely. Would she be satisfied? And how would she adjust to living in Australia? She hardly knew anyone apart from my family. Would she make friends in a strange land?

Bill told me how he believed God had revealed to him that he was to marry Jo Anne. In his euphoric state he enthused, 'My marriage to Aldwyn was a 27-year honeymoon.' Well, this next one won't be, I thought, knowing how different Jo Anne was from the first Mrs Dennett. She certainly wouldn't fit the submissive, evangelical spouse paradigm.

Three months later the excited bridegroom returned for the wedding. His boys came with him. The nuptials were held in the SIM chapel, followed by a reception in the Webi Shabelle Hotel. Mr Modricker, our Somali leader, gave the bride away. The ever-generous bridegroom had sent Jo Anne's older sister, Esther, the fare to attend the wedding. She performed the role of Matron of Honour. Margaret Jehan, who had cared for Jo Anne during her illness, and I were the bridesmaids. Missionary friends made our dresses. Jo Anne was 48 years old. Another missionary lent her a satin wedding dress and pillbox hat with a veil.

'Who's going to drive us from Margaret's house to the chapel?' I asked the day before the wedding.

'I'll drive the VW Beetle,' Jo Anne announced.

'You will not!' I exploded. 'Do you want the whole show to be a circus? Can you imagine a bride of your age getting out of a VW at the church in a satin wedding dress? If you drive, I'm not going.'

Thankfully, one of the missionaries who owned a blue station wagon transformed it into a bridal car. Still, there was a churning deep inside me wondering how the ceremony would develop. We had a middle-aged bride who was moving forward anchored by some Bible verses but certainly not in love and a bridegroom with stars in his eyes, dreaming of a relationship similar to his first marriage. I had to admit, though, that the dresses were becoming, and our hair, arranged by Mary Amalia, looked elegant.

The Matron of Honour, Esther, made a dignified entrance. Margaret and I never managed to achieve the special step we had been taught. We were certainly not in step with each other. We valiantly hung on to our bouquets but they were a disaster. Beautiful pink rose buds succumbed to the heat and limply hung their heads. 'Were you playing "He loves me, he loves me not" during the prayer?' our chauffer, Verne Black, asked me as we were driving to the reception. He had opened his eyes and seen me pulling off the worst of the curled-up petals while people were praying.

Another glitch was when Jo Anne's mind went blank when she attempted to sign the register. 'How many t's in Dennett?' she whispered to Bill. He looked amazed as she had been writing to him regularly.

God gave me special strength at the reception to propose the toast to the bride and groom. It was an opportunity to share the way Jo Anne and my friendship had been blessed and some history of the work in Somalia. The next morning, saying goodbye at the airport, the person who had spoken so bravely the day before was an emotional wreck.

'God helped you yesterday,' Jo Anne said as we prepared to part.

'Well, he's not helping me now,' I sobbed.

Bill saw what was happening. Leaving the people he was talking to, he strode over, took Jo Anne's hand and pulled her through the departure gate. That was that. She had left on her honeymoon and I was left to face the mission Sunday church service.

Bill also paid for Esther to accompany them to Kenya. She was revelling in her first opportunity to travel outside America. I believe she was the only person who enjoyed the honeymoon! Suddenly Bill and Jo Anne realised how little they knew about each other.

The next three months was the time I spent at language school at Debra Berhan learning Amharic. I grieved for Jo Anne as though she had died. I loved language learning, which helped, but there was a deep ache inside me for the loss of my friend.

Jo Anne was also having a hard time. The details of the first years of the marriage, plus the eventual good years, are written in her and Bill's book *An Unusual Marriage*. My conclusion, as I heard about their struggles, was: 'If God has a husband for you, he can bring him from the ends of the earth, but if it's not part of God's plan, you wouldn't want it!' In spite of the difficult adjustment they both experienced, neither of them ever wavered in their belief that God had brought them together.

In Bill I gained a beloved brother who always welcomed me into their home.

Three months after the wedding, the Twidales and I launched into the Kelafo saga.

(Note: I am over 80 years old now. I never married and feel a pang when I observe contemporaries with their grandchildren. However, when I look at my life and compare it with others, I would not swap with anyone. With a grateful heart I can say amen to the psalmist's words: 'No good thing does [the Lord] withhold from those whose walk is blameless' (Psalm 84:11b). Because God sees us as blameless, clothed in the righteousness of Christ, we can only take with open hands that 'good thing' he chooses to give. I also accept that as a single midwife and nurse among the Somalis, I was able to stay with people when they needed it and not have to worry about the waiting family.)

32

HERE WE COME, KELAFO

Suddenly I heard a familiar voice: '*Nabat miya walaaliyalo* (is it peace, my brothers and sisters)?'

We all turned to see Abdi Warsame, a Somali friend who had worked with us in the clinic in Bulo Burti. A tall, handsome, charismatic young man, he was one of the Christian Somalis. Abdi had a confident, easy style of relating in almost any situation. We had rejoiced as we observed how easily he shared his Christian faith in conversation. Somehow, on some boundary-crossing Somali grapevine, he had heard that we were on the plane and had come to meet us.

We had travelled by train from Addis Ababa to Dire Dawa and then by plane to Gode, way down in the Ogaden Desert. We had no idea how we could go the rest of the way to Kelafo. Now the outlook that had seemed like a brick wall with no known way ahead suddenly revealed a gateway.

Abdi told us he was working for a retired Presbyterian missionary, Dr Donald McClure, who was away trying to gain support to provide a hospital for Gode. We knew the doctor. Typical of his kindness was the news that he had left a message saying we were welcome to stay in his house until we found transport to Kelafo. Abdi drove us in the doctor's Land Rover to his lovely home. There was no electricity because of a broken generator, but there was a place to sleep and food to eat. After the plane trip and our glimpse of the bleak, desert landscape, this was luxury.

But how were going to reach Kelafo? Abdi and John scoured the town. It seemed impossible to find a truck for hire in Gode. As a last resort they tried the army camp. Even to talk to the officer in charge was a diplomatic adventure. Each time they inquired they were challenged.

'But why do you want to see the colonel?'

'We want to ask him a favour.'

'What kind of favour?'

'We want to borrow a truck to go to Kelafo.'

Unbelieving laughter followed this remark. That was impossible!

However, at last they gained an audience. The Ethiopian colonel was also amazed. Even to see an Englishman and a Somali walking together, conversing with each other in a mixture of English and Somali, was a new phenomenon. His first response was negative. There were absolutely no trucks available to transport people to Kelafo. Then John said, 'We would be willing to pay, of course.' After more abject begging and some weakening on the colonel's part, it was agreed: if the petrol there and back was paid for, an army truck could be made available for this last lap of our journey. The price of the gasoline was extortionate. We were about to find out that nothing here in this backwoods was cheap.

Early the next morning we heard the brakes of a heavy vehicle groaning as it came to a standstill outside. I rushed out to see our transport, racing back inside to report, 'There's a bunch of soldiers on the back of the truck.' A cohort of uniformed men with metal helmets on their heads and rifles held at the ready stood at attention waiting for us. The colonel, who arrived in an army jeep to see that we really left, announced, 'I am sending these men to protect you on the road.'

'From what?' I asked. No answer. Perhaps it wasn't appropriate for a man of his rank to answer inane female questions.

With no more small talk, Ruth, her six-year-old daughter Heather and I, plus two kittens, climbed into the cabin with the driver. John and the luggage joined the cohort in the back. Our adventure began.

What a journey! Only 95 kilometres but there was no road to be seen. The driver, Bereke, simply followed the tyre marks of a previous truck. Every now and then we bounced down dry creek beds. Keeping the vehicle upright as we crossed the deep gullies caused Bereke to grimace and his biceps to bulge. Whether the soldiers in the back were maintaining their upright stance was left to our imagination.

Our thirst raged as the heat intensified. The water we brought from fridge-less Gode was tepid and did little to satisfy. 'Let us be glad we are really on our way,' we kept reminding each other. We needed to think of something positive because the bouncing and bumping on the hard, springless seat while hanging on to the frightened kittens did not make for a comfortable ride. Needless to say, there were no seat belts to hold us steady.

Figure 32.1 – Camels by the Webi Shebelli, mid-1960s.

The desert landscape was familiar, similar to Somalia except for strange barren mountains on the horizon adding a lunar aspect. Sporadically, when passing a clump of thornbush, we saw gazelle, baboons and one stately ostrich couple.

Our goal was a mission property built by the banks of the Webi Shebelli on the outskirts of the town of Kelafo. The previous workers, including a doctor, his family and some teachers, had left in 1966 when the river had flooded and inundated their buildings. They never returned. Now the Twidales and I had been given the task of restoring the buildings to recommence the medical work and other ministries.

Suddenly we were there. Bereke drove over a hump, which we later found was a manmade dyke. There in the dip was our destination, our future home and place of ministry.

'Look at the trees!' we exclaimed. Because of the river nearby, there had been plenty of water for the previous workers to plant Neem trees, which were now as tall as the buildings.

As soon as we descended from the truck, the soldiers unloaded our luggage and left to return to Gode. It was mid-afternoon and we three adults and a child, surrounded by suitcases, surveyed our new home.

Nearest the river were three cement-brick, two-bedroom houses in a row. Through the trees we could see another building, which had been a two-roomed school. In the distance was a small hospital plus a home for a Somali family. They had cared for the property while there were no foreign workers. Daqani and his wife with their five children were to become our best friends.

I looked at the three houses. 'I like the first one,' I announced. John took out a bunch of ancient keys. He chose one and said, 'Here you are, Dear Lady, see if you can get in.' Dear Lady was his regular name for me. Perhaps this was because his wife was Ruth too. I liked it.

I went to my house, climbed three steps and inserted the key in the lock. It turned. I put my shoulder to the warped wood of the door, pushed and went hurtling inside my new domain.

The cement floor was mud caked, evidence of the 1966 flood. The only furniture in the lounge room was a wooden rowing boat that filled the room. The height of the flood was evidenced by the walls being denuded of plaster for the first three feet.

Figure 32.2 – The Twidale family arriving at Kelafo, 1973.

Figure 32.3 – John and Ruth Twidale, c. 1979.

As I stood wondering how we would ever get the boat out, my stomach rumbled and I realised I had not eaten since a meagre breakfast. I was very hungry. We did not have any food. We had brought hardly anything with us and had no idea what the village was like or what would be available.

Not expecting to find anything, I looked in the kitchen cupboards. 'Look!' I called to Ruth and John. 'Tins of beetroot!' They had been there since before 1966.

'Do you think they'll be OK?'

'Let's try.'

They were fine. We made quite a meal of what we found, with no ill effects. Since then I take very little notice of 'use by' dates. I would rather go by the 'sniff' test. It has never let me down.

So there we were, safely settled in Kelafo. What lay ahead was waiting for our goods to follow us, making friends, cleaning, painting, planting gardens and, eventually, resurrecting the hospital and teaching ministries – and seeing God work his own purposes out in and through us.

33

SHAFI'I:
UNUSUAL HOUSE HELP

'*Hodi! Hodi!*' A loud voice thundered through the screen door, echoing through every room in my house.

Somalis never knock; they always call out '*Hodi*'. But rarely had I heard the confidence and authority of this voice. I responded with alacrity, curious to see the owner.

Framed in the doorway was a tall man of about 40. My immediate impression was of a wide, beaming smile and strong bandy legs.

'*Nabat miya* (is it peace)?' I said as a greeting. He responded in the customary way, looking me up and down as I was doing to him.

It wasn't polite to ask 'What do you want?' in Somali, so I waited for him to share the purpose of his call.

'I have come to work for you,' he announced. 'I will be your houseboy.'

I swallowed hard. Would it be appropriate for a single woman, living alone, to allow this assertive, unknown man to have the run of the house? I had only been in Kelafo a week. Although the truck had arrived from Addis Ababa with our furniture and other supplies, a monumental task of cleaning, plastering and painting loomed ahead. Houses, school building and hospital all needed serious attention before we could begin the medical and teaching ministry.

'What do you know about being a houseboy?' I asked. I had already tried a village girl. Through her I discovered that most of the local people had had very little to do with Westerners. She spent the whole morning gaping at me, failing to respond to anything I asked her to do. Her main interest seemed to be finding empty tin cans, which she asked for. By midday I was ready to scream. I gave her some money and said goodbye.

'I know everything!' declared Shafi'i. 'I worked for Misterr Scheel and I worked for Misterr Grreen.' The Scheels were the doctor's family and Ethel Greenlie, whom Shafi'i called Misterr Grreen, had been the nurse. 'I washed their floors and I washed their clothes.'

'OK,' I ventured dubiously. 'We could give it a try.'

When I had a chance, I told John Twidale that I had tentatively employed a guy whose name was Shafi'i.

'I have bad news for you, Dear Lady,' John said the next time we met. 'I made some inquiries and Shafi'i did work for the Scheels, but they let him go for some misdemeanour, and in retaliation he came back and burned down their chook house.'

I was sorry to hear that because Shafi'i had been impressing me with his enthusiasm as he attacked the mud. He threw himself into the clean-up with prodigious results. I was loath to let him go after my previous experience.

So I ventured to ask him, 'It is being said you burned down the Scheels' chook house. Is that true?'

He scratched his stubbled head, caressed his chin and after a long moment said, 'No! That wasn't me. That was another fellow.' I didn't believe him, but I was so happy with the way he was working I let it go. Besides, I didn't plan to have chooks.

Figure 33.1 – Shafi'i at work scrubbing the tiled floor.

Shafi'i, a widower, was engaged to be married to a teenager. He had two sons in their teens from his first marriage. 'Next time you send an order for supplies, could you get me some black hair dye?' he asked. 'My fiancée is very young and I don't want to look like an old man beside her.' I ordered black hair dye for him and later beheld his joy when he looked in the mirror at his tarry pate.

Speaking of hair, one of my ongoing challenges over the years was to find a hairdresser when I was appointed to isolated situations. For 13 years Jo Anne had done a magnificent job in Bulo Burti, but who would do it now?

Searching for information one day, I said to Shafi'i, 'Who cut Misterr Grreen's hair?'

'I did,' he said.

'What?' A villager who had been all his life in a small village, having never seen a hairdresser, cutting an American woman's hair was hard to believe.

'Could you cut my hair?'

'Of course I can. Where are the scissors?'

I didn't have much choice. So with scissors and comb in hand and a towel around my shoulders, I sat on a chair under a tree. Watching in a mirror, I said, 'It's all yours.' He held the scissors like an orchestral conductor's baton. After three dramatic snips in the air he clipped some hair. It took a while with the continual air snips between clips, but the finished result was surprisingly nice. I still marvel at the fact that, with three days' Land Rover journey to the nearest hairdresser, I managed to be attractively coifed all my time in Kelafo.

Six months after our arrival the plastering and painting were completed, the pawpaw trees were thriving and the hospital was open, with a constant stream of outpatients and some maternity cases. We had come through the transition, overjoyed with the transformation. My house and clothes were well looked after by my very unusual 'houseboy'.

Outside Kelafo there was a bumpy, fairly primitive airstrip. When the weather was good and there was no other hindrance, an Ethiopian Airlines DC6 arrived weekly with mail and passengers, sometimes including a visitor for us. A friend, Queenslander Dawn Bryce, working in another part of Ethiopia, spent some of her holiday with me. One afternoon, sitting in the lounge room at afternoon tea time, Dawn had a long-range view of the floor under the kitchen sink. 'I can see caked mud under the sink cupboard,' she pointed out. 'Have a look.'

Sure enough, in the dim light under the cupboard was a layer of dried mud that had been missed in the clean-up.

'Shafi'i,' I said, 'look at the dirt under that cupboard.'

With his usual enthusiasm he got down on his knees and peered at the offending heap. He stared for a while. Then, still on his knees, he looked at me and said, 'Ya, that's not our dirt, that's Misterr Green's dirt.' He couldn't understand why Dawn and I thought that was hilarious. We didn't remind him that Ethel Greenlie had been gone for six years.

Another time, tired of the lack of fresh food in the market, I asked him what Misterr Green had for the evening meal. 'Aas kreem,' he said, 'always aas kreem.' I didn't argue, but knowing Ethel, I knew she didn't eat ice cream every night. Later the mystery was solved. I was making cinnamon rolls, and when Shafi'i saw them he said, 'Oh, aas kreem.' And I realised that 'aas kreem' covered anything sweet that Westerners ate.

One disaster was biscuit making. Mixing dough for Anzac biscuits, I showed Shafi'i how to roll little balls for baking. Impatient with the process, he decided to make the balls bigger, ending up with only about six biscuits. Because the ingredients had to be flown in and were very expensive, I was irritated when I saw what he had put in the oven. He couldn't believe the result. Repeatedly kneeling down and looking through the oven glass, he kept saying, 'My God, they are all joined up together.' We ended up with one huge Anzac.

Others on our missionary team marvelled at how I tolerated my unusual house help. He was outspoken, blunt and no respecter of persons. But I liked him. Besides, we were not in the house together very often. He was working while I was in the clinic. He was clean and mostly thorough, apart from the episode of Mr Grreen's dirt.

As we worked together one afternoon in the kitchen, we chatted companionably until he said, 'You know, Anab, we get on well together and I will never lie to you. You can be sure of that.'

'But you already have,' I answered.

'When?'

'You told me you didn't burn Mr Scheel's chickens, but I think you really did.'

After a long silence and a scratching of the once-again piebald hair,

he said, 'Well, perhaps it was me, but I didn't burn them very much.
Just a little bit.'

We stayed together until the war which caused our precipitous
departure.

One challenge Shafi'i unsuccessfully tried to help me with was cleaning
and lighting the kerosene refrigerator. I never learned how to relight it
after cleaning and filling. Someone told me it was because the cement
floor wasn't quite level. In memory of that trial I wrote a poem.

ODE TO A KEROSENE REFRIGERATOR
A SONG OF THE BLUES

O kerosene fridge decked out in white
With exotic chrome trim, polished and bright
You graced my kitchen with regal disdain
And cared not at all that you caused me deep pain.

I already knew you were there to taunt me
And your expectations were going to haunt me
O despotic waster of my day-off pleasure
You thwarted my hopes of longed-for leisure.

Because weekly I faced the dreaded routine
Of filling your tank with fresh kerosene
Trimming the wick was part of my duty
And shining the glass to transparent beauty.

The steps to follow were clearly written
Why would I then with such stress be smitten?
Because, no matter how keenly I tried,
Success in the project was always denied.

Firstly I'd strike a match to light
The tricky wick, now clean and bright
And push the tank back into its place
And say a prayer for an act of grace.

Success is marked by a flame of blue
And no sign of smoke from out of the flue
A yellow flame would spell disaster
And the smoke would rise blacker and faster.

With my cheek to the floor and my rear in the air
I'd stare at that flame with utter despair
It's yellow and red with a blackening wick
And I shout at the fridge, 'You make me sick!'

A kerosene fridge from Satan is sent
To cause people like me to moan and lament
That's how it felt as I fought week by week
Prostrate on the floor a blue flame to seek.

Without a blue flame the thing wouldn't freeze
That's why so often I was down on my knees
And when in the end no joy for my labour
I swallowed my pride and got help from my neighbour.

Figure 33.2 – The kerosene fridge.

34

LONELINESS

The work of renovating was finished. The reopening of the hospital, after a closure of eight years, caused the village to buzz with excitement. The governor in charge of the town administration and all the town elders came to the ceremony. The new plaster and paint shone. The people came back for medical treatment in their droves. Women began coming into our maternity ward to have their babies.

One afternoon I was enjoying the peace of my house after a busy morning in the clinic. I sipped my coffee and allowed the lush green branches brushing against the lounge room windows to add to my sense of well-being. Then I saw two crows mating. Not wishing to intrude on their privacy I turned to the other window, and there were two turtle doves in a similar relationship. It must have been the Kelafo spring. Everyone was twitterpated!

'What about me, Lord?' I questioned. 'The birds have each other. John and Ruth have each other. And here am I on my own. Is that fair?'

For the first year of our time in Kelafo, the Twidales, their daughter Heather and I were the only missionaries in an isolated situation.

'You know, I really like Ruth and John,' I continued, voicing my complaint. 'But Ruth is not the chatty sort. I need someone to talk to. I am lonely. Do you want to see me here pining away like this?'

We had special meals together and we visited in the village homes together. For a garrulous extrovert it wasn't enough. The evenings were long. When I entered my house at about 6.00 pm it was already dark. There was no twilight and no electricity. I would light a lamp, have my evening meal and then settle down to write letters. But because there were no screens on the windows, the bugs would come to investigate the lantern and find me sitting beside it. My hot, sweaty skin was delectable to the local insects. Soon they would crawl, some stinging, over my arms, down under my dress, under my glasses and in my hair. I did not last very long.

'I can't stand these bugs!' I would explode, turning the light out and going to bed. Sometimes it was as early as 7.00 pm.

My companion in bed was John Stott, a gifted English preacher. I possessed some audio-cassettes of his sermons, which I loved. I would lie listening to the tape recorder in the dark. When John prayed at the end of the message, I would feel like crying because I felt he was praying just for me. Even then I had to ration this indulgence because batteries were expensive, brought in by air.

The morning after the bird-mating episode I rose early. Early rising was one thing I did share with the birds. I sat on the top step of my front verandah to read and pray.

As I meditated, my mind drifted to Jesus' time on earth, and I began to think about how lonely he would have been. It was not until after the resurrection and Pentecost that his closest friends really began to understand who he was and the inner meaning of his message. I let my mind dwell on those 33 years – how he must have longed for his Father and the fellowship he had enjoyed through all eternity. Jesus regarded his body as given to him in order to carry out his Father's will. How painful it must have been for him when his closest companions argued over who would have the best places in the coming Kingdom. Even the three in the inner circle were unable to stay awake in the Garden of Gethsemane.

I realised how pathetic my grumbling was in the light of his experience.

I was also reminded in one of my devotional books that it is only in this life that we have the privilege of suffering with Jesus. In heaven we will serve him more perfectly and will have unbroken fellowship with him, but we won't be called to suffer with him. We will never be lonely; we will be surrounded by love. As I contemplated these things, I prayed that I would not waste this precious opportunity and that I would learn all he wanted to teach me. In an act of worship, like the woman with the alabaster jar (Mark 14:3), I offered my loneliness to God and accepted his will for me at that time. There were other times when I really longed for a companion, but the bitter struggle was over.

On another occasion I was struck by Ephesians 1:11–12, which reminded me, with fresh impact, that our appointment is to live to the praise of God's glory.

APPOINTED

Appointed to live for the praise of your glory!
How can it be, Lord?
Teach me I pray,
To understand that your calling for me
Is to reign in Christ Jesus, day after day.

Appointed to live for the praise of your glory!
No higher appointment
There ever could be.
You chose me for this before earth's foundation,
That I should be holy and blameless. Yes, me!

Appointed to live for the praise of your glory!
I read it with joy,
But joy becomes pain.
My perpetual failing and weakness still tempt me
To doubt my vocation again and again.

But appointed to live for the praise of your glory
Is here in your word
So I know it is true.
You have appointed and you will enable
Yes, the One who will do it, Lord Jesus, is you!

35

HANDS AND FEET

On a quiet Sunday afternoon, as I enjoyed pottering in my kitchen, our gateman, Abdulahhi, appeared at the screen door with a man from the bush beside him.

'*Nabat miya* (is it peace)?' I said.

'*Haa waa nabat* (yes, it is peace).'

'What can I do for you?'

'*Naag waa foolinaysaa* (there is a woman in labour).'

The bushman could contain himself no longer. '*Soo daqso* (hurry up)!'

'Is she close?' I asked.

No one, including me, knew whether I meant the distance we had to travel to pick her up or the time to delivery, but the caller uttered an emphatic '*Haah!* (Yes!)' and then again, '*Soo daqso!*'

Being called to a woman in labour in the bush was a rare occurrence. When it happened we always accompanied the husband with a sinking heart – firstly because we had no idea how far we had to travel or what the track would be like, and secondly because these people would not ask us to come for anything less than a crisis. Bush people were self-sufficient, failing to see having a baby as a reason to get outside help. Especially from a foreigner.

'Why didn't you bring the patient with you?' I asked.

'She can't walk! And it's too far.'

These were delaying tactics on my part. I didn't want to go. I knew I was going to face a situation that would be very difficult. Reluctantly I climbed into the Land Rover, beckoning the worried husband to climb in beside me. He indicated the direction with his chin, as is the Somali custom. Pointing with the outstretched finger is rude.

'Where is the place?' I asked.

My guide answered, 'See that tree?' There were hundreds of trees in our line of vision. 'It's just beyond it.' That was encouraging. However, over an hour later the guide was still saying 'That tree ahead.' I realised he was not referring to a tree I could see but one in his mind.

Long, long after I gave up trying to decide which tree he meant, he suddenly said, 'This is the tree. Turn right!'

There was no sign of habitation. We were heading into deeper scrub on an even narrower path. By the time we reached a small group of *aqals* (Somali huts), I had long given up protesting about the distance, resigning myself to driving through bush forever or until the petrol gave out. It was now late afternoon.

Female relatives were waiting for us and in no time had the labouring woman in the back of the Land Rover, yelling at me, '*Daqso! Daqso!*'

These women had never before been in a motor vehicle or seen a foreigner close up. They were obviously desperate. I felt slightly more positive about the return trip. I knew how far we had come; I was no longer expecting our destination to be the next tree so there was marginally more predictability. But as I listened to the talk in the back of the vehicle, I was gripped by a new horror. I heard one woman say the baby's hand was out.

Oh no!

I had read the chapter on hand presentations in Professor Bruce Mayes' *Textbook of Obstetrics* only recently. To manage a hand presentation the directions were very brief. 'Prepare the patient for surgery and alert operating theatre staff. A hand presentation is undeliverable by any means other than caesarean section.' No beating around the bush, I thought. That seemed a little ironic. I had been beating around the bush for hours.

My distracted mind composed a little ditty:

> *Bump, bump, bump, down the track*
> *Women talking in the back*
> *Guide beside me points his chin*
> *Undeliverable! Undeliverable!*

There was another song I also thought of, this one found in Psalm 55:6–7: 'Oh, that I had the wings of a dove! I would fly away and be at rest. I would flee away and stay in the desert; I would hurry to my place of shelter, far from the tempest and the storm.' I believe that many a missionary midwife, both before and after me, has longed for the wings of a dove when faced with a difficult case without a doctor, operating facilities or any way of transferring the patient.

We arrived at the hospital at dusk. There were no other in-patients. I had a bed ready in the labour ward. After experiencing her first journey in a car and her first contact with a foreign woman, Weris, the pretty little girl from the bush, heavily pregnant, now faced climbing a few steps and entering a cement-rendered, white-painted building with tiled floors, beds and lanterns. Her only homes had been transportable huts made of woven mats tied to a wooden frame, with a dirt floor and mats on the ground to sleep on.

Pushed and pulled by her relatives, she unwillingly went in and lay on the bed to let me examine her. Sure enough, a little hand was showing. Her contractions were sporadic. She was obviously exhausted.

Ruth Twidale, also a midwife, had no more idea than I did as to what we should do. In my desperation I decided on a plan of action. I would give Weris an injection of pethidine so she could get some sleep. Then we would all try to rest. In the morning I would radio for a plane owned by Missionary Aviation Fellowship to come and take her to Addis Ababa for surgery.

I told the waiting Somalis this. You should have seen their faces. After their first car trip, there was no way they would contemplate flying through the air. The plan was never going to work, but it allowed us all to survive the night.

Philippians 4:6–7 had been much in my mind in the previous days. I lay down and prayed, 'Lord, I commit this whole situation to you with thanksgiving. It is beyond me. I now claim your peace that passes understanding to keep my heart and mind in Christ Jesus as you have promised in your word.' The next thing I knew it was daylight. A sporadic sleeper at the best of times, this was definitely not normal for me in the middle of a crisis.

My thoughts flew to what was happening in the hospital. I found that Weris had slept all night too and was now in strong labour. Obviously, there was no way the aeroplane plan was feasible. Even if an aircraft were available, the ten-hour flight to and from Addis Ababa was out of the question. No, we could not fly away like doves, and neither could our problem. We had to do something.

Then I was met by a group of men who had walked the long, thornbush-lined track we had driven the night before. 'Weris and her husband are from different tribes,' an old man, obviously the spokesman for the group, explained to me. 'Because of that we have witnesses from both tribes to make sure there will be no trouble afterwards.' Never before or since had I been in such a situation.

'Here we are,' I groaned to Ruth. 'We're new here. The news of what happens will spread like wildfire.' Stretched beyond our experience and expertise, we prayed for wisdom.

I gave instructions that the bed containing Weris be placed in the middle of a large room and told the men to sit on the floor against opposite walls in their tribal divisions. As far as I could tell the baby had died, and I decided that the only thing I could do to save the mother was to amputate the arm at the shoulder and turn the baby around. Everyone from both tribes gave me permission to do this. We prayed in Somali. Everyone understood our prayer. Then we put Weris to sleep with ether on a mask, and Abdi, a Somali dresser (male nurse), continued the regular dripping while Ruth and I attempted the delivery.

Cutting the little arm off was heart-breaking. I saw Ruth turn her head away. I just prayed constantly and did what I believed was the only option. Then together we turned the baby into a breech, enabling it to be delivered without difficulty.

A relieved Weris was soon awake and enjoying a cup of tea. I looked at her talking with her relatives and felt so grateful to the Lord that we had been able to save her life. Everyone in the room knew that had she continued in labour she would have died. She was young and healthy and hopefully would have more babies.

News soon spread around the bush and the town that the new *gaals* (infidels) knew what they were doing. It was only partly true. I have been told since by those who know better that what I did was a dangerous procedure. The uterus could have ruptured. We really had no choice. I thank God for a successful outcome – and that I never faced a hand presentation again.

I had cut off the arm of the baby to save Weris, but another pivotal moment in my time at Kelafo involved saving a hand.

In the clinic I was the boss. I never saw myself as a first-class nurse. I knew that others were more precise, more careful about details and more dedicated to following best medical practice. I was always a big picture kind of a person. However, I really enjoyed running the show. I was good at delegating, training Somali helpers and keeping people entertained as well as treated. Others had to look after the fine tuning. I suppose the reason I was in charge was because I had been there the longest, had the most experience in Africa and was better at the language.

For most of the time in Kelafo I lived in a house by myself. That meant I had no one to remind me to take anti-malaria tablets. Without openly admitting it, I secretly believed that after being in Africa for many years I was immune to any attacks from the ever-present mosquitoes. I didn't make a decision not to take malarial prophylaxis – I just let the weeks and months slip by without swallowing that weekly dose.

It was foolhardy. Living near the river, in an area where malaria was rampant, the inevitable happened. I woke up one morning feeling ill.

'You never get sick,' I told myself. 'This is going to be a busy day, so pull yourself together.'

I was the only trained nurse there at that time. I struggled to keep going for as long as I could. Then, as we reached the last few patients, I said to my helpers, 'You finish. I have to go home. I think I have a fever.'

Staggering through the trees to my house, I made it to the bedroom, threw myself on the bed and a rigor commenced. In the heat of the tropics I shivered and shook. A rarely used blanket flung over me made no difference at all. I felt freezing cold.

Then I heard a knock at my bedroom door. Someone's come to see how I am, I thought. But no, someone had come to tell me I was needed back at the clinic.

'I can't!' I groaned through rattling teeth.

'You have to. A man has had his hand caught in the grain mill. It is torn to ribbons.'

I thought standing upright would be impossible, but somehow I left my bed and walked back to the clinic. As soon as I saw the patient I pigeonholed my symptoms for a later date. I don't know how but that's what happened.

In Kelafo there was no town electricity but there was a grain mill with its own generator. The people brought their millet and corn to the mill to be ground into meal, which they then cooked into a thick porridge. For many this was their staple diet. The man with the ripped up hand, whose name was Mahad, was the boss. That morning a helper had activated the motor before he was ready and the result was a bloody, shredded mess of mangled fingers and torn palm. The most ominous injury was the index finger, which was dangling uselessly.

In the fog of my mind I remembered that in Paul's letter to the Ephesians he mentions supporting ligaments and I reminded myself that the One who created the body would guide me through this impossible task. Praying for strength and skill, I swabbed the hand with antiseptic and injected it with local anaesthetic. As I began the task of mending the tears, I was able to find the two ends of the severed ligament belonging to the dangling finger and bring them together.

As soon as I made the join with a catgut suture, Mahad moved his index finger again. The onlookers gasped with relief and encouraged me to keep going.

Slowly and carefully I sutured the lacerations. It meant working up and down repairing the sides of each finger as well as the tears on the main part of the hand. It was a prolonged and tedious operation, but my hand was steady and my concentration improved as I went. After about an hour the repair was complete and the hand neatly bandaged. Mahad, who was a brave and excellent patient, thanked me. He need not have said anything. The expression on his face was enough. His job was his family's means of survival. If we hadn't been there, his hand would have ended up a useless, rotting mess.

Leaving the others to clean up, I returned home. This time there was no shivering and shaking. My temperature was over 105°F. It was time to throw my bedclothes off and try to cool my burning body.

The malaria had to run its course, which included rigors and temperatures. But with the right medicine and some rest, I was well in a few days. At regular intervals I was able to see Mahad's hand. It was clean and healing well. We both made a complete recovery. We both thanked God for answered prayer. From that time on I found it easier to remember to take the anti-malarial tablets.

Paradoxically, after the two cases involving hands we dealt with a foot saga.

Ruth Twidale and a few Somali workers were helping me on another busy morning in the outpatients' clinic. A noisy crowd of patients and relatives were in the waiting room. Ten had been called in and were seated in the treatment area. I questioned the new patients, jotting down notes so my helpers could look after them. Almost always it was action-packed drama laced with a sprinkling of comedy. Most

Somalis are inveterate extroverts and interested in everyone else's business. As each newcomer told their story, there would often be exclamations, comments or advice from the onlookers. It was nothing like the poker-faced atmosphere in Australian doctors' waiting rooms where people tend to whisper to their companions and refrain from staring at fellow patients. Our Somali clinic was loud and invasive.

One man from the bush, Jama, poked his gnarled, weather-beaten foot at me, pointed to a tumour the size of a small apple and asked, 'Can you cut that out?'

Gingerly I felt the hard, knotty protuberance. 'No!' was my definite response.

Looking around the room and seeing Ruth Twidale standing near the medicine counter, he said, 'Ask your mother if she can.'

Ruth, a few years older than I but nowhere near my mother's generation, roared laughing as I said, 'No, she can't either.'

Undeterred, Jama left, arriving back soon after with a traditional rural doctor. 'This man knows how to do the operation and he will show you,' he announced.

'I can't let him operate in my hospital.'

'I'll just show you how to do it,' said 'Dr' Ali.

'But your instruments are dirty,' I objected, pointing to a woman's handbag dangling from his arm. Ali opened his bag and showed me his tools of trade: a couple of metal scoops hammered out like miniature soup spoons. As the two men continued to beg, I thought, 'Well, I suppose I could sterilise his scoops and see what he does.'

I was reasonably sure that none of my missionary nurse friends would think this was a good idea, but I had been working with the Somalis for so long I was bordering on the unconventional. I didn't need to tell anyone about it anyway. So we boiled the scoops, Ali and I scrubbed our hands and we both donned sterile gloves. I sanitised Jama's foot and injected local anaesthetic, which is what he really wanted from me anyway. After making an incision with my sterile scalpel, Ali guided me in carefully separating the glistening, knotted ball from the healthy flesh and removing it. I then sutured the wound.

The procedure was a resounding success, and Jama and Ali went off laughing.

After they'd gone, I opened the tumour and out spewed what looked like tiny black wood chips. In my indispensable *Merck Manual* I found a chapter on Madura foot. There I read an exact description of Jama's tumour. The scientific term is *mycetoma pedis*, a fungal disease. The spores, present in the soil, enter the skin through a minor trauma such as a thorn prick. Safe inside the warm body, the tiny spores work together to form an initial tumour, which eventually ruptures. This allows the spores to spread, causing further tumours to develop and multiply, eventually resulting in destroyed limbs. Excising the tumour while still intact can save a limb and often a life.

Never would I recommend learning from traditional Somali bush medicos. I had been shocked and saddened many times by treatments that resulted in increased suffering and often death. However, this was an exception to the rule. Using more conventional instruments, I was subsequently able to excise many of these tumours and save a multitude of limbs. Thank you, Jama and Ali, for your persistence.

36

THE DEATH OF DOUG HILL

It was 3 June 1975. I was home on my third furlough. My parents were living in Parkes and I was staying with them. The phone rang. At first no one spoke and then I could hear sobbing. As I listened, wondering who it could be, Bill Dennett's voice came over the sound of weeping.

'Ruth, Jo Anne wanted to talk but she can't. We've just heard that Doug Hill has been killed in the Ogaden.'

I held the phone, stunned. Doug Hill, a talented young doctor from Tamworth, who had gone to work in Africa for a short term, was now dead. I heard the full story from Bob and Anne Burcher, who were on the team Doug was helping. I am sharing the fine details from Bob's notes.

Doug had accompanied two Canadian nurses, Mary Amalia and Judy Frazer, to the village of Merkan in the Ogaden Desert. A Somali helper was also with them. Early in the morning they had left a camp established to help famine victims and driven for about an hour across the arid, dusty land. Their goal was to set up a temporary clinic.

As the Land Rover ground to a halt, a crowd gathered. Mothers with babies on their breasts and toddlers clinging to their sarongs mingled with old men leaning on sticks, young warriors, middle-aged matrons and everything in between. Medical help was rare. There were always sick people to treat. The village people knew the visitors brought medicine and welcomed them with open arms.

But before the medicine was unpacked, unbelievable tragedy struck. A young man, a stranger to the village people, lunged at the white visitors clutching a dagger. The crowd pushed one nurse out of range, but as the other ran, they heard an anguished cry of 'Why? Why?' Looking back they saw Doug, aged 26, lying on the ground dying.

Doug, whose lifeblood stained the desert sand, had only three weeks to go before he was to return home to Australia after 18 months in Africa. He had delayed his departure to fill an urgent need in an Ogaden

Figure 36.1 – Bob and Anne Burcher, 1975. Used with permission.

famine area. As he died, a village woman took off her shawl and placed it under his head, saying, 'You came in peace. We said "Peace" to you and now you are dead.'

The Ogaden is rough savannah country, varying from red earth and sand to rock. It lies within Ethiopia, west of Somalia and north of Kenya. The population consists largely of Somali nomads subsisting almost exclusively on the products of their herds of cows, camels and goats, and their crops when it rains. But water is always short, and if the rainy season is brief or fails, famine ensues.

In times of famine the dry ground cracks and the animals starve – and so do many of the children. Where missions or aid organisations set up feeding stations, the workers were daily confronted with hollow-eyed children arriving with swollen bellies and limbs like dry sticks. Babies and toddlers were brought sucking on leathery, empty breasts. Adults arrived with heartbreak in their eyes. They had seen their crops fail and their animals die, and now they feared losing their children as well. Suitable food usually resulted in full recovery.

Doug had arrived to give medical help and to support the missionaries who were temporarily living in Bokh, an Ogaden village, to be near the worst famine areas. The team leaders, Bob and Anne Burcher from Australia, were typical Aussies: practical, supportive and generous. Bob, a Vietnam veteran, had a quirky sense of humour combined with a deep love of reading and Reformed theology. Anne was creative in every way.

They could be summed up as 'Bob the dreamer' and 'Anne the dynamo'. Together they formed a wonderful, synergistic partnership. Mary, Judy and three Somali men made up the rest of the team.

The Bokh team had welcomed Doug with open arms and loved him for his willingness to delay going home, his deep spirituality and his extroverted heartiness. In the Land Rover on their way to Merkan on the day he died, he said to one of the Somalis, 'Jama, it doesn't matter if something happens to us – just as long as you are all right.' The Somali workers had heard a rumour that there were plans to kidnap a white person. During devotions before they left on the trip that day, Doug had read the 23rd Psalm, stressing the verse, 'Yea, though I walk through the valley of the shadow of death, I will fear no evil.'

The Land Rover left Bokh at 7.30 am. Before two hours passed, the thrust of a double-edged Somali knife into Doug's chest killed him.

Stunned with grief and shock, the remaining team members, who had left Bokh with excited anticipation, now faced the task of fitting the body back into the vehicle. Village men helped as the unwieldy remains were manoeuvred onto the back seat. There was not enough room. The seat was inadequate. One of the Somali men had to edge in and stop Doug from falling between the front and back seats. Numbly they did the best they could.

'Could the assassin return and finish us all off?' their dazed minds wondered as they worked.

Once they were away from the village, Mary broke the news to the Burchers by two-way radio. Then began the hour-long trip over a desolate gravel road with the sun scorching down on them from a pale sky. Judy and Jama sat beside Mary as she drove.

Back in Bokh, they laid Doug on a bed in the tent. Bob and the girls washed his bloodstained body with buckets of water from the well. His hand had been slashed as he tried to stave off the fatal blow, and his bare feet had been scratched when his body had been dragged through the thornbushes to the vehicle. The dried blood clung tenaciously to the white skin. Heaving with sobs, Bob, Mary and Judy worked until the body was clean. 'Why? Why?' was a constant refrain. Night came to them, but sleep did not.

The next morning the body was manhandled into the pod of a single-engine Cessna to be flown away. And so Doug Hill left the desert, not to return home to his waiting family but to a lonely grave in Addis Ababa.

The only time I had met Doug was when I was in Australia on leave in 1965, ten years before.

'Ruth, we want to sing you a song in Somali,' he said to me when I visited Tamworth Baptist Youth Group. He was in his late teens and leader of the group. 'Come on, guys, let's show Ruth how we can sing in Somali!' With that the whole group had opened their mouths and sang 'Alhamdulillah' (Praise the Lord), one of the most popular Somali songs, with gusto.

'Joy Newcombe taught us that,' Doug said. It was obvious how proud they were of Joy, who was a loved member of the church and who had been home the year before. 'We also know "I have decided to follow Jesus" in Somali,' he said, and off they went again, confident in both words and music. I was fascinated. Among her friends, Joy was famous for not being able to sing in tune, but now I found she had taught the young people in her home church two Somali songs which they sang melodiously!

Tamworth Baptist had been Doug's church from early childhood. For many years he had a sense of mission, and the decision to follow Jesus was truly the theme of his life. After schooling in Tamworth he trained in medicine at Sydney University. On graduating, he worked as a resident in Perth, and then as a locum in Tamworth for two years. In 1974 he and his friend Brian Taylor, an engineer, set out for Africa.

For five months Doug joined Dr Ken Elliott, an Australian farmer turned missionary surgeon, working among the Fulani in Djibo, Burkina Faso (formerly Upper Volta). In the mornings they worked together in medicine and in the afternoons they worked with Brian and the Africans, building the hospital. Dr Elliott, with his wife, Jocelyn, continued in Djibo as the only doctor and expat in the hospital he built himself.

After Djibo, Doug and Brian visited Piela, also in Burkina Faso. He later shared in a letter to his family the pull he felt between the medical needs of the people and their need for evangelism and Bible teaching. He finished by saying, 'I'm torn between these two callings, but time will tell – God will tell.'

Later his parents received a letter after he and Brian had driven across Africa from west to east in their Land Rover. He said he was delaying coming home by a few weeks to help meet the need in the Ogaden. 'I hope the news isn't too great an anticlimax for you after my previous letter,' he wrote. He went on to say how he would like to return to Africa eventually, but that for the present he was happy to spend a few more weeks to help in a current need. 'I am only sorry that my stay in the desert will be such a short one.'

It was indeed a short stay. In a few days he was dead. His last words of 'Why? Why?' have been echoed by all who knew him and by the many thousands of others who have heard the story. There is no answer to why, except for Doug's own words which he wrote home before he died on hearing of the death of a key missionary figure in West Africa, Roland Pickering, in a motor accident: 'One cannot but wonder why such a man was taken in such circumstances, but God's ways are not our ways and we are inclined to forget that his ways are perfect in the long term.'

Doug's death would be described by the press as a 'lone-wolf' murder. Much more common in Somalia now are multiple killings by a group of terrorists known as Al-Shabaab. We worked among the sick and needy in relative safety in the 1960s and 1970s. Those days are gone. Murderous rampages are common now and there is no safety for those who go to alleviate the suffering of the needy. The losers are the ordinary people, who are dying without the humane aid of many who would willingly give it.

Figure 36.2 – Doug Hill, 1975.

37

KELAFO FLOOD

The time had come for me to return to Kelafo after being back in Australia on another leave. 'I am not sure if I want to go this time,' I kept saying to myself. 'What will we do if there is a war?'

It was February 1976 and I was 42 years old. In a few more days I would be leaving home again and there were disturbing rumours of the Somali armies of President Sayyid Barre being determined to win the Ogaden area back from Ethiopia to become part of greater Somalia. Kelafo, where we were working, was in the eastern, Somali side of the Ogaden, situated on the Shebelli River which ran into Somalia.

My father was postmaster in Parkes, western New South Wales, and I was spending the last weeks of my time at home with my parents. I did not share my fears with them.

One night before going to sleep I opened my Bible. The reading for that night was Psalm 27. I read these words:

> The LORD is my light and my salvation –
>   whom shall I fear?
> The LORD is the stronghold of my life –
>   of whom shall I be afraid?
>
> When the wicked advance against me
>   to devour me,
> it is my enemies and my foes
>   who will stumble and fall.
> Though an army besiege me,
>   my heart will not fear;
> though war break out against me,
>   even then I will be confident …

For in the day of trouble
   he will keep me safe in his dwelling;
he will hide me in the shelter of his sacred tent
   and set me high upon a rock.

Little did I know how prophetic these words would prove.

'Why do you keep going back?' my father asked each time I was preparing to face Africa again. 'Surely you've done your share.' I would talk to him about obedience to God's will. He would scratch his head and sigh. I guessed he thought I was sacrificing my opportunity to marry and have a family. My mother understood and never mentioned me staying at home.

The family always came to Mascot Airport to wave good bye. As I left Australia and progressed towards Kelafo, the planes grew smaller, requiring a prayer for courage to board. Leaving Sydney in a Jumbo Jet was luxury. Dire Dawa to Kelafo was a nightmare. That leg involved a DC3, better known by foreigners as the Vomit Comet. What a relief to feel its wheels hit the tarmac, coming to a shuddering stop on the red desert sand of the Kelafo airstrip.

'Thank God we made it,' I whispered to myself. My main concern, as the Somali attendant opened the only door and let down the ladder, was whether I would be able to get my legs to work again. The turbulence over the desert had resulted in a tension that made my whole body feel as though rigor mortis had set in. The circulation had been cut off in my lower legs because of the iron bar in the bucket seat pressing behind my knees. I stood shakily. Gratefully I found that I could still walk, even though my gait might have been better described as a drunken stagger.

The flight had not been worse than usual. But 'usual' in a DC3 over the desert is a grim experience. To be back on solid ground always engendered a profound '*Alhamdulillah*' ('Praise God' in Arabic) from the hapless passengers. This time the praise was hindered by a goat losing its footing as the plane descended, causing it to hurtle from the rear to the front. The owner had found it impossible to control his animal as he struggled to remain in his seat.

The intense heat engulfed me as I stepped down the three steps from the plane onto the tarmac. Missionary and Somali friends surrounded me with hugs of greeting.

Everything was dry. This was desert, normally barren, but worse than usual. The rains were late. The time for planting crops was passing. The locals were crying out to Allah for mercy and to send the rain. We missionaries prayed to our God. We had experienced the devastation of famine in other years and knew the extent of the suffering.

It seemed as though the rain had been waiting for me. Two nights after my arrival we heard the sound of thunder followed by a torrential downpour pounding on the tin roofs of the houses. The deluge continued all night and for the next two days and nights.

We were well aware of the cycle of severe flooding in the area. Hadn't we, with Somali helpers, spent almost a year replastering and painting the houses, school and hospital after the 1968 flood? Was it all going to be washed away again?

On the third afternoon there was a lull. Grasping the opportunity, I ventured outside to see for myself what was happening.

'The floodwater always comes from that dry lake bed behind the hospital,' Daqani, our main worker, told me. I walked through the eerie stillness. The sodden trees shared drops of water with the perennially dry ground, now turning to mud. I reached the indentation he said would become a lake should the rain continue. The water in it, barely an inch deep, was spreading outward like a giant amoeba, slowly but surely moving in the direction of our property.

There we were, three single, 40-ish women alone on the outskirts of a Somali village in Ethiopia. We were Gwen Carter from Alma, Georgia, Christel Voll from Germany and me. We had no communication with the outside world and no electricity. The Twidales, with daughter Heather, had boarded the plane I so gladly disembarked from to go for a holiday.

What would happen if there was a flood? We had no idea. What I had seen did not look threatening, but because of the area's history we began to lift medicines and valuable equipment in the hospital and houses as high as we could.

As darkness fell, so did the rain. It began with even greater intensity. Gwen and Christel were in one house, I was alone in another. I lit a hurricane lantern as I listened to the drumming on the roof, trying to decide whether to eat or join the others.

Without any warning the torrent came. In one gigantic whoosh the whole world changed. One moment there was no water outside apart from the rain-soaked ground and the next it was three feet deep in my house. Dazed, I watched the kerosene fridge float and lie down flat, totally submerged. The bed began floating out the bedroom door and other treasures bobbed and danced while I stood waist-deep, silent and amazed.

Before I could do anything there was a loud knocking at the back door. Outside was a boat manned by two of our workers.

'Get in, Anab,' Daqani ordered in Somali, 'you can't stay here. You might drown.'

Speechlessly I climbed in, uncharacteristically silenced by the shock of what had happened.

The boat was a leaky relic from the last flood: the vessel that had filled my lounge room the day we arrived. There were no oars, but my rescuers were able to punt the unwieldy vessel to Gwen and Christel's house and then to the huge granite hill beside the airstrip. They had come for us before their own families.

'Quickly, get out,' one of the men ordered. 'We have to go back.' We had no shoes and the sharp terrain of our rocky refuge cut our feet. Painfully we managed to climb to the top while we heard the boat go and return in the darkness with its precious cargoes of families.

The rain stopped falling. The burning red ground where the plane had landed four days before was a lake.

Eventually someone brought us a blanket. The three of us shared it, lying down with sharp stones poking into us, but very relieved the rain had let up. The turmoil in our minds forbade sleep. The night was long and the mosquitoes were many and vicious, but we were safe.

We kept wondering about the village people. Had many drowned? There were only five families with us on the rock. Where were all the others?

We spent four long days and nights on the rock. We frizzled in the day and froze at night. Some food and more blankets were brought from the houses, but it was survival living. Toilet arrangements were basic. There were no trees. A hole could not be dug in the rocky ground. At night, darkness gave some privacy. In the daylight two women held their long skirts out while the third squatted between. Fortunately we had adopted ground-length dresses years before because the Somalis found seeing women's bare legs offensive.

Our Somali friends, always hospitable, coped better than we did and sometimes brought us some of their food. We heard that no one had drowned but 20,000 from the village and surrounding areas had been forced to leave their homes. They had gone to higher ground on the other side of the village.

After four days we were rescued again. A plane owned by an aid organisation, Mercy Airlift, had been sent by our leaders to collect us and landed about four kilometres away on dry land. Our faithful Somali friends were able to take us to the plane in the boat. We floated across high trees. The usually dry, barren land was several metres underwater.

Three sunburned, unbathed, exhausted women gratefully climbed out of the boat and up the steps, collapsed onto the comfortable private plane seats and were flown to Addis Ababa.

Two days later, safe in the mission HQ in Addis Ababa, I bumped into Gwen Carter looking magnificent. 'How come you only look like that when you're flying to America?' I teased.

'Now you huuush,' she drawled in her soft Southern brogue. She was dressed in her best and had visited a beauty parlour for a fancy hairdo. That night she was boarding the plane for home in Georgia on leave.

Two days earlier she had emerged onto the Addis Ababa tarmac from the Mercy Airlift plane with Christel and me. The three of us were bedraggled and smelly. When I tried to hug one of my best Addis friends, who had come to meet us, she recoiled. 'Wait until you've had a shower,' she begged.

'This is wonderful,' I purred soon afterwards as the hot water flowed over me. There was a new appreciation as I remembered dreaming of a hot shower as I sat on the rock.

The next morning the mission director called Christel and me to his office. 'What a relief to see you unscathed after such an experience,' he said. 'We here had no idea what was happening to you. We only had general news from the government radio.'

After listening to our story he asked if we would be willing to return to Kelafo almost immediately. 'The news is that there will be severe suffering for the local people and that there's sure to be an outbreak of all kinds of diseases,' he explained. 'We want to do all we can to help. The need for medicine is vital.'

'Our houses are full of water!'

'We'll make sure the water is gone,' he assured us.

The next day a team of men travelled to Kelafo to survey the situation. A dyke built around the mission compound after the previous flood, which had failed dismally to stem the torrent, was now blocking the water from running away. With local men helping, the dyke was breached. The water immediately flowed out of the houses, hospital and other buildings. Only the ubiquitous smelly mud and slush were left.

We prepared to return. Loaded with medicine, the Twidales, Christel and I boarded a single-engine Cessna and flew back to Kelafo, landing on dry ground at the edge of the shrinking lake. The same old leaky boat arrived to take us home. 'Welcome back!' chorused our Somali boatmen. 'We were afraid we would never see you again.'

When we asked how things were, their faces fell. 'There are millions of mosquitoes,' they said. 'There is no sleep. Our houses are ruined. There is still much water in the village. The children are all sick.'

And so we arrived home. Home meant floors caked in mud and walls with the new painted plaster washed away to waist height. All the restoration work had been undone. Everything above the flood height was intact. Most things below were ruined.

Figure 37.1 – Flooded street and houses in the village of Kelafo, March 1976.

Slowly I picked out of the water the lovely new dresses my sister, Rhonda, had made for this new term of service. Most were indelibly stained by mud. I sadly remembered the fun we had choosing the material and the hours Rhonda had spent sewing. Then I found my brand new Pentax camera, ruined by the water. But the sadness was fleeting. My losses were replaceable. For the Somalis, their mud-and-stick homes had been destroyed, and finding the money to rebuild for many would be impossible.

When I walked out of my house to escape the smell, I saw John Twidale crying. The unflappable John Twidale, who had masterminded the repair work two years before, resulting in every building being restored to pristine condition, was reduced to tears when he saw their cat. The beloved puss had been up a tree to escape the water for a week. It was starving. As soon as it hit the ground, it pounced on a green pawpaw and attacked it with gusto. The pawpaw trees, laden with green fruit, lay in the mud, their short roots unable to hold against the rush of the torrent. They lay there, another reminder of hopeful sowing and nurturing destroyed by an overabundance of the precious liquid we had used to keep them alive and help them grow.

A tent had been pitched on the other side of the river, ready for our clinic to begin the next day. So began a routine of carrying our medicine along a road still knee-deep in water. We crossed a bridge to higher ground and, seated on low stools in the tent, treated sick people all morning. No one had drowned in the flood but the aftermath took many. We saw babies with croup and whooping cough and children and adults with malaria, ear infections and diarrhoea. We treated all who came. Many were beyond our reach. These were the irreplaceable losses.

The walk to and from the tent was a daily adventure. The thick mud sucked our thongs off. We had to reach down and dig to find them. We were afraid the murky water hid broken glass and branches from thorn trees. One day a crocodile came out of the river and was sunning itself on a half-submerged jeep. It barely opened its languid eye as we crept past.

Once home, the work of cleaning began. The scraping and washing of floors and walls with the help of Somali friends was interrupted by many visitors. World Health Organization workers and other aid organisation representatives were regular visitors. We were the only

Figure 37.2 – Tent housing the medical clinic in Kelafo after the flood, 1976.

Figure 37.3 – Crowds waiting for medicine after the Kelafo flood, 1976.

people able to offer hospitality. It was a challenge to our resourcefulness to find food and cook it on a charcoal stove for strangers who were invariably interesting world travellers, well accustomed to visiting disaster areas. An older man from Germany, known as the Red Baron, continually kept us spellbound with his stories of the war and his other flying adventures.

'We would never have met people like these if it weren't for the flood,' I said in awe to Christel. 'This is like something out of a story book.' Our drop-in celebrities were grateful to have meals and a bed. I kept pinching myself to be sure it was all really happening.

One unforgettable, frequent visitor was a Swiss gentleman called Ernie Tanner, the founder and director of Helimission. This was an organisation established to provide helicopters for disasters such as floods and famines. Ernie was a volatile extrovert with a temper bordering on the volcanic. In our area he was flying food across the flooded areas to stranded villagers.

One afternoon I was talking to John Twidale outside my house. 'Ernie asked me if you would like to have a ride in the helicopter,' he said.

I immediately thought it was a thank you gesture for all the meals we had fed him. 'OK, that would be nice,' I answered. But it was a trick. After flying across the water, we landed near a large pile of 25-kilogram bags of macaroni guarded by four Somali men.

'This food is for another village,' explained Ernie. 'I want you to supervise the men. They must stack 12 bags at a time on this rope cargo net and one man must stand on top and loop the net onto the hook on the helicopter.' I surveyed the men and the pile doubtfully.

Without waiting for agreement, Ernie demonstrated how to place the bags criss-cross on the hammock and flew off. We did what he said, gathering the rope ends to make a loop.

'You hook it on, Isaac,' I told one of the men. He looked apprehensive but climbed on to the stack as the helicopter made its descent. Just as contact was imminent, the entire structure collapsed with Isaac sprawled spreadeagled on top. I frantically signalled to Ernie to back off and then doubled up in mirth. The scene resembled a first-class comedy movie.

This infuriated Ernie. He emerged from the helicopter, red-faced and shouting.

'Everything's a joke to you, Root,' he screamed in his thick Swiss accent. 'This is life and death. You don't play with helicopters.'

It wasn't fair. We had little idea of what we were doing. But there we were, unwilling victims of his program, inexperienced and inadequately instructed. He flew off again with a muttered, 'Do it properly next time.'

Somehow we did 'do it properly'. He flew over the water with load after load. The giant cargo net swung beneath the helicopter like an outsized baby carried by an overweight stork. We worked like beavers to be ready for each return. Fortunately there were no other collapses. Lifting the 25-kilogram bags was exhausting, but we succeeded.

On the way home Ernie was smiling. 'You did a good shob, Root, a really good shob.'

I didn't answer. I kept my peace until I met John Twidale again. I could tell by the twinkle in his eye that he was aware of the purpose of my 'joy ride'!

Ernie Tanner was a genius. He and the organisation he established helped thousands. But as one missionary pilot said to me once, 'Working with Ernie is like working with a crocodile. You never know when you're going to be snapped at.' In my heart I agreed, but I continued to feed him nourishing meals whenever he came. He may have been snappy, but his inspiration and Helimission brought relief to a multitude in crisis situations.

38

OGADEN WAR

The weeks in the tent clinic were exhausting, as were the cleaning and restoration of the houses and hospital. Weariness was an antidote to mulling over possible dangerous situations. One result of the flood was the erosion of the airstrip. This prevented planes from landing and so any mail from home was only received when helicopters came or an occasional four-wheel drive appeared. We had the two-way radio to communicate with our headquarters in Addis Ababa, but the comfort of news from home was infrequent and sorely missed.

Kelafo was an Ethiopian government outpost. A resident governor and a small contingent of police were stationed on a hill overlooking our compound. We were aware that there were sporadic visits from military vehicles and rumours of Somali soldiers attacking Ethiopian government facilities in other places, but we were not warned of imminent danger. The constant stream of sick people needing treatment, along with other activities such as an agricultural and English teaching program, occupied our days.

We were shaken into sharp reality on 18 March 1977 when a WHO helicopter landed near the hospital. Our area was the last bastion of smallpox in the world. World Health Organization doctors came regularly to examine the patients we reported. On this occasion a South American medico, Emilio, who was also a helicopter pilot, sprang out of his machine, extremely agitated.

'Are you crazy?' he shouted. 'Don't you know there's a war on? This is the only place that hasn't been attacked. What are you doing still here, and with children?' With that he jumped back into his helicopter and took off.

Our group consisted of five adults and two little girls. We were left in a quandary. The Twidales and three nurses were away on holidays. Remaining were John and Pat Warner with Michelle, aged four, and Robyn, a toddler of 18 months; Christel; Geoff Clarke, a young

Australian university student, who was supervising an agricultural program; and me.

'Even if we wanted to leave, how would we?' puzzled John. He described the situation, which we all knew. 'No planes have landed on the airstrip since the flood a year ago. We don't have enough petrol to go far and we've been told the roads are mined.'

'We're safer where we are known,' we all agreed.

'Everyone knows we are here to provide medical help for the Somali population. Why would they want to hurt us?' I asked myself. And so we continued with our day's work, hoping Emilio was exaggerating.

Two days later I was awakened from a deep sleep by the sharp crack of bullets hitting the iron roof of my house. I had been dreaming that patients were dropping coins in the clinic money tin, but the reality was that the Ethiopian police on the hill were firing down onto our houses, which were surrounded by Somali insurgents dressed in camouflage fatigues. I looked out my bedroom window to see Ali, our night guard, being dragged along by the strangers.

Figure 38.1 – John and Pat Warner with daughters Michelle and Robyn, 1982.

'What's happening, Ali?' I called.

'They want you to open your door,' he answered.

I grabbed a kaftan, hanging on the wardrobe door, always ready for night medical calls. Then I went to the backdoor and opened it. My thought was that here were Somali men, whose language I knew and who would understand that I was there to care for the village people. But it was not like that at all. These men were wild eyed and frantic. I panicked and slammed the door in their faces.

The response was pandemonium. They shot at the door with their machine guns and stabbed at it with bayonets. Aware that the wooden door was too fragile to stand against such treatment, I opened it again and cowered against a wall.

They burst in shouting for money, food, cameras and tape recorders. Their behaviour was out of control, nothing like the Somali people I was used to. They were either drugged or manic from lack of sleep.

I vacated the house as they trashed the bedroom, having found no valuables in the kitchen. Standing outside, I was aware I was in danger of being shot by the police on the hill. I was in a quandary. Inside the house were wild-eyed freedom fighters and outside was a constant bombardment of bullets from the government outpost.

This is what terror feels like, I thought. My heart was pounding, my mouth dry and my bowel in a knot. I felt a desperate urge to go to the toilet but couldn't re-enter the house. I eventually climbed into some bushes.

Then I saw John Warner emerge from his house next to mine. 'Come over here with us, Ruth,' he called. 'Christel is here too.' We all gathered in the Warners' house. Everyone was pale with shock.

We had no time to talk before a crowd of soldiers burst in with their machine guns aimed at us. 'Money! Money! Where's the money?' they shouted.

'You already have it all,' John said. With that, one fired his gun in our direction. John hit the floor as the heat of the bullets seared his ear. No one was injured. There were bullet holes in the wall behind us. We were only a few feet away. They could have easily killed us. Why didn't they? They obviously had other plans.

Eventually they all left the house again, and, hidden among the trees, they continued shooting up towards the Ethiopian government buildings. After some discussion, we decided to lie on the ground outside with the Warners' house protecting us from the government shooting. Nothing could protect us from the Somali soldiers. We were totally at their mercy. From time to time one of them would approach and threaten us.

'You have drunk the blood of our people,' one said. 'You deserve to die.'

'If we find one Ethiopian person on your land, we will kill you all,' another threatened.

We had given permission for two Ethiopian smallpox workers to camp the night. Would that have fatal consequences for them or us? No. We heard later that at the beginning of the attack the two young men had escaped by swimming across the river, which ran alongside our property.

I lay on the ground near Christel with four-year-old Michelle Warner between us. There was a nightmarish sense of unreality. It was the 16th birthday of my nephew, Andrew, at home in Australia. My family would be celebrating with no idea of what was happening to me. The Twidales' chooks were loose, scratching around with contented clucks. Birds flew into the trees above and stayed awhile. Much of life was continuing as normal while we wondered if it was our last day on earth.

At one stage John climbed in the window above us, emerging with a Bible. He read Psalm 46, 'God is our refuge and strength, an ever-present help in trouble. Therefore we will not fear …' We prayed for protection and talked from time to time with the soldiers who came over to us. Several had our backpacks, which we had prepared for such an emergency, on their backs.

'Our runaway bags are running away without us,' I quipped, and we laughed.

'What will happen if they shoot us?' Michelle whispered to Christel and me.

'We will go to be with Jesus forever,' Christel answered.

'I am not sure I will go.'

'Have you asked Jesus into your heart?'

There and then, lying on the sandy ground shielded from police bullets but vulnerable to the Somali machine guns, the three of us prayed and Michelle was at peace.

After midday it was too hot to stay outside and we sought the coolness of the house. Presently a few soldiers joined us and asked who was the mother of the children. On hearing it was Pat Warner, they ordered Christel and me to leave the house with them. Without a word of protest we obeyed.

We were led to Christel's house. One soldier, Musa, took me into one bedroom. More than one accompanied Christel into the other. I sat on the bed feeling absolutely bereft. I knew what was going to happen.

'What difference does it make that I am here in your service?' I said to God. 'You are not looking after us. You know what this man is going to do and then he will probably kill me.'

'If he kills you, whose body is it?' were the words that entered my heart.

I remembered the familiar verse in Romans 12:1, 'Therefore, I urge you, brothers and sisters, in view of God's mercy, to offer your bodies as a living sacrifice, holy and pleasing to God – this is your true and proper worship'. I had committed myself to God's service years before.

'It's your body, Lord,' I said, and with that I experienced a measure of peace.

'Take off your clothes!' the solider ordered.

'I have not been with a man in this way before,' I said. 'If I were your sister, would you want this to happen?'

With his bayonet pointing at me, he motioned to me to obey and to lie on the bed. He placed a dagger beside my head. It was useless to struggle. The desire to go on living was much stronger than a pointless refusal.

He did not treat me viciously and, to a certain extent, the memory of God's peace keeping my heart stands out in my mind more clearly than the details of the rape. Lying there knowing it could easily be my last few moments on earth, I felt the Lord's presence around me.

When Musa had finished, he told me to get dressed. As I pulled the kaftan over my head, more soldiers burst in, ordering me to undress again. I felt I couldn't bear it. Terror gripped me.

'Leave her alone!' Musa ordered. 'Let her go!'

Without waiting another moment, I walked through these other soldiers, left the room and the house, and returned to the Warners' house. I passed Ali, our watchman, sitting between the two houses. He knows what has happened, I thought as I looked at his handsome face marked by deep concern and fear on our behalf.

As Pat, John, Geoff and I waited in the house, Christel joined us. 'Two men raped me,' she said. 'One was very cruel.'

For some strange reason, John Warner had not understood why the soldiers took us. I believe God kept him from jumping to the obvious conclusion. Undoubtedly he would have fought to protect us and there could have been bloodshed. John spent sleepless nights afterwards believing he had failed us. I am sure there was nothing he could have done.

The level of our apprehension rose dramatically as the afternoon wore on. We had no access to electricity and we dreaded to think what darkness would bring. Then our faithful watchman, Ali, came to the door.

'You must leave,' he urged.

'How can we? They will shoot us.'

'They have all gone into the hospital. They have found the medicines. They are filling their sacks. Go now.'

It was a 100-metre walk to the gate of our compound. Beside the gate was our Land Rover on its side. One of the soldiers had tried to drive it and had been shot by the Ethiopian police on the hill. We walked past it into the deserted village. It seemed as though a giant vacuum cleaner had descended and sucked up all the people. Aware that we could be shot from behind at any moment had the soldiers seen our escape, we struggled with shaking legs up the stony hill to the government offices.

'You're alive! You're alive!' people shouted as we reached the summit where the Ethiopian administration was situated. Somali villagers and government employees emerged from offices and other buildings. 'We thought you were all dead. The police have been shooting down on to your houses all day.'

The governor, whom we had met several times, came to welcome us and took us to his office. 'You can have this room,' he said, and ordered some mattresses to be brought. The room was already occupied by most of the town's prostitutes. They outnumbered us and could have treated us as intruders. But there we all were, escapees from grave danger, recipients of the governor's hospitality and thankful for a place of safety.

When the mattresses were arranged, I found there was one narrow one for Geoff Clarke and me to share.

'That's funny,' I said.

'Why funny?' someone asked.

'Well, in SIM a single male missionary and a single woman missionary are not even allowed to travel on a bus journey on the same day.'

'Why not?'

'Because they might be seen getting off together and the wrong impression be given. Now we are to share this mattress that isn't even as wide as a single bed!'

We all laughed.

'We'll sleep with our heads at opposite ends,' I told Geoff. Even in hair-raising situations my bossiness seemed intact.

Our stomachs growled for food but the raging thirst was worse. We took sips each from our tiny amount of boiled water, doing our best to ignore our burning throats. The only food available was biscuits prepared for famine victims, sent from the Netherlands. They were rock-like and dry, almost impossible to swallow without liquid.

When the lights went out, I lay on my side on the narrow mattress. The discomfort of heat, thirst and the constant biting of sand flies were overshadowed by the knowledge that the Somali insurgents could easily overpower the small Ethiopian contingent of police.

Eventually I dozed off, only to be suddenly awakened by Geoff grabbing my leg.

'What's this?' I asked as I sprang up.

'Sorry,' he said, 'I dreamt you were a crocodile.' It was funny in retrospect. However, that was the end of sleep.

The police outside our open window spoke Amharic. They talked loudly to each other while taking sporadic potshots at the intruders down below, still hiding among our trees. Although I only understood some of their words, the apprehension in their voices conveyed a more sinister message. They were no match for the enemy raging below them. The Somalis were armed with submachine guns augmented with belts of bullets around their chests. The Ethiopians were equipped with ancient .303 rifles.

To my horror, I also understood from their conversation that their ammunition was pitifully inadequate. 'How many bullets do you have left?' I heard them asking each other. I didn't hear the answers. I didn't need to. The fear in their voices was enough.

The next morning we saw the situation for ourselves. Suddenly there were shouts of joy. We looked down the road to see a cloud of dust approaching which gradually materialised into a column of army trucks. The Ethiopian military had heard of the invasion and sent reinforcements. A large canon took pride of place on the back of one vehicle.

A policeman standing beside me murmured, 'Praise God!' I turned towards him.

'Were you running out of bullets?' I asked. It was a question I had hesitated to put into words before.

'Look.' He opened the pouch on his belt to reveal one solitary cartridge. His fellow officers were the same.

With the arrival of the military the visitors on the mission compound vanished. We heard no more shooting. Again, as in the flood, we spent four days and nights on a rock. This time it was the rocky hill that held the Ethiopian administration.

'These people must have done a *dembi wayn* (big sin) to be sent to work here,' Somali friends often said to me. Being sent to Kelafo was a dreaded assignment for Ethiopian staff. They were far from home, with limited finance and a hostile local population resentful of Ethiopians being in charge of what they believed was their land. The Somalis were adamant the Ogaden belonged to them.

The military visitors were a source of great interest. We watched them use their metal helmets as basins for washing their socks. Then they would rinse them out and line up for their ration of stew. They were friendly, cheerful, ready to help in any way they could. Their arrival probably saved our lives.

Life on the rock was uncomfortable. Although we enjoyed the shelter of the governor's office, toilets, bathing and food were all a challenge. Our hosts were kind but facilities were limited. Emotionally traumatised, cut off from our homes, with uncertainty ahead, we longed for news from our leaders. At last, on the fourth day, John Warner was able to visit the mission compound. Accompanied by soldiers, he succeeded in using the two-way radio. Once our leaders knew our situation they were able to arrange a mission plane to pick us up.

The initial attack had occurred on Monday 21 March 1977. On the following Friday we were able to return to our houses and collect a few belongings. 'Here's my passport!' I shouted as I scrabbled through my trashed possessions. Moments later I found my pendant made of Somali gold. This has ever since been a symbol to me of how we were looked after.

Soon, with a double row of soldiers on the airstrip, their rifles at the ready, the single-engine Cessna landed. Without wasting a minute we were all aboard and away. The missionary pilot was literally risking his life. No one knew where the terrorists were hiding.

And so our work in Kelafo ended. We left almost everything behind. There had been no time to say goodbye to our friends. The buildings, so painstakingly made habitable twice in four years, were left empty again. Most of the Somali population was taken to refugee camps in Somalia.

Ninety kilometres north-west of Kelafo was Gode, an American Presbyterian mission station. We decided we had better stop to tell the folk there what had happened. Our friend Dr Don McClure, who had been working there with his wife for some years and was now in his 70s and due for retirement, was packing their belongings with the help of his son Donnie. His wife was waiting in Addis Ababa. Their plan was to return to the United States permanently. His was the house we had sought refuge in when we first arrived in the Ogaden. I thought he was one of the kindest people I had ever met. Also occupying the post at Gode were New Zealanders Graeme and Pam Smith and their four children. They were working with World Vision and were relative newcomers to Africa.

We had lunch with the folk at Gode and told our story. 'Try to get a plane and leave as soon as you can,' we urged.

Later we heard they were attacked two days after we saw them. We don't know if they tried to leave. Pam Smith sustained a bullet wound to her leg and Dr McClure, smiling and friendly as usual, was shot dead. A life of sacrificial service ended there in a desert place. Donnie was left to take the devastating news back to his mother. After a most wonderful, God-glorifying memorial service, Mrs McClure and her son returned to the United States and the Smiths went back to New Zealand. We will never know whether the intruders were the men we had encountered. It is very likely they all died too because the Ogaden war ended with the Somali insurgents defeated by the Ethiopian army, supported by Russian intelligence and equipment and thousands of Cuban soldiers.

Once we were safely back in Addis Ababa, we reported to SIM's East African field director. While grateful to God for our safe escape, he suggested that Christel and I keep to ourselves details of the abuse we had suffered. 'We don't want other women missionaries to hear about this. It will make them frightened. I want you to keep quiet about it,' he said. We agreed, but for me it was an impossible request. I did tell some of my closest friends.

The only other mission official to speak to me was the headquarters doctor. 'Hi Ruth,' he said, 'I want to see you in the morning.' When I turned up he greeted me with a syringe full of penicillin. 'This will make sure you don't get an infection,' he stated simply.

In 1977 'debriefing' was unknown. It was not common parlance until after the Iranian hostage crisis in 1981. Then the world heard that before those hostages were united with their families there was a professional debriefing. Since then the process has been developed into a regular practice in a wide variety of situations. Most missionary organisations arrange for their workers to undertake a professional debriefing after every term of service, especially when there has been a traumatic event. One of the greatest satisfactions I have experienced is being trained in debriefing and seeing its positive effects.

In 1977 none of this happened. The only message was: 'Don't talk about it!'

I returned home to Australia for a break before being assigned to a new project. One afternoon I went with Jo Anne and Bill Dennett to see *The Hiding Place*, the story of Corrie ten Boom and her family being arrested and imprisoned by the Nazis as punishment for hiding Jews in Holland. I had read the book years before and loved it, but I felt nervous about the film. I sat in the theatre, my heart pounding, my mouth dry, on high alert as I watched the German soldiers push their prisoners out of the army truck and towards the prison gates. The moment they prodded Corrie's father with their bayonets I started crying.

'I have to go,' I said to Jo Anne. That was the only time I wept over the war in Kelafo. My reaction to seeing the bayonets in the film was my debriefing. As I sobbed, the knot of my emotions unravelled, bringing relief. The only remaining symptom was an increased startle response when a car backfired near me or there was some similar sound reminiscent of gunshots.

39

MEETING KATH

'I don't want to be in a room with my mother,' I informed Daisy Griffiths, the women's convention organiser. 'She snores loudly and I won't sleep a wink.' Being a guest speaker with pre-performance nerves, I would find sleep difficult anyway.

'No, no, we're not putting you with your mother,' Daisy assured me. 'She will be in a dormitory with other campers. We're arranging for you to share with Dr Kath Donovan, a missionary from Papua New Guinea, who is another speaker.'

I had heard of Kath and was sure I would enjoy meeting her. It was 19 November 1977. I was still in Australia after the Ogaden war. I was 43 years old.

Our accommodation was a room in the building where students from St John's Theological College, the Anglican theological seminary in Morpeth, were usually housed. It felt like a monk's cell. My memory is of stone walls and floors. It was cold and forbidding. My mother and I arrived on the Friday night, which was the beginning of the conference, but there was no sign of Kath. I endured a restless night alone. Nervous about speaking the next day, cold and aware of the strange atmosphere, I tossed and turned and waited anxiously for morning.

Kath arrived after breakfast, accompanied by two old friends, all packed into her VW Beetle. At morning-tea time one of her friends came to make Kath's bed. I started wondering, 'What is this Kath Donovan like? She brings servants with her to make her bed.' I met her at the prayer time before the session when we were both speaking. It was perfunctory. We were both preoccupied with what we were going to say. Throughout the day we spent no time together. All we knew about each other was from our public presentations.

After the evening meeting I returned to the room. No sign of Kath. Perhaps she didn't want to share a room with me. I got into bed and was reading when my mother came to say goodnight.

'Kath Donovan hasn't even been in the room once,' I said. Big mistake! My mother was an incorrigible problem solver, always ready to deal with any difficulties her children may meet.

As she left, to my horror, I heard her meet Kath on the other side of the door and say in her school teacher's voice, 'I'm Mrs Myors, Ruth's mother, and she's wondering why you haven't been to the room.' My first reaction was to put my head under the bedclothes and pretend to be asleep.

'Hello, Mrs Myors' daughter!' Kath said, typically seeing the funny side. Without small talk she changed into pyjamas, jumped into bed and said, 'How do we manage the light?'

What? I had been warm in bed for some time, but I had to climb out, gingerly cross the freezing floor with bare feet, switch the light off, find my bed in the pitch dark and climb in once more.

Strangely, it was the icebreaker. As soon as we were in the dark we began to talk. We knew the basics from our individual public addresses and now we filled in the details, some of which would have been inappropriate in a public address. I had not told anyone in Australia what personally had happened to me during the raid in Kelafo, but I opened up to Kath. She in turn shared a painful experience related to her mission administration. In a special gift from God there was an immediate trust that broke away any barriers. We talked until 2.00 am.

I knew this was not a casual meeting. This was a life changer. I felt sure I had found a new and special friend. We had touched one another deeply.

Standing in the auditorium after morning tea next day, I heard the putt-putting of a VW Beetle starting up. Daisy Griffiths leaned towards me and whispered, 'There goes Dr Donovan.'

'What!' I muttered to myself. 'Come on, Kath. After all that sharing you didn't even say goodbye. You didn't tell me you were leaving early before the conference ended. Come late, leave early. How strange!'

In spite of her precipitous leave-taking, I didn't let her go. At least she had given me a phone number. The next morning, back home in Belmont, I rang her and said, 'It's me.'

'Hello, Me! How nice to hear your voice,' she answered.

Kath was due to return to Papua New Guinea. 'You need a holiday. You look like Morticia Addams,' I helpfully pointed out.

'I don't know her but I can imagine what she looks like,' said Kath. After consideration, she rang me back agreeing to delay her return to PNG by a week. We decided to spend her extra time together. Our holiday accommodation was an onsite caravan in a park near Redhead Beach. We spent the time relaxing and talking, talking, talking. So much to share.

Unbeknown to us, some of Kath's friends in Balimo Hospital in PNG's Western Province, where she worked, had been concerned for her health and refusal to have a reasonable holiday. 'We prayed that Kath would find a friend and enjoy some time off,' Mairi Kerr told me years later.

I know now it was part of a plan God had for both of us. This was not my regular time for leave. It was special leave granted to me by our leaders because of the raid. The timing meant that Kath and I met and cemented a friendship, the synergy of which was to be used in valuable ministry.

Kath returned to Balimo. I began a new assignment in Nairobi. Letters crisscrossed over the 11,000 kilometres and the sharing continued. During that term of service the one-bedroomed house next to my parents' property became vacant. The sale price was $12,000. We bought it. In 1980 we both returned home for leave and spent the time in our own cottage. Again we returned respectively to Balimo and Nairobi. Again the letters flew over the ocean.

Eventually, in 1983, Kath's doctor would tell her she was not well enough to continue to run a one-doctor hospital, and she would come home permanently. I would also return to chase a dream. But until then I was committed to a task that stretched me, taught me self-discipline and opened my eyes to the exciting impact of Christian radio.

Figure 39.1 – Kath Donovan in 1980.
(Source: Worldwide Photos. Used with permission.)

40

RADIO PRODUCER

Missionaries who have a role that suits their gifts and work within a compatible, supportive team tend to stay longer in their overseas work. I have observed that for today's missionaries these are the two main ingredients determining missionary longevity, along with their faith and sense of call.

After the Ogaden war I was appointed to work in Nairobi as part of the Somali radio program *Codka Nolosha Cusub* ('Voice of New Life'). My Nairobi sojourn began in early 1978.

What a change! From isolated Kelafo and the hurly burly of the outpatients' clinic, where I was regularly challenged way beyond my training and experience, to busy, urban, sprawling Nairobi. There I sat in an office all by myself. From being surrounded by a noisy, demanding crowd of bush and village people, I spent my days in solitude, writing radio scripts and learning to type them in Somali. The clinic was a scene of drama, challenge, satisfaction, laughter, tears, relief and sadness. It was never, ever boring. Radio work involved quiet, tedium, prayer for inspiration and a constant need for perseverance and commitment to the task. The outpatients' clinic was a venue I was uniquely equipped for. Writing and typing radio scripts was a foreign environment for an extrovert.

Another adjustment was driving. In Kelafo, manning the Land Rover to pick up women in labour often involved bush dirt tracks, thorn trees, punctures and unreliable navigators, but few other vehicles on the road. Driving in Nairobi meant crowded roads, crazy drivers, crammed-full buses, unpredictable pedestrians and taxis honking continually. Driving in the Kelafo environs was frustrating and slow; in Nairobi I was more likely to be paralysed with fear. Clinging to the steering wheel, with sweaty palms and aware of a dry mouth and racing heart, I prayed for safety as I wove through the congestion, wondering how the African drivers were so carefree.

Small vans with seats in the back called *matatus* (English translation: 'three pennies') were ubiquitous. Used as minibuses and loaded with probably three times the legal number of passengers, they careered across lanes and cut corners. Their name came from the fare demanded many years ago. It was not unusual to see one overturned, adding to my mental discomfort. Most of my co-workers took driving in Nairobi in their stride. Unfortunately, I didn't have the same confidence.

The redeeming factors in working in Nairobi were a wonderful team of known and loved friends, who had also moved from Somalia, and my conviction that this was a job well worth doing. Radio waves reach places foreign missionaries can never go. The government had robbed us of our work in Somalia, but the message over the airways was not limited by passports and visas or any other kind of red tape.

The Voice of New Life reached the hitherto unreachable. Listening to a tiny transistor radio, which most people had, could often be undertaken in safe privacy. In contrast, regular visits with a foreign missionary immediately brought suspicion.

The role was not ideal for me. I could do what was required but was always far more fulfilled working with people. The compensations were firstly that my colleagues from Somalia were there to encourage me (even though chatting while I was supposed to be writing or typing was discouraged), and secondly that I had the joy of teaching newcomers the Somali language. There was a constant trickle of young people wanting to work in Somali-speaking areas. I revelled in relating to them. A gentle, long-suffering Somali informant, who corrected their pronunciation, tempered my propensity to be impatient.

In Nairobi we lived in a suburb known as Eastleigh. Even though this placed us in proximity to a huge, spreading slum known as Mathare Valley, we were also close to where the majority of Somalis lived. We made friends with our neighbours. They were responsive and generous and impressed that we knew their language. However, because we could not tell them about our actual work, in order to protect our Somali employees, there were limitations in our relating. The value of medical work, which drew people to us in droves in our previous situations, was missing.

The voices on our programs were all Somali voices. We had a very bright young man, Faraax, who translated our scripts into Somali and who did most of the reading. Then we found a gifted songwriter who wrote Somali 'scripture in song' choruses and sang them beautifully while he strummed on his guitar. Besides music, the programs comprised some health information, learning to use an English word and a Somali proverb. The climax was invariably a Christian message and an invitation to undertake Bible correspondence courses. The programs were broadcast every night from the Seychelles by means of antennas on the coral reef. The organisation responsible for the transmitting was the Far East Broadcasting Company.

Our recordings of the program needed to arrive at their destination six weeks ahead of the broadcast date. This meant constant deadlines hovering over us. The programs were recorded in a studio belonging to Africa Inland Mission, manned by helpful and competent Kenyan Christian technicians.

My missionary colleagues in the radio work in Nairobi were my special friends Albert and Tina Erion. The friendship had been consolidated through the ups and downs in Somalia, and their three children, all born in Bulo Burti, helped compensate for being so far from my own nephews. Another blessing was a new Australian worker, easily young enough to be my daughter, Bev Harris (now McGregor). She was the bookkeeper, appointed to keep track of our finances.

'Ruth, I have balanced the books early and have time to help with your typing,' she would regularly announce.

'You are a darling! Go for it,' I would answer, thanking the Lord for another provision to help me keep going.

While it was difficult to make many Somali friends, we formed warm relationships with Kenyans. I employed a cheeky lady called Margaret, who helped in the house and added humour to my days. Spiritual ministry was provided by running a weekly Bible study for Kenyan women. Those who came were either neighbours or those who worked in our homes. I have never forgotten the prayer times after the study.

'O God, Joshua needs new school shoes. The soles are falling off his.'

'Father, we need maize meal for our food tomorrow. The money is all gone.'

'Dear Lord, please help my husband to understand. Keep him from beating me and the children.'

One afternoon I visited one of the homes. A room the size of an old-fashioned railway carriage was home to two families, each with half

Figure 40.1 – Bev McGregor (nee Harris) in Wyoming in 2016.

*Figure 40.2 – Albert and Tina Erion with their children
Alan, Rhonda and Glenn, c. 1974.*

a dozen children. It was immaculately clean. I have no idea how they slept or how the children did their homework, but I do remember that the two older boys I knew at the time both finished high school and were eventually well employed.

Whenever I see food being wasted, I remember those women and thank God for what I learned from them and how my own attitude to careless squandering of any kind of resources has been educated.

Then we started a Sunday school. Beautiful, smiling children who lived in the neighbourhood arrived every Sunday morning and sang all the old Sunday school hymns we learned at their age. They stole green passionfruit from our vine as they left, but we always felt better for having the time with them. It was an important outreach and helped fill the gap left by our inability to mix with many Somalis.

Our property was guarded at night by a Maasai tribesman called Marunga. In the manner practised by many of his people, his earlobes had been stretched into dangling loops. One day, concerned for him being outside all night, I gave him a pair of warm socks. The following morning Marunga came to Sunday school. Just as I rose to tell the Bible story to the children, Bob Burcher, one of the missionaries, whispered to me with a twinkle in his eye, 'The socks have it.' Following the direction of his gaze, I saw our guard looking magnificent with a sock knotted through each earlobe. Warm feet were sacrificed. Ear embellishment triumphed.

The poverty of many of Nairobi's residents contributed to one of the city's most serious problems: crime. Because of this, we needed Marunga to be our guard. We lived in a property surrounded by high stone walls topped with broken glass and protected by padlocked iron gates. We heard stories of muggings, carjackings and violent robberies. Murder for something as small as a cardigan or a few shillings was common. Desolate slums spread in the shadow of upscale neighbourhoods and world-class wealth. Chauffeur-driven Mercedes shared the roads with overladen *matatus* and, in the outer suburbs, donkey carts.

My self-discipline in persevering in writing and typing radio scripts was lightened by attractions that brought people to Nairobi from all over the world. Nairobi National Game Park was only seven kilometres away. With the skyscrapers of the city as a background, we could visit the animals grazing in their own domain. A further 200 kilometres south-east of the city was Amboseli Game Park. Unforgettably etched on my mind is my first view of snow-capped Mount Kilimanjaro towering over the grassland, 5895 metres above sea level. Like one in a dream, I drank in the beauty of the mountain, with gazelle, giraffe, zebras, wildebeest, elephants and other breeds of animal grazing around the base adding to the wonder. With holidays in Mombasa, visits to lush agricultural areas and snorkelling at Malindi and other unique locations, I was aware there were many compensations. The anticipation of regular breaks visiting places others had to travel across the world to see helped me persevere.

However, the joy of the game park adventures paled in significance compared to the delight we experienced when we began to receive letters in response to our radio programs.

I remember clearly the day Albert returned from the post office with the mail and announced, 'There's a letter from Somalia!'

Figure 40.3 – Ruth typing the scripts, 1978.

We had waited six months for that first response to the programs. We read and reread each word, thrilled at the evidence that our message was reaching its target. Gradually the stream of correspondence increased. People began requesting Bible correspondence courses. There were also negative, abusive reactions including threats to find out who we were and bomb us.

However, the positive, affirming requests predominated and convinced us that our labour was not in vain. Today, as I write, I am hearing that the numbers of letters and hits to *The Voice of New Life* website are increasing exponentially. In Isaiah 55:11 God promised that his word would not return to him empty. That promise has been confirmed repeatedly through Christian radio ministry. For me, the five years I spent in the radio ministry meant doggedly keeping my nose to the grindstone, but I am convinced it was more fruitful than anything else I ever did.

At 6.00 am on 1 August 1982, I was reading in my lounge room. My concentration was jolted by reverberating explosions outside. I thought they were from the backfiring tankers that regularly serenaded us. But when I turned on the radio, I heard that the air force had attempted to overthrow the government of President Daniel arap Moi. Looking out the window I saw that the racket was from trucks filled with armed men shooting into the air.

Memories of the war in Ethiopia came flooding back. I groaned, 'I can't go through it all again.' Then a still small voice spoke in my ear: 'Yes, you can. Remember the peace that passes all understanding.' I reminded myself that the God who had been with me through other trials was still there, and quietness of spirit returned.

Then came a call asking us all to meet in the Lairds' house. We numbered about ten, including an American couple who were visiting. Bro Laird, our director, asked the visitor to pray for us. He began, 'O Lord, it is possible we are all going to die today.' I can't remember any more of the prayer. I switched off. The visitor was new to Africa. He had no idea what some of us had already endured.

The looters continued in an unending stream past our house. We knew that at any moment they could attack us. We were unarmed in the midst of a completely African neighbourhood. Most other Westerners lived on the other side of town.

The most vicious attacks during the time of anarchy were against the Indian population. All their shops and many of their homes were wrecked. Women were raped until some of them died. The Indians, who had been brought to Kenya to help build the Mombasa Railway in the 1890s, had become the wealthy class, and as employers they were often racist and autocratic. From my balcony I had witnessed my Indian neighbour in his motor repair business knock employees to the ground with a blow. That day, people in the Indian population of Nairobi, both good and bad, bore the brunt of Kenyan anger.

The coup, however, was short lived. The army took the side of the government, successfully gaining control. A curfew was put in place at 6.00 pm. This saved us from a night invasion. Anyone seen on the streets after the curfew was to be shot. The official estimate of casualties that day was 145. In reality, over 2000 were dead.

Two weeks later, my early morning peace again was disrupted by the shout of '*Kufungua malango* (open the door)!' This angry, autocratic Swahili shouting was followed by loud banging on my apartment door. With a dry mouth and legs threatening to give way, I undid the lock and faced the visitors. They were four uniformed Kenyan soldiers, unsmiling and impatient.

'Let us in,' the leader commanded. 'We are here to search your home for stolen goods.' With that they pushed past me and without apology began flinging open cupboard doors and pulling out drawers. Finding nothing, they then invaded my next-door neighbour's flat, making her cry with their brashness.

I hadn't stolen anything so I should have been totally at ease. But I had a guilty secret. 'Are we all going to gaol because I'm stupid?' I anguished.

The people from the slums and from many other areas had embraced the chaos of the short-lived coup, pouring into the CBD and vandalising every shop. We watched from an upstairs window as hoards from the nearby Mathare Valley ran down our street, laden with luxuries. A constant procession of TV sets, rolls of expensive textiles, lounge chairs and other items from exclusive department stores passed by on the shoulders of the hilarious looters.

Now the soldiers were searching for the plunder and punishing the guilty. Although I had not stolen anything, I had taken a risk. Our next-door neighbours, a Somali family, were special to us. They spoke the language we knew and reminded us of all the Somali friends we had left. One of their daughters was soon to be married and they had accumulated rolls of expensive material for the celebration outfits. The bride's mother came to me and said, 'Anab, the soldiers will come and accuse us of stealing. They won't come to the house of *wazungu* (foreigners), but they will search our house. They hate Somalis. Will you hide it for me?' With some misgiving and without a word to my fellow missionaries, I took the suitcase, secreted it in our storeroom and forgot all about it until the soldiers came.

I followed them through our offices, my mouth too dry to talk. Room after room they savaged, and then they left. They walked straight past the storeroom. They even grunted an apology in farewell. To cap it all, they bypassed our Somali neighbours.

Doing the job in Nairobi, which in many ways did not fit my gifting and personality, taught me patience and a new way of thinking of worship, as in Romans 12:1–2.

WORSHIP

Worship is obedience.
Worship is acceptance.
Worship is trust.
Worship is giving you my body as a living sacrifice.
Worship can be pecking at a typewriter.
Worship can be patience in a traffic jam.
Worship can be housework done with joy.

Worship is reading your word with an open heart.
Worship is prayer.
Worship is all that I am; all that I have;
All that I dream; all that I love; all, all, all
Given back to you because I love you.

Worship is accepting each circumstance that comes
My way as from you and saying, 'Thank you, Lord.'
Worship is looking at love praying in a garden
With sweat as great drops of blood, and saying,
'Not my will, but thine be done.

41

UNIVERSITY STUDENT

'Ruth, here's an exercise we are asking everyone to do,' said Bro Laird, handing me a piece of paper. He was our SIM leader in Kenya at the time. A warm, extroverted Irishman, his real name was Vivian, but because he had a habit of addressing people as 'Bro', the name had become his. No one but his wife, Merilyn, called him 'Vivian' in my hearing.

The 'exercise' was an invitation to take time to dream and write about what I would like to be doing in five years' time. It was late 1982, over five years since I had begun working in Kenya. What could I see myself doing in another five years?

As various images sprang to mind, one in particular developed a sharp clarity. 'In five years' time,' I wrote, 'I would like to be living in a large, comfortable home on the outskirts of a city. Tired missionaries on leave would come to rest, receive counselling and then resume their ministry with healing from any wounds sustained from their previous term of service.'

I handed the paper back to a surprised Bro Laird. I then began to pray this dream into reality.

Most difficult was sharing with my friends in Nairobi that I was contemplating returning to Australia permanently. I struggled with the decision. I had applied to be a missionary in Africa until death or retirement at 60 years of age, and here I was planning to leave at the age of 48. Was I a quitter because I didn't like my current job, even though it was reaching out to Somalis for Christ? I prayed for guidance. Was I being led by God or by my own selfishness? For many years I had had a keen desire to study psychology in order to be better equipped to help people at a deeper level. Another question was whether someone who hadn't completed secondary school be acceptable in a university.

My brother Peter was the purchasing officer at Newcastle University. He talked to the professor in charge of the English Department, giving him a thumbnail sketch of my history. 'Tell her to come and apply, bringing evidence of all her qualifications,' the professor said. 'There's a good chance she will be accepted without doing a bridging course, even though she hasn't matriculated.'

I accepted that as a green light, excitedly booking my passage home. It was a wrench leaving my friends, but I was comforted in knowing that there was a replacement in the radio work. I was not sad to leave Nairobi. It had never been 'home' in the way Bulo Burti and Kelafo had.

I arrived back in Australia in the beginning of February 1983. Before the month had ended I was a university student. Like someone caught up in a dream, I wandered around the campus, remembering the pain I had felt leaving school prematurely.

I imagined that a middle-aged lady, two years short of 50, would be seen as somewhat of an oddity by the students who had graduated from secondary school the year before. But it wasn't like that at all. In no time I had made friends of all ages. We formed groups to help one another. My maturity was an asset. While the youngsters juggled their social lives with their studies, I spent most of my time working on the assignments and studying for examinations. Apart from occasional speaking engagements and writing a weekly script for the Somali program, I was totally absorbed in the course.

Soon fellow students were phoning me, wanting to discuss a current assignment. Age and background were irrelevant. We were all together focusing on how to survive the course. One little Malaysian girl always sought me out to sit with in lectures. I loved it. The four years spent gaining an honours degree in psychology are one of my special memories.

Kath, home now from Papua New Guinea because of her health, began doing research into stress and coping. She was particularly interested in how this related to cross-cultural missionaries. Before her medical studies Kath had completed a doctorate in microbiology, so research was her natural domain.

She was also well-versed in statistics, an area of my course that was initially incomprehensible to me. I sat through the first lecture in a dream – or a nightmare. I wondered what on earth the lecturer was talking about. He seemed to be using a foreign language. Don't worry; Kath will help me, I thought to myself. But it was not that simple. 'Work at it yourself and see how you go,' she would say. It was not until I cried that she would relent, saying, 'Now, now, what's the problem?' I needed to resort to tears regularly to gain the help with statistics I needed.

One evening before an exam, I remember listening to Kath trying to explain a certain graph. There was a curved line coming from the middle of the diagram. 'What's that line?' I asked.

'Why are you such a genius at irrelevancies!' Her response was unusually irritable, so I kept quiet and listened humbly. I never found out what the line was. However, because of Kath's tutelage, I ended up with a distinction in statistics in the final exam. This borders on the miraculous, because my grasp of the subject is still limited. Not my cup of tea at all.

For financial reasons I needed to study at Newcastle University so I could live at home. The psychology course was research based rather than majoring on people-oriented skills such as counselling. For example, when we studied stress, we observed rats' reactions to various stimuli and counted the number of droppings as an indication of their stress response. I wondered how this would equip me for a ministry to missionaries. I don't know about the rats' stress (although there were lots of droppings), but I clearly remember my own stress when told to grab the rat by the tail, take it from its cage and put it on the observation equipment, known as the 'open field'.

'Don't worry,' said our teacher. 'No student has ever been bitten in this course.' Trustingly, I grabbed the long, curling tail and the rat bit me.

'Not another psychology student bitten by those rats!' said the nurse at the clinic as I arrived, requiring antiseptic. When I asked if many came, she answered, 'Oh, all the time.' I didn't mention this to the lecturer when I returned to class, and of course he didn't say anything to me.

'This course is not relevant to what I want,' I complained to Kath as I wrote an essay on the stress response of laboratory rats to external stimuli on the open field.

'Don't worry,' she replied. 'You are being educated in psychological thinking. From now on you will be able to read scientific journals and understand them.'

I'm not sure that was true, but I loved the challenge of the course and gained the qualifications needed to use psychometric tests and so be equipped to do psychological assessments of missionary candidates.

One vital requirement was to be accepted as a member into the Australian Psychological Society (APS) and to be registered by the NSW Board of Psychologists. To gain postgraduate experience, I completed the Graduate Diploma in Counselling at Charles Sturt University. A great course! It involved practical counselling experience, excellent lecturers, interesting fellow students and no rats.

At the time I was attending Belmont Presbyterian Church, accompanying my mother. A satellite of the Charlestown congregation, it was a tiny gathering with hardly a dozen regulars meeting in a preschool kindergarten. The members were mostly my mother's vintage. An aged piano was played by a lady nudging 90, and on gala occasions a man, slightly younger, played the ukulele with her. Most of the people had known each other for generations. They were each other's closest friends. One Saturday a month they invited other friends to join them to play crazy whist.

Then there was a surprise. One Sunday morning a young family joined us for the service. A father, mother and two little girls! 'They won't stay,' I thought. 'Next Sunday they'll be looking for a church with young families.'

I was wrong. Enjoying a cup of tea together after the service, the husband, David McKie, told me they intended to come regularly and had dreams of bringing other children together for a Sunday school. It happened! We visited families in the neighbourhood, inviting the children to come to Sunday school. This was followed by a letterbox drop and soon we had a keen group of children attending every Sunday. On special occasions their parents came.

The relevance of the Sunday school to this memoir is because its development was the tip of the iceberg in the story of my life. That same morning, as David told me his plans for a Sunday school, he also mentioned he was an educational psychologist. He was most interested to hear I had recently graduated with honours at the age of 52.

At that precise time, I was facing the challenge of applying for state registration and acceptance into the APS. I needed a guide through the tortuous maze of requirements. David led, supported, supervised and introduced me to others who could help. He read my reports on the missionaries I interviewed and helped me develop the skills I needed. When the time was right, he recommended me for registration and acceptance with the APS. The day the news arrived of my success, he seemed as excited as I was.

The process took two years. Just as the goals were reached and I was fully qualified to sign my name as a registered psychologist and member of the APS, the McKies were moved to Wagga Wagga for David's work. As in the story of Esther, as far as my life was concerned, David was brought to Belmont for just that time.

42

CHRISTIAN SYNERGY CENTRE

My graduation from Newcastle University was in May 1986. 'Let's organise a Stress Management Seminar for missionaries soon,' Kath suggested shortly after. To me that was an ambitious plan, especially as I'd only learnt how stress affected rats by counting the number of droppings. How could that be relevant to our prospective audience? But instead of pointing that out, I decided to wait and see what Kath had in mind.

'As a base for our seminars, we'll form an organisation called the Christian Synergy Centre,' Kath announced another day.

'What's synergy?' asked the psychology honours graduate.

'It means 1+1=3. The sum of your gifts combined with mine results in something greater than the individual parts.' It became one of my favourite words.

Again I felt doubtful. Kath was confident we were doing something good. All the time I had been studying she had been developing her theories on stress. We booked the facilities belonging to Bethshan Mission at Wyee, New South Wales, and sent brochures announcing the seminar to various mission agencies. When 20 applications arrived in the mail, my response was: 'What if it's a fizzer?'

But Kath's confidence was justified. There were no problems with the program. She dealt with the issues of stress. She was brilliant. Her emphasis was that we have been given a stress response, fight/flight, not only for our survival but also for our growth in maturity as we learn to deal with the response and deal with the situation in a godly way. (Her full teaching was later published in her book *Growing Through Stress*.[6]) My task was to bring balance with exercises in communication and illustrations in ways we can change our thinking concerning what is causing the stress, always in the context of scripture.

---

6. Kath Donovan, *Growing Through Stress* (rev. edn), Institute of World Mission, Andrews University, 2002.

Throughout the weekend there were opportunities for the missionaries to share with one another, as well as in the group as a whole. No matter where the person had been working overseas or with what missionary society, many of the stressful situations were similar. As the ice broke, a transparent honesty emerged that enabled the participants to share deeply. That sharing was the therapeutic element of the time together. Humour was a constant ingredient as we learned to laugh as memories were shared.

That first weekend was a resounding success and the beginning of a ministry that continued for over 15 years. The Bethshan staff were always supportive and never refused our bookings, although we rarely reached the number of guests they required as a minimum for other groups.

Gradually we added other subjects for running weekend and day seminars. We dealt with major adjustment issues, grief, depression, conflict resolution, healthy relationships and factors around returning home permanently. Besides weekend gatherings, we developed an annual ten-day retreat at the Church Missionary Society guesthouse in Katoomba and a biannual five-day intensive in Sydney. It is difficult to find adequate words to describe the joy it was for us to deal in depth with people who had given their lives to serve the Lord in all sorts of difficult situations. We used to drive home to Belmont exhausted, but so grateful for the time we had spent with these 'cream of the crop' people.

Soon we were invited to run church weekends and speak at Christian women's functions, clergy wives' retreats and a variety of other groups. We held day retreats for Anglican bishops' wives and even ran one afternoon seminar with the bishops. During the 1990s, we were invited to Bolivia, Pakistan, Ethiopia and Papua New Guinea to run seminars and speak at annual conferences.

'What on earth possessed us to say we'd go?' Kath groaned, holding her head in her hands the night before we left for Bolivia. Plane travel was something she avoided when at all possible. Now we were facing a long trip to Los Angeles and then another south to Cochabamba's high altitude (2500 metres) and even higher to Candelaria (3300 metres), where many of our meetings were to be held.

There was no way out. We had agreed to go. Bookings were set in concrete. Unsurprisingly, we loved it. We met missionaries from 13 different home countries, heard about their work and returned home thankful for the experience.

It was the same each time. Kath dreaded the plane trip, bravely faced each one and always returned home enthusiastic about the country we had visited. Highlights were travelling to former beloved venues in Ethiopia (for me) and Balimo in Papua New Guinea (for Kath). We were able to show each other our previous workplaces, as well as minister.

On the way home from Bolivia, we broke our journey in New Zealand and spoke at an orientation course for missionary candidates who were applying for overseas ministry under the auspices of SIM. We immediately clicked with the SIM New Zealand director, Murray Dunn, and his wife, Pam. Consequently, for the next ten years, we made an annual pilgrimage to Auckland to speak at the orientation course and carry out psychological assessments of the candidates. Murray was always one of our greatest supporters. We loved our New Zealand trips, even though the packed program precluded any time for sightseeing.

Teaching pastoral care at SMBC for several years was another privilege. The girls sat with the boys – there was no gender apartheid now. Nineteen-fifties era 'stockings and built-up shoes and dresses with sleeves' were replaced by jeans or shorts, joggers or thongs, but the students were similar, wanting to learn, laughing at jokes, seeking guidance for future ministry.

We were definitely seen as elderly even though our course was popular. Because I had graduated from SMBC, one of the students asked me to point out my class graduation photo on the dining room wall. When she saw it was 1958, she said, 'My mother was only six years old when you were a student.'

The trip from Belmont to Croydon, where SMBC was situated, meant either leaving at 5.00 am for a morning lecture or returning home at midnight after an evening lecture. When we had both passed our 70th birthdays, we told David Cook, the principal, we were resigning. He did not think our age was a legitimate reason to leave, saying that his mother was still engaged in interior decorating at 84. We weren't moved by that information. One of our determinations that we strictly adhered to was to leave jobs while people still liked us. We missed the students. We never missed the trip on the freeway.

In 1997 we were invited to speak at a forum of world mission leaders where the reasons for missionary attrition were addressed. What a privilege to be the keynote speakers. Mission executives from all over the world gathered together to think about why many missionaries were leaving their work prematurely. This was a regular four-yearly conference of the World Evangelical Fellowship. The chairman of the fellowship, Bill Taylor, an American and a former South American missionary, had heard Kath and me speak when he was in Australia. The three of us had clicked and thus we were invited.

The most memorable occasion for me connected with my ministry with Kath was speaking at a ReachOut weekend at Katoomba. ReachOut is an annual conference aimed at exposing young adults to teaching about foreign missions. Our topic was 'The Effect of Generational Differences on Missionary Work'. The audience had been sitting in meetings all morning and our slot was mid-afternoon on the Saturday. We arrived during the first session after lunch, a deadly time for any speaker. To make it worse, the topic was 'Missionary Financial Support'.

It was a cold, dull day and the auditorium was packed with approximately 1100 young people. All we could see were coat collars pulled up around ears and chins on chests while people snoozed gently. I nudged Kath and whispered, 'How are we going to wake this lot up?' Her response was a nervous grimace.

Driving up the mountain we had composed a song to the tune of 'Old Macdonald Had a Farm'. Each verse described qualities of the three generations we were going to address. But even before we had a chance to sing it, our introduction was greeted with whistles, clapping and foot stamping. Bible college students, missionaries we had spent time with and others who knew us gave us a heart-warming welcome. The session, with pertinent overheads and illustrations, went well. There was lots of laughter and a standing ovation at the end. We drove back down the mountain on the way home thrilled, in fact overwhelmed, by the response.

Not everything was a resounding success. Some event assessment forms contained negative comments. There are some memories that cause a cold sensation in the pit of my stomach and I wish we could have another go at using what we had learned from our mistakes. However, on the whole, I know that when the Lord brought Kath and me together, he gave us a privileged ministry, and the synergy was clearly evident. Working with Kath was an experience beyond anything I had ever dreamed of. I remind myself often that I might not have met her if I had not come home to recover from the Ogaden war experience.

My degree in psychology gave me a pioneering role among the various missionary societies as well. When I graduated, I had the privilege of working with John Neal, a former missionary to the Ibo people in Nigeria, then the Australian director of SIM. John, with a degree in psychology himself, began conducting psychological testing with all SIM candidates. I worked with him to gain experience. He then passed on all his materials to me. He was my mentor and great encourager.

When John retired, I was appointed counselling coordinator for SIM, which meant conducting all the testing and debriefing for candidates within that organisation as well as arranging ongoing counselling when needed. Gradually, most of the other interdenominational missions decided to use the service too. By the time I retired, I believe the vast majority of missionary societies were convinced of the value of using trained professionals.

So the paradigm shift, from simply trusting the call of God to using a combination of the call with professional testing and interviewing, gradually evolved. Psychological testing was useful in suggesting potential problem areas that could hinder cross-cultural adjustment. The test results and interview also helped people to gain valuable self-awareness. Instead of diminishing the spiritual aspect, the opportunity to prepare people more thoroughly before going overseas was provided.

How I wished I had gone to Somalia better prepared! I remember Jo Anne praying for me one day, reminding the Lord that I was a Sanguine and needed help in mood control.

'What's a Sanguine?' I asked after her 'amen'.

Her response was to give me Tim LaHaye's book on the Four Temperaments.[7] I was fascinated. That was my first taste of personality differences. Ever since I have found it an absorbing study, both in reading and in observing behaviour.

Last but not least was the admission of Valmai Gallard, who had worked in Papua New Guinea with Asia Pacific Christian Mission for

---

7. Tim LaHaye, *Spirit-Controlled Temperament*, Tyndale House Publishers, 1962.

27 years, into the Christian Synergy Centre. When Valmai could not return to PNG after her last home leave, we invited her to work with us. She was skilled in all avenues of clerical work. What a relief it was to have someone to write the letters, organise the testing materials, make appointments, collect fees and so on. Valmai was the opposite in personality to me in every way. She was concrete and detailed and very particular about how things should be done. For those who are familiar with the Myers-Briggs Temperament Indicator, Valmai was ISTJ, Kath was INTJ and I was ENFP.

One example of our different ways of seeing life occurred after I had been for a walk. When I returned, I began to tell Kath and Valmai what I had seen.

'I just saw a miracle!' I began.

'What?' asked Valmai.

'Yesterday that new house on the corner was surrounded by bare dirt. Today there is lovely grass and shrubs and sprinklers. It's a miracle.'

'No, it's not,' said Valmai. 'Men bring the turf on a truck, roll it out and buy the shrubs and plant them. That's not a miracle.'

'It seemed like one to me.'

'It's just the S and the N,' Kath said to me when we were alone. 'Don't argue.'[8]

ENFPs like me are intent on telling a good story. They want to inspire and surprise. ISTJs like Valmai want factual, realistic renditions. They interrupt a story if they sense a detail like a date or the number of people is inaccurate. They ruin the story, and the ENFP is left wondering what on earth was so important about that detail.

In spite of these differences I learned so much from Valmai, who was with us for seven years. My test papers are still in the order in which she taught me to place them. We could not have managed without her. Our friendship remains strong. Her contribution was another part of the Lord's wonderful provision.

I didn't have a big house where groups of missionaries could come and stay for long periods, although we had plenty of visitors. The retreats and seminars were held in a variety of venues. But the main ethos of the dream I wrote down in Kenya was fulfilled. It was exceedingly, abundantly more than I ever asked or thought (Ephesians 3:20).

---

8. See Myers-Briggs Temperament Indicator (MBTI Basics). The S and the N indicate different ways we process information.

Figure 42.1 – Ruth and Kath in Pakistan for ministry with missionaries, November 1995.

43

LIGHT AND DARKNESS

'What on earth possessed you to say that to our guests?' Kath asked one evening when the front door closed after we had waved our visitors goodbye.

'I thought they looked fidgety, as though they wanted to go and didn't know how to make the move,' I answered.

'It's better to let people make up their own minds.'

After a leisurely meal and interesting conversation, I tried to put myself in our guests' shoes, thinking they may want to go home. Perhaps they were tired or had things to do before bedtime. So I thought I would ease the way.

'If you want to go home, that's OK,' I ventured. Within minutes they were gone. I was right, I thought. They were dying to leave.

Kath disagreed. She thought that what I said was not appropriate for a hostess.

A major difference between us was our ideas of what was appropriate and what wasn't. Kath was a reserved conformist with a disciplined tongue. I was the opposite. As a result, 'What on earth possessed you?' was heard often in our house.

In spite of the differences, knowing Kath and sharing a home and ministry with her were major highlights of my life. She taught me so much. She loved me. I often wondered why, since she was so clever and above me in many areas. Yet both of us expressed frequently to one another how blessed we were to know each other. The strength of our relationship was in sharing ideas, working together, presenting seminars, running enrichment retreats.

'We are just a couple of song and dance men,' Kath would often say as she introduced one of our presentations. 'I'm the song, Ruth's the dance.' That was true. She was the brains and I lightened the program with humour and illustrations.

Through our relationship, our friendship circle expanded

exponentially. Kath's group of friends from the past met my friends from the past and all liked each other. Every year we took holidays with a mixture of co-workers from Somalia and Papua New Guinea.

The differences in our personalities and backgrounds were not wasted. They were our best resource in finding helpful illustrations to use in our seminars. One area of contention between Kath and me was her obsession with *The Sydney Morning Herald*, which she insisted on having delivered every morning. My problem was that she often had no time to read it. Her work schedule prohibited a leisurely read, resulting in the paper remaining rolled up in its cellophane wrapper when she went to bed.

'Someone has to read this,' I would say to myself, resignedly sitting up in bed half asleep, trying to hold the unwieldy pages open and muttering to myself. Eventually sleep would overcome me. The paper would drop as I dozed off with the light still on.

In my counselling training, I learned how to address difficult issues, to listen and not attack. 'Let's have a practice,' I said to Kath one day after describing what I had been learning.

'What topic will we begin with?'

'*The Sydney Morning Herald.*'

'OK.' Kath wasn't aware that her failure to take time to read the paper was an issue for me. Her theory was that she paid for it and so why should I mind what she did with it.

'You start by saying to me, "I would like to hear why you have a problem with me having *The Sydney Morning Herald* delivered and not always having time to read it",' I told her. 'Then you listen to my explanation. You don't interrupt or attack, and when I finish, you respond, "I heard you say …" and report back what you think I said. Then we reverse the process.'

'OK, here we go. I would like you to tell me why you have a problem with me buying *The Sydney Morning Herald* and not always reading it.'

I responded by telling her that I was worried about all the gum trees that were being sacrificed for unread papers and what a waste of money it was buying it and not reading it. She could have easily interrupted saying it was her money, but she refrained and repeated what she had heard me say, then gave me the opportunity to reverse the process.

'Why is it so important to you to get the *Sydney Morning Herald* delivered instead of going to the newsagent and buying it when you have time to read it?' I asked.

'*The Sydney Morning Herald* has always been part of my life. Right until the day I left for Papua New Guinea it was delivered to my home. Everyone in the generation before me has died. This is one thing from my past that has continued. My grandfather, Charles Brunsdon Fletcher, was editor for many years. It is something that has been an integral part of my life. Most things have gone.'

As I listened, any resistance I felt melted away. I understood.

It was not a major issue, but it showed us how facing it together without rancour or attack gave us a much better understanding of each other. We role played this in many of our seminars. Often couples reported afterwards they had been enabled to face up to a topic they had been skirting around, not knowing how to address.

'Kath, do you want a fish sticker on your car rear window?' I asked her another time.

'Definitely not,' she responded.

'But you should have one,' I argued, ignoring her tone of voice. 'A fish sticker on the rear window tells others you are a Christian. You don't know where it could lead if the service station man or your mechanic asked you about it.'

'You have one on your car, that's your choice. I don't want one on my mine.'

But I had already bought one for her, for $4. Serious money in 1984. When she went out I stuck it on her VW Beetle thinking she wouldn't mind when she saw how good it looked. How could she mind? It was a Christian witness. Besides, it was a psychedelic fish!

Big mistake! Her reaction was explosive and uncharacteristic of my mildly spoken, academic friend. Although we rarely experienced conflict, we were verging on it. If I'd had a tail it would have been tucked well between my legs as I fled for cover.

But because I enjoy living dangerously, after a reasonable cooling off period, I tried another tack. 'Kath, why were you so angry about the fish on your car?' I asked.

'First of all I don't like fish stickers, and secondly I have an aversion to being manipulated. All my life I've been surrounded by manipulative people.'

I was studying psychology. Hearing Kath admit to being sensitive to manipulation set me on a psychoanalytical investigation. On one of our interstate work trips, using a caring, person-centred approach, I said, 'Could you explain what the word "manipulation" means to you?'

'My mother was a champion manipulator.'

Wow, I thought, here's a Pandora's Box to take the lid off. 'Tell me about it,' I continued in my carefully modulated, empathic tone of voice.

For the next hour or two, as we drove down the Hume Highway with the Paterson's Curse blazing purple in the hillside paddocks, Kath described the painful relationship she had had with her mother. As she talked I noticed a gradual softening in the tenor of her voice.

'Do you know, as I've been reminiscing, something has crystallised,' she said eventually. 'For the first time ever, I have been able to get into my mother's shoes and understand a little of why she acted the way she did.'

Enhancing long car trips with discussion of deep issues was a regular practice for us. This time had particular significance. Kath's older sister had died soon after Kath's birth. Her mother never recovered from the loss. One outcome was the dysfunctional way she related to her other two girls. That day Kath entered into her mother's pain and began to understand.

So there were at least three outcomes from this testing of the relationship. Firstly, I learned to be a little less pushy. Secondly, we explored a painful topic with therapeutic results. And thirdly, the VW rejected the fish and it peeled off.

These examples, among many others, had the effect of deepening our understanding of one another and enriching our friendship. I can honestly say we never went to our beds angry with one another. We dealt with our differences as they arose, and from the beginning we were open and honest in our interactions.

Sometimes Kath would sniff the milk and say it was off. Then I would give it a sniff and disagree, saying, 'It's OK.'

'I did a PhD in the serology of milk and I know when it's off!' she would respond. I had no match for that.

In 2000 I was diagnosed with bowel cancer. My attitude to illness has always been to make light of it, whereas Kath tended to see the worst possible outcomes, both for herself and for others. Even my specialist accused me of not taking the implications seriously. But I didn't need to; the tumour was removed without any spread. I didn't have a colostomy or need chemotherapy. However, the surgery was a shock. I felt much worse than I expected. Then, to live forever after with the uncomfortable effects of a large piece of bowel missing, has been an ongoing challenge.

Some years after my surgery Kath began saying she was losing her memory.

'Everyone has trouble with names as they age,' I responded, denial taking over.

Next she began emerging from her room in the morning saying there had been a crowd of people sitting looking at her in bed. 'They weren't frightening,' she said. 'They were like Salvation Army types and they were all smiling at me.'

Still, I tried not to take it seriously. But the symptoms increased. On holidays she became disorientated in the new house. She could not find her bedroom. A cold hand gripped me in the pit of my stomach as I accepted the growing awareness that the signs of progressing dementia were adding up.

Kath shared her fears with our GP, Stephen Harvey, who also tried to make light of it. Once at a large medical conference Stephen had heard one of the speakers, Dr Bernie Hudson, an infectious diseases specialist, describe Kath in glowing colours. Bernie and Kath had collaborated in writing a book on malaria. Stephen said to himself, 'He's describing my patient!' Stephen loved spending time with Kath and mentally baulked at accepting the signs of increasing dementia.

Eventually, however, he could not ignore the evidence. Towards the end of 2007, he referred her to a gerontologist, who ordered psychometric testing and an MRI. Then came the diagnosis. We were sitting in the specialist's office waiting. The CAT scan was illumined on the display screen.

'See those black spaces,' Kath said to me, pointing to the picture of her brain. 'They indicate that the neurones have shrunk.'

'Dr Donovan, I have to confirm that you do have Alzheimer's disease,' intoned Dr Walsh entering his office and sitting down, 'and I am afraid it is the type that advances rapidly.'

I cried as Kath discussed the implications with the specialist as though she were conferring about one of her patients. I could not believe that my friend, the brainiest person I had ever known, the person I loved most in the world, was going to lose her mind.

From then on we had regular appointments with Dr Walsh to discuss the progress of the disease and to report on how I was coping as Kath's carer. At first he was gentle and patient, but on one visit I sensed he was cross. He implied that I had not done enough about arranging full-time care for Kath or even day-care. 'If you're not careful she will end up in Scone or somewhere!' he snapped, referring to a small town two hours' drive north-west of Newcastle. Grabbing a piece of paper, he scribbled a few words on it and handed it to me.

'That is the address of the East Lake Macquarie Dementia Service [ELMDS],' he said. 'Go there and have Dr Donovan enrolled for day care.'

'I'll go next week. We're having visitors this weekend.'

'You will not wait until next week. You will go there on your way home today,' he barked with blazing eyes.

We somehow made it out to the car before I dissolved in tears. Sobbing all the way, I found the place he described.

'Don't cry. It will be all right,' Kath kept murmuring.

The woman who opened the door to us at ELMDS took one look, opened her arms without any questions and hugged me. 'Don't worry, we'll work it out,' she whispered in my ear. Her name was Julie. I will never forget her. She introduced us to the charge nurse and Kath was enrolled.

I was wrong. Dr Walsh was right. I thought Kath would hate a day-care place but she loved it. As I saw her interacting at ELMDS, I decided she believed she was in charge of a hospital again. When she arrived in the morning, she would greet the other guests and ask them how they were. She was interested in each one. She would also sit in the office chatting with the charge nurse.

On three days a week the ELMDS bus would pick her up in the morning and bring her home in the afternoon. On the days the bus didn't arrive, Kath would be disappointed and accuse me of cancelling it without consulting her. Explaining that it was the weekend or a 'men only day' made no difference to her belief that I had somehow interfered with her doing her work.

At first the progress of the disease was gentle, almost imperceptible. Then, as if it had arrived at the brow of a steep hill, it gathered pace and began racing pell-mell down the slope, crashing at the bottom with a fall in the shower and the need for full-time care. On the corner of our street was a nursing home for residents with dementia called Nazareth, under the administration of Calvary Care. How wonderful to be able to find a place so close to home where Kath could be lovingly cared for.

One day when browsing through the documents on the computer, I found Kath had written some of her thoughts on being diagnosed with Alzheimer's.

> How are we to respond to an illness which carries with it loss of ability to do things which we were previously able to do well? For example I used to be good at cryptic crosswords but now I can hardly do them at all; I often find it hard to discover the time after I've looked at my watch and two other clocks and still feel a little uncertain; I used to be able to give talks to people but mainly I can't do that and so it goes on. But I'm not saying it out of self-pity. What I am saying is how am I to respond to this major loss in my life?

> I've been reminded of Albert Schweitzer's statement, 'It's not what we experience that counts, but how.' 'How am I to experience Alzheimer's?' I frequently ask myself … As I thought about this, I realised more than ever that my responsibility as a person with Alzheimer's is to hold on to my faith. I do not in any way consider that God has given me this disease, but I believe He has given me 100% confidence that he is the God of all comfort who comforts us in all our troubles so that we can comfort those in any trouble with the comfort we ourselves have received from God (2 Cor 1:4). I also believe that the end of this illness 'is not death but the glory of God' (Jn 11:4). In our working together, Ruth and I have often reminded ourselves and our students that pain can lead to growth and growth to ministry. Even more significant is Paul's comment in writing to the Corinthians, 'having this ministry by the mercy of God, we do not lose heart' (2 Cor 4:16).

During the time Kath was a resident in the nursing home I visited her daily to feed her lunch. She always smiled when I arrived and appeared content. Once more it seemed as though in her mind she had returned to the hospital at Balimo. She would use words like 'theoretically speaking' and discuss resources but never respond to anything I said. Nor did she show any interest in our dogs. It seemed as though our years together had been erased.

While Kath was in Nazareth, I gained permission to run a weekly service for interested residents. Every Wednesday afternoon we met and sang old hymns, prayed together and considered a short portion of Scripture. A friend, Margaret Sumner, a gifted pianist, played the keyboard. Others came to support, including my brother Peter and his wife, Betty, and friends from church. It was a ministry provided by our heavenly Father and brought blessing to us all. I was aware of strong opposition by the enemy of souls. Every week I experienced opposing forces but always came home rejoicing that we were serving the victorious Lord Jesus.

Kath had a beautiful singing voice. Right until the end she sang alto and when appropriate the descant to hymns such as the 23rd Psalm. One of the helpers, Lily, has continued the ministry since I left.

On 6 January 2014, after two-and-a-half years in care, Kath died of a short, sharp attack of pneumonia, one month after our beloved dog, Tilly, also left us. Her death was a release to a far better place. Much of my grieving had been done. I had lost her years before. I had dreaded seeing her descend to a vegetative state, so death was, in one way, a relief. The manager of the nursing home said to me, 'This place received so much from Kath.'

After her death I found my mind was obsessed with the seven years of dementia. Where were the good memories?

'They will return,' my sister Rhonda said. She had been through a similar experience when her husband died.

She was right. Gradually the sad memories of the Alzheimer's disease faded and the richness of the other years resumed their rightful place. Through diaries, letters, other writings and reminiscences, I have found again the treasure we shared. Kath will not come back to me; I will go to her. But until then I have precious treasures, such as her Bible, to reflect on.

One day after her death I stood near the recycling bin battling with ambivalence. 'What should I do?' Kath was gone. Her room and her possessions had to be dealt with. Decisions, decisions, decisions! Grief fogged my mind and confusion reigned.

I was holding her favourite Bible, which after years of constant use was in tatters. The spine was broken, the cover was detached and some pages were loose. I didn't need another Bible. But how could I treat something she loved as garbage? As I vacillated, the writing inside the back cover caught my eye. It was typical. I could hear her speaking. The words pierced my heart.

'I can't throw it away. This is part of Kath,' I decided. My mind was made up.

I visited the Belmont Copy Shop and asked the owner if he bound books.

'No, but I know someone who does,' he replied, and he gave me the details of Sue's Book Binding at Rutherford.

I rang Sue and asked how much to rebind a Bible. Without hesitation she said, '$180.'

'Is it ever any cheaper than that?'

'It can be, but it can also be more.'

On the agreed date I drove to her workplace. Sue's Book Binding studio is well signposted. Besides an eye-catching notice in the yard there was a van decorated with lurid advertising in front of the house. Sue herself is a technicolour person, a bustling, buxom, confident lady who wastes no time on small talk. When I handed her Kath's Bible, she took one look and said, 'Bloody hell!' and then added, '$250.' I gulped, but I was not going to change my mind. I left it with her. She promised to phone me when the job was done.

The cost of the Bible restoration was not really a concern. I had decided not to keep the ashes from the cremation. That saved more money than Sue charged. When planning the cremation with the funeral director, I broached a subject I had often wondered about.

'How do the mourners know they are getting their loved one's ashes,' I asked, 'and not a jar of sawdust from the coffin?'

'Because the only thing that does not burn during the cremation is the skeleton,' he answered. 'Everything else is completely demolished. The urn only contains ground up skeleton.'

'Well, I don't want it,' I said. 'I don't want any ashes at all.' I had already checked this decision with Kath's relatives. One nephew, Pete, said, 'We still have Jim's remains in the bottom of the wardrobe.' His father-in-law had died years ago.

Ashes and cemeteries have no interest for me. I rarely visit my parents' graves. I prefer photos, old letters, daydreaming and memories. Sue's restoration of the Bible fits into this category and is magnificent. Kath's notes are on almost every page. Daily, her comments enrich my reading. The book I almost threw in the recycling bin has become one of my most precious possessions.

Without Kath a light has gone out of my life. Nothing on earth can replace what we shared. I thank the Lord for the 30 years of companionship. I also thank him that the missing causes me to depend on him more consciously.

O friend, my bosom said,
Through thee alone the sky is arched,
Through thee the rose is red;
All things through thee take nobler form,
And look beyond the earth;
The mill-round of our fate appears
A sun-path in thy worth.
Me too thy nobleness has taught
To master my despair;
The fountains of my hidden life
Are through thy friendship fair.

Ralph Waldo Emerson (1823–1882)

44

HOUSE OF DREAMS

Before I bring this memoir to a close I need to complete the saga of the house Kath and I bought in 1980. Occupying a block of land next to where my parents lived, it overlooked both the Pacific Ocean and Lake Macquarie. The price was $12,000.

Our mansion was a little wooden building with one bedroom, a kitchen-dining room and a parlour the size of a railway sleeping compartment. The toilet was outside, close to another ramshackle building that contained an ancient bath. These rooms had no electricity and there was no way to heat water. As soon as possible we had the toilet enclosed and enlarged and a shower and hot water service installed.

As missionaries, Kath and I had survived on a living allowance adequate for our needs where we were working. But Kath had $6000 from shares left by her father and my father agreed to lend the money for my contribution. We were both in Australia the year we became homeowners and were able to occupy our property and then rent it to a young couple when we returned overseas. In 1983 it became our permanent residence.

For seven years we lived in the little wooden house. We even had friends come to stay. Guest accommodation was a sofa in the lounge room and a tiny verandah that held a camp bed. Later we bought an old caravan. During those seven years, I trained as a psychologist and counsellor. Kath did research on stress and wrote her first book.

Then we both had aunties die. We individually inherited money. With other donations there was enough to build a brick extension: two bedrooms, a bathroom and two offices attached to the front of our little wooden house. Ten years later a neighbour, who was our friend, died suddenly, and incredibly we were her sole beneficiaries. So the little wooden house was pulled down and the other half of the brick house was built. It was complete. Now we had four bedrooms, two bathrooms and two offices.

Over the next 20 years, that home was the base for the fulfilment of our dream. There was an office where I saw people. Kath had an office where she worked on medical issues and wrote. We had plenty of room for visitors to come and stay. Whenever we had to go away for work, we never tired of the joy of coming home again. As we crossed the bridge over the Swansea Channel on the road to Belmont, one of us would be sure to say, looking at the sparkling blue-green water, 'We haven't seen anything more beautiful than this anywhere!' Then we would pick up the dogs from wherever they had been staying and head for home.

To write about the dogs would take too long. Sufficient to say there have been six furry friends over the years, usually two at a time. Reuniting with them after being away was a tail-wagging, rapturous ecstasy.

Our house was a gift from God. We heard other people talking about mortgages. We never had one. Now I am leaving. The House of Dreams and its yard are too big. It is lonely on my own. Along with the sadness of the losses there is the excitement of a new adventure. With the blessings of the past in mind, I look forward to the road ahead.

Figure 44.1 – Joy Newcombe, Pat Warner, Jo Anne Dennett,
Anne Donaldson and Ruth (behind) in 2006.

Figure 44.2 – The 'pack gently aging': Jeff, Ruth, Peter and Rhonda gathered for Ruth's 80th birthday in 2014.

'*For age is opportunity no less*
Than youth itself, though in another dress,
And as the evening twilight fades away
The sky is filled with stars, invisible by day.'

Henry Wadsworth Longfellow (1807–1882).

EPILOGUE

As it sinks into my consciousness that this book, so long dreamed about, is at last finished, there is a sense of relief and also ambivalence. I know there have been many failures in my life that are not included. Have I painted myself more saintly than I really am? On the other hand, there are successes I have also deliberately omitted. Just as in moving house there is drastic culling while deciding what to load into the removal van, so in writing a life story similar choices are necessary. Some things have to be left behind. There just is not room.

If I ask myself, 'Why did I go to the trouble of writing a memoir?' several reasons come to mind. Firstly, I have had an interesting life. I think my friends will enjoy reading about it. Secondly, writing has been a therapeutic experience for me personally. Healing has come in areas where, as I remembered, I became conscious of scarring and pain.

But most of all I wanted to share my experience of the faithfulness of the Good Shepherd who has gone ahead every step of the way. Though the path has been rocky at times, the shadows have always been lightened by the never-failing presence of Jesus, the Light of the World. If you have read this book and still do not know him, I have a question for you that you need to answer:

What will you do with Jesus?
Neutral you cannot be;
Someday your heart will be asking
What will he do with me?

A.B. Simpson